food network kitchens

# get grilling

Meredith Books
Des Moines, Iowa

Editor: Jennifer Dorland Darling
Contributing Editor: Lisa Kingsley
Senior Associate Design Director: Mick Schnepf
Graphic Designer: Joline Rivera,
idesign&associates, inc.

First Edition. Printed in the United States of
America.
Library of Congress Control Number: 2004112905
ISBN: 0-696-22213-2

This is the third book in our continuing effort to give Food Network viewers the type of recipes they ask us for on our website, foodnetwork.com. This time (you asked for it), we've brought the Food Network Kitchens outdoors to grill.

Since it is actually against the law to grill outdoors over an open flame in the city of New York, we have a lot of people to thank for opening their backyards to our testers and shooters! Thanks to Mory Thomas and Nick Caballero for sharing their yard—for months—with our crack development team (Suki Hertz, Santos Loo, Rob Bleifer, Jay Brooks, Miriam Garron, Bob Hoebee, Andrea Steinberg, Allison Ehri, and Mona Ming), who ferried across the Hudson daily and returned home smelling of fresh air and hardwood charcoal!

Test Kitchen Director Katherine Alford oversaw development of these wonderful recipes and diligently timed the ferry schedules to her tastings. Thanks also to Jonathan Milder for his great research and Caitlin Francke for putting words to our food. Stacy Meyer and Derek Flynn provisioned many locations with great food. And Miguel DeLeon, Athen Fleming, and David Martin tirelessly loaded and unloaded endless location vans.

As ever, our Food Network family headed up by president Brooke Johnson has been a great support, and our partners at Meredith have been a pleasure.

Finally, the barbecue gods were with us for two rainless weeks in August in my backyard as we shot photos with uber-stylists Krista Ruane and Bob Hoebee and back-kitchen grillers Angie Ketterman, Lisa Schoen, Lynn Calamia, and Allison Ehri (you all rock).

Photographers Mark Ferri and Robert Jacobs and stylist Francine Matalon-Degni gave us these gorgeous shots and helped us eat our way through the book. Special thanks to my husband, Rick; Robert Jacobs; and my neighbors Elyce, Rob, Justin, Ryan, Laurie, Walter, Joanna, Ed, and Katie, who graciously opened their gardens to us to celebrate the appetite you get only in the outdoors.

I hope you'll enjoy every bite!
Susan

*Susan*

Susan Stockton
VP, Culinary Production
Food Network

# who's who

FRONT ROW: Santos Loo, Suki Hertz, Stacey Meyer, Harriet Siew, Susan Stockton, Krista Ruane, Katherine Alford, Andrea Steinberg. MIDDLE ROW: Susan Maynard, Jay Brooks, Eileen McClash, Bob Hoebee, Miriam Garron, Lissa Wood, Miguel DeLeon, Lynn Kearney, David Martin. BACK ROW: Mory Thomas, Jonathan Milder, Robert Bleifer.

Food Network Kitchens is the passionate team behind all the fabulous food you see on Food Network cooking shows. We are cooks, writers, researchers, recipe developers, shoppers, and stylists. If it has to do with food, we do it. And just like you, we say grilling is one of our favorite ways to turn out a meal. Over the years at Food Network, we've fired up a lot of grills and learned a lot about cooking out. You name it, we've cooked it—from basic burgers to tailgating extravaganzas. And we've grilled in some pretty unlikely places: Air Force bases, ostrich farms, beaches, trout streams, boats, mountains, driveways, docks, football fields, theme parks, tarmacs, and backyards. The one thing all these places have in common is the results: the unmistakably fabulous flavor of the outdoors. We think you'll agree—the food just tastes better!

# table of contents

# we're grill-crazy

At Food Network Kitchens, we love to grill. We love those days when the sun calls us and we just have to move the kitchen outdoors. Fresh air always adds extra flavor to dishes. What is more fun, after all, than being with friends, eating tangy barbecued chicken, and kicking back with an ice-cold limeade or margarita?

For more than a decade, Food Network Kitchens has been grilling with the most talented grillmasters in America. In this book you will find a wide range of our own original recipes, along with tips and ideas to turn out meals from simple but utterly delicious hot dogs to downright elegant lobsters with tarragon butter. There are dishes you can whip up after a long day of work or linger over on a Saturday. There are recipes for all grillers and all taste buds—from authentic melt-in-your-mouth North Carolina-style pulled pork to Thai Curried Scallops in Banana Leaves.

We get you started with nibbles such as Spinach & Artichoke Dip. (It's not grilled, but you gotta eat something while the grill is heating up.) Then we send you into the main event with recipes such as Jerk Chicken, Peach-Mustard Pork Chops, and Hog-Tied Cheese Dogs. We finish off with great desserts, including a Blueberry Buttermilk Bundt Cake and even a grilled banana split.

This book is crafted with you in mind. Through our website and viewer mail, we hear from you all the time. We also meet a lot of you. Because the shows we do are taped all across the country, we travel a lot. We've been in your supermarkets doing cooking demonstrations and have sampled your hometown fare. You tune in to our shows, and we tune in to your taste buds. Think of us as your own personal cookout cheerleading squad—we love the food you love, have created thousands of recipes, and just want to get you grooving at the grill.

We love it when people put our recipes to work. When we were in a Minneapolis supermarket on a book tour recently, one woman bought our book, went out to her car, and spotted a recipe she liked. She came right back inside to buy the ingredients. She was thrilled—and so were we.

So dig into this book and get that fire started. We've got ideas for you on how to throw a party with menus ranging from burgers to paella, and sides going from good ol' coleslaw to zippy Watermelon & Baby Arugula Salad—all washed down with drinks as homey as an old-fashioned limeade and as exotic as Pomegranate Margaritas.

Have fun!

5

# the art of the grill

How many times have you eaten charred chicken that is practically raw inside? Or had black bits stuck in your teeth from gnawing on ribs that had been torched by flames? There is an art to grilling, but it's flexible. Nail down a few essentials and you are on your way. It's all about playing with heat, making sure it is not too high or too low. Someone a long, long time ago figured out that long, slow cooking makes meat so tender that it melts off the bone. So we encourage you to play and be creative—but we also want to share what we have learned in creating this book to make you the talk of the neighborhood.

We gathered ideas from around the country, gave them our own twist, and put the recipes to the test. In a Jersey City backyard—the home of one of our cooks—we set up a grilling laboratory. We had five grills blazing at all times. After two months of testing, ferrying dishes across the Hudson River for tastings by the whole staff in Manhattan—sometimes in 105-degree heat—we settled on the recipes and techniques we believe are the best.

## GETTING COOKING

**Equipment:** There are two types of grills, charcoal and gas. While we believe that charcoal grills impart the best grilled taste, we appreciate the ease and convenience of gas grills. Why not have both? We do. Don't worry, though—all the recipes in this book are cross-tested on charcoal and gas grills, so both will work for any dish.

If you are a gas griller, you should know that many grills are calibrated so that they are hotter at the back and cooler in front. Get to know your grill—it's smarter than ruining food. In addition, we believe that the more burners you have, the more control you'll have and—obviously, more heat you'll have.

**Fuels:** There are three main types of fuel for grilling—charcoal briquettes, which burn slowly; natural hardwood lump charcoal, which burns quickly but has great flavor; and propane for gas grills, which imparts little flavor but delivers consistent, easy heat. All are available at home improvement or barbecue stores. We believe the best technique for live fire is combining lump

**1.** Charcoal briquettes burn slowly and steadily.   **2.** Hardwood lump charcoal burns quickly but has nice flavor.   **3.** We like to combine the two in a chimney starter and wait until it is nicely ashed over for the best of both worlds and a darn easy fire.   **4.** Wood chips added to your fire lend another dimension of smoky flavor. First, soak them for half an hour to keep them from igniting.
**Opposite:** For optimum indirect heat control on a gas grill, you need at least two—but preferably three—burners.

1.  2.  3.  4.

1. A direct-heat fire with coals spread evenly across the grill. 2. An indirect fire with coals banked to one side. 3. An indirect fire with coals on both sides. 4. An indirect fire using the "ring of fire" method.

hardwood charcoal (to give the dish great flavor) with charcoal briquettes (to sustain heat longer).

**How to start a fire:** Starting a charcoal fire used to be a challenge. Behold the chimney starter, an inexpensive aluminum canister available at any home improvement or barbecue store. It makes measuring and firing up your charcoal foolproof. Other options include building a fire underneath the charcoal—which can be a tricky undertaking— or using lighter fluid, which can leave a chemical taste if it does not burn off completely.

**How to use a chimney starter:**

**1.** Fill the chimney with the briquettes.

**2.** Stuff newspapers underneath the grate and light them. If you can, find quick-light cubes for the chimneys—they make lighting the fire a snap. (But, as with lighter fluid, make sure they burn off fully or they will leave a telltale taste.)

**3.** Wait for 15 to 20 minutes until the briquettes turn an ashen color all over, then dump them into the grill. Lightly oil the grate, put it on the grill, and preheat it for 5 minutes. You are ready to go.

Our preferred method combines natural hardwood charcoal and briquettes. To do this, first lay the hardwood charcoal in the grill, then pour the heated, ashen briquettes on top. Wait about 10 minutes for the hardwood to catch fire and you will have the best of both worlds: hardwood heat and flavor, and the longevity of charcoal.

If you are using a gas grill, turn all the burners on high, close the lid, and let it heat up for at least 10 and up to 30 minutes. Then adjust the burners to whatever heat the recipe specifies.

**Judging the temperature:** Some grills these days come with nifty temperature gauges to tell you how hot the grill is inside, but we like the old method for figuring out if your flame is ready. Hold your hand about 5 inches from the heat. If you can stand the heat only a second, it is a very hot fire; if you can hold on for 2 seconds, it is a hot fire; if you can bear it for 3 or 4 seconds, it's a medium fire; 5 seconds is a medium-low fire; and 6 seconds is a low fire.

## DIRECT VS. INDIRECT HEAT

Remember all that charred meat you have eaten? We want to show you how to manipulate the heat on your grill so that you end up with moist, scrumptious food. You don't bake hamburgers for an hour or broil a whole chicken. Why? Because some dishes need quick cooking over high heat, while others need long, slow cooking over low heat. You can control the heat on your grill as easily as you can on your stove or in your oven. Mastering the techniques of direct and indirect heat will get you on the road to becoming a grilling superstar. You're playing with fire—literally.

**Direct heat:** This is big-fire cooking. The briquettes are spread evenly across the grill, and the meat or vegetables are placed directly on top of the grate. They cook quickly. It's good for dishes such as chicken breasts, pork chops, scallops, and anything else that's less than 2 inches thick.

For gas grills, preheat the grill with all the burners on and adjust to the temperature called for in the recipe.

8

**Indirect heat:** In this method, the briquettes are piled to one side—or on opposite sides—of the grill and the food is placed on the grate so it is not directly on top of the heat. This is good for whole birds, ribs, and large pieces of meat that need to cook longer and more slowly.

For gas grills, preheat the grill with all the burners on, then turn off the one directly underneath the food. For optimum control on a gas grill, you need at least two—but preferably three—burners.

Using both direct and indirect heat allows you the greatest flexibility and control in cooking on the grill. You are creating different heat zones, which means you can move things around the grill as you see fit. If something needs to be seared quickly, zap it over the hotter, direct heat side, then keep it warm on the cooler, indirect heat side. If something is cooking too quickly, zip it over to the cooler, indirect heat side for a while.

## TOOLS OF THE TRADE

Here's a list of things you need—and things that can come in really handy—at the grill.

**Photo 1, below:** A long spatula with a wood handle that doesn't get hot; wooden skewers (make sure you soak them for at least 30 minutes before using so they don't ignite); metal skewers for kebabs; tongs for easily moving things around the grill; and a rotisserie attachment, which comes with some souped-up gas grills.

**Photo 2, below:** A fire extinguisher (hey, you can never be too careful); heavy-duty foil for wrapping up hobo packs; quick-light cubes; a chimney starter; aluminum drip pans—great for catching grease at the bottom of the grill to prevent flare-ups and for covering food on the grill; a spray bottle to tame your fire and to nail your neighbor (NEVER SPRAY WATER INTO A GREASE FIRE); a wire brush to scrub your grill before and after every use; and a heavy-duty mitt.

**Photo 3, below:** A cast-iron grill pan for those midwinter nights when it is just too darn cold to grill outside; pastry brushes for basting thick sauces on meats and veggies; a barbecue mop for slathering thinner sauces onto meats (it applies thin sauces better than brushes do); and a squeeze bottle for squirting on sauces or just filling with ketchup to put on the table.

**Photo 4, below:** A fish basket so your fish won't flake apart like crazy and stick to the grill; a vegetable basket to make turning the veggies a snap (How many slices of red pepper can you stand to flip?—and it's good for small stuff such as scallops and shrimp); a rib rack to hold ribs in an upright position so they cook evenly; and cedar planks. If you want to give your food a different flavor, put these on the grill (soak them in water first) and lay your fish or meat on top of them. (Just be careful they don't catch on fire; we admit it, we incinerated a couple.)

# *outdoor* style

GRILLING IS ALL ABOUT EASY, KICK-BACK FUN. The sheer pleasure of being outside is a party-starter in and of itself, so make it easy on yourself. Hot dogs or lobster—anything goes on a glorious day or a tender night. If you want to deck out your backyard like a scene from Provence, go for it—or just lay a blanket on the grass and have a picnic. Move a table next to your garden and admire your blooming flowers. Settle into the chairs on your porch and watch the world go by.

Here are some tips to setting the stage:

When eating outside at night, think of light—you need enough so you can see your friends, the fire, and the food. Put votive candles all around the serving table in small glasses, jelly jars, or painted punched-out coffee cans. You can also use unscented oil lanterns (they're good for more than emergencies) or buy some battery-powered lamps. Drape bushes with white holiday-style lights, or rig up some fun paper lanterns.

If you don't have a picnic table, why not take your kitchen mainstay outside? You can even make a table by putting a slab of plywood—or an old door—on two sawhorses. Collapsible card tables or small TV tables draped with fabric can easily be transformed into nice serving pieces. Make fun tablecloths from burlap bags, straw beach mats, or even colorful sheets. For a kids' table, use funky shower curtains. (You can hose those right off—and maybe the kids too.)

Centerpieces can be flowers snipped from your garden or small potted plants such as petunias or geraniums, which can be planted in your garden after the party. One bright gerbera daisy in a simple vase makes a cheery statement. Lay a blooming branch down the center of the table. Try taking

tendrils of ivy and anchoring or taping them under a center plate, letting the vines cascade down the sides of the table. Make bouquets from blooming herbs. Fill bowls with lemons or colorful stones and shells. Fill baskets with fragrant peaches or colorful cherry tomatoes on the vine.

Buy sturdy dishwasher-safe plastic plates—you can use them again and again. The same goes for plastic glasses. Look for inexpensive silverware at discount stores so you don't have to use the flimsy plastic stuff you'll throw away. Don't feel as if you have to set the table. Put a pail full of knives and forks next to stacks of plates and napkins. Set food out on large platters. Let your guests serve themselves—it makes them feel comfortable and at home.

To make sure everything goes off without a hitch, write a quick game plan for yourself. Jot down your menu (so you don't forget anything), gather serving utensils, and make sure you have enough fuel for the fire, ice for the drinks, and libations aplenty.

The fun about being outside is that you really can create your own environment; you are not limited by the walls of your dining room. One person we know has three separate seating setups in her yard: one with two chairs under a tree; one with four under an umbrella; and one with eight under an awning on the patio. Honestly, each one feels like a totally different room. You know you have achieved success when the sun goes down, the candles flicker, and you are oblivious to anything but the beautiful night and your friends' satisfied smiles after eating a delicious dinner.

11

# nibbles & noshes
## one

# summer rolls
## WITH CHILE DIPPING SAUCE

Makes 12 rolls

DIPPING SAUCE

- 1/4 cup water
- 3 tablespoons rice vinegar
- 1 tablespoon sugar
- 2 teaspoons kosher salt
- 2 tablespoons finely grated carrot
- 1 clove garlic, minced
- 1 scallion (white and green parts), minced
- 1/2 to 1 serrano chile (with seeds), stemmed, halved, and thinly sliced crosswise

ROLLS

- 2 ounces Vietnamese-style rice vermicelli (glass noodles)
- 1 medium carrot, peeled
- 3 medium radishes
- 1 Kirby cucumber, quartered lengthwise and seeded
- 2 scallions (white and green parts), very thinly sliced
- 1/3 cup fresh cilantro
- 1 tablespoon peanut oil
  Juice of 1/2 a lime

- 1 1/2 teaspoons kosher salt
- 12 to 16 6-inch round Vietnamese-style rice spring roll skins
- 12 medium cooked and peeled shrimp, halved lengthwise (about 4 ounces)
- 24 fresh mint leaves (about 1/4 cup)

**1.** Whisk all sauce ingredients in a small bowl. Set sauce aside.
**2.** Bring a pot of water to a boil over high heat and salt it generously. Add the noodles, cover, and turn off the heat. When noodles are soft but not mushy (after about 3 minutes), stir with a fork to separate the strands. Drain in a colander and rinse with cool water. Shake the colander to remove excess water. Put noodles in a large bowl.
**3.** Cut the carrot, radishes, and cucumber into long, thin, matchstick-size strips with a knife or hand-held mandoline. Toss the vegetables with the noodles along with the scallions,

cilantro, peanut oil, lime juice, and salt.
**4.** Fill a large bowl with cold water. Dip a spring roll skin in the water, soaking just until pliable. Place the skin on a work surface and pat very dry with paper towels. (See photos, below, for remaining instructions.) Place roll seam side down on a serving platter and repeat with remaining ingredients to make 12 rolls. Serve with sauce.

## ■ SHOPSMART
Vietnamese rice spring roll skins are also called *galettes de riz* and *banh trang*. They're available in Asian markets, specialty food stores, and online.

## ■ COOK'S NOTE
The rice spring roll skins are very fragile, so having a few extra on hand helps if some tear or soak for too long.

1. Mound 1/4 cup of the vegetable mixture across the bottom center of the spring roll skin and top with 2 shrimp halves and 2 mint leaves for a pretty finish. 2. Fold the edge of the skin closest to you over filling and fold in the sides. 3. Roll tightly to seal.

# edamame
### HUMMUS

Makes 1¼ cups

½ pound frozen shelled
  edamame (green soybeans),
  (about 1½ cups)

⅓ cup water

¼ cup tahini

½ teaspoon finely grated lemon
  zest

  Juice of 1 lemon
  (about 3 tablespoons)

1 clove garlic, peeled and
  smashed

1 teaspoon kosher salt

½ teaspoon ground cumin

¼ teaspoon ground coriander

4 tablespoons extra-virgin
  olive oil

1 tablespoon chopped fresh
  flat-leaf parsley

  Sliced cucumbers, celery sticks,
  cherry tomatoes, or other raw
  vegetables, for dipping

**1.** Boil the soybeans in salted water until tender, about 4 minutes, or microwave, covered, about 2 minutes.

**2.** Puree the soybeans, water, tahini, lemon zest and juice, garlic, salt, cumin, and coriander in a food processor until smooth. With the motor running, slowly drizzle in 3 tablespoons of the olive oil and process until smooth. Transfer the hummus to a bowl and stir in the parsley. (If the dip seems too thick, thin it with a tablespoon or two of water.) Cover and set aside at room temperature about an hour to let the flavors develop. Before serving, drizzle with the remaining olive oil. Serve with the suggested dippers.

*No one will ever guess these delicious dips are so shockingly healthful.*

SMOKY

# eggplant dip

Makes 1 to 1½ cups

2 globe eggplants (about 2½ pounds)

1 clove garlic, peeled

2 teaspoons kosher salt

Juice of 1 lemon (about 3 tablespoons)

¼ cup extra-virgin olive oil

2 tablespoons chopped fresh flat-leaf parsley, mint, basil, or a combination

Grilled pita wedges, sliced cucumbers, bell pepper strips, or sliced fennel, for dipping

**1.** Prepare an outdoor grill with a medium-hot fire.

**2.** Pierce the eggplants six or seven times with a fork. Grill the eggplants, with the grill cover closed, turning occasionally, until completely soft and the skin chars, for 30 to 40 minutes. Wrap the eggplants in foil and set aside to cool. When cool enough to handle, peel the skin and discard. (This can be done a day in advance.) Drain any excess liquid or the dip will be too thin.

**3.** Smash the garlic clove, sprinkle with 1 teaspoon of the salt, and, with the flat side of a large knife, mash and smear the mixture to a coarse paste. Whisk the eggplant, garlic, lemon juice, and the remaining salt in a medium bowl until evenly mixed but still a little chunky. Gradually whisk in the olive oil, starting with a few drops and adding the rest in a slow, steady stream. Stir in the herbs. Cover and refrigerate about an hour to let the flavors develop. Serve with the suggested dippers.

## COOK'S NOTE

Take advantage of a cooling grill. Place a couple of eggplants on a hot grill after you have cooked a meal and close the cover. The eggplants cook slowly as the grill cools, and you don't need to fuss over them. Refrigerate the cooked eggplants for a day or two until you are ready to make the dip.

## SHOPSMART

Globe eggplants are the familiar purple pear-shaped ones. Choose eggplants on the smaller side—they tend to be less bitter. Lightly press the eggplant with your finger. If it bounces back, you've got a ripe one; if it leaves an impression, it's too ripe.

## SPICY THAI-STYLE
# pineapple wraps

Makes 12 wraps

    Juice of 2 limes (about ¼ cup)

2  teaspoons sugar

2  teaspoons chile paste, such as *sambal oelek* (see ShopSmart, right)

2  teaspoons fish sauce

2  cups roasted peanuts or cashews, roughly chopped

⅔  cup roughly chopped fresh cilantro (leaves and stems)

12  Bibb lettuce leaves (about 1 head)

    Half a medium fresh pineapple, peeled, cored, and cut into bite-size chunks (about 3 cups) (see page 274)

    Kosher salt

**1.** Whisk the lime juice, sugar, chile paste, and fish sauce in a bowl until the sugar dissolves. Add the peanuts and cilantro and stir until evenly dressed with the sauce.

**2.** When ready to serve, arrange the lettuce leaves on a large platter. Put about ¼ cup of pineapple in each leaf and season with salt to taste. Top the pineapple with the nut mixture. Serve, letting your guests wrap (or fold) each lettuce leaf to enclose the filling.

### COOK'S NOTE

It is important to chop the nuts by hand—not in a food processor. Machine-chopped nuts will be overworked and pasty. The dish is so much better when the nuts have a distinct texture.

### SHOPSMART

*Sambals* are potent Indonesian condiments packed with chiles. There are different kinds, but the slightly tangy *sambal oelek* is a blend of hot red chiles, salt, vinegar or tamarind, and sometimes garlic. Other Asian chile pastes are suitable substitutes.

We like to get guests snacking while we set up the grill, and this dish is ideal. On a hot day it is totally refreshing with a cool drink. Friends get into wrapping and rolling while we get prepped for grilling.

# pool party

Limeade

Summer Salsa

Guacamole

Tortilla Chips

Jicama Sticks

Asparagus & Endive

Skordalia

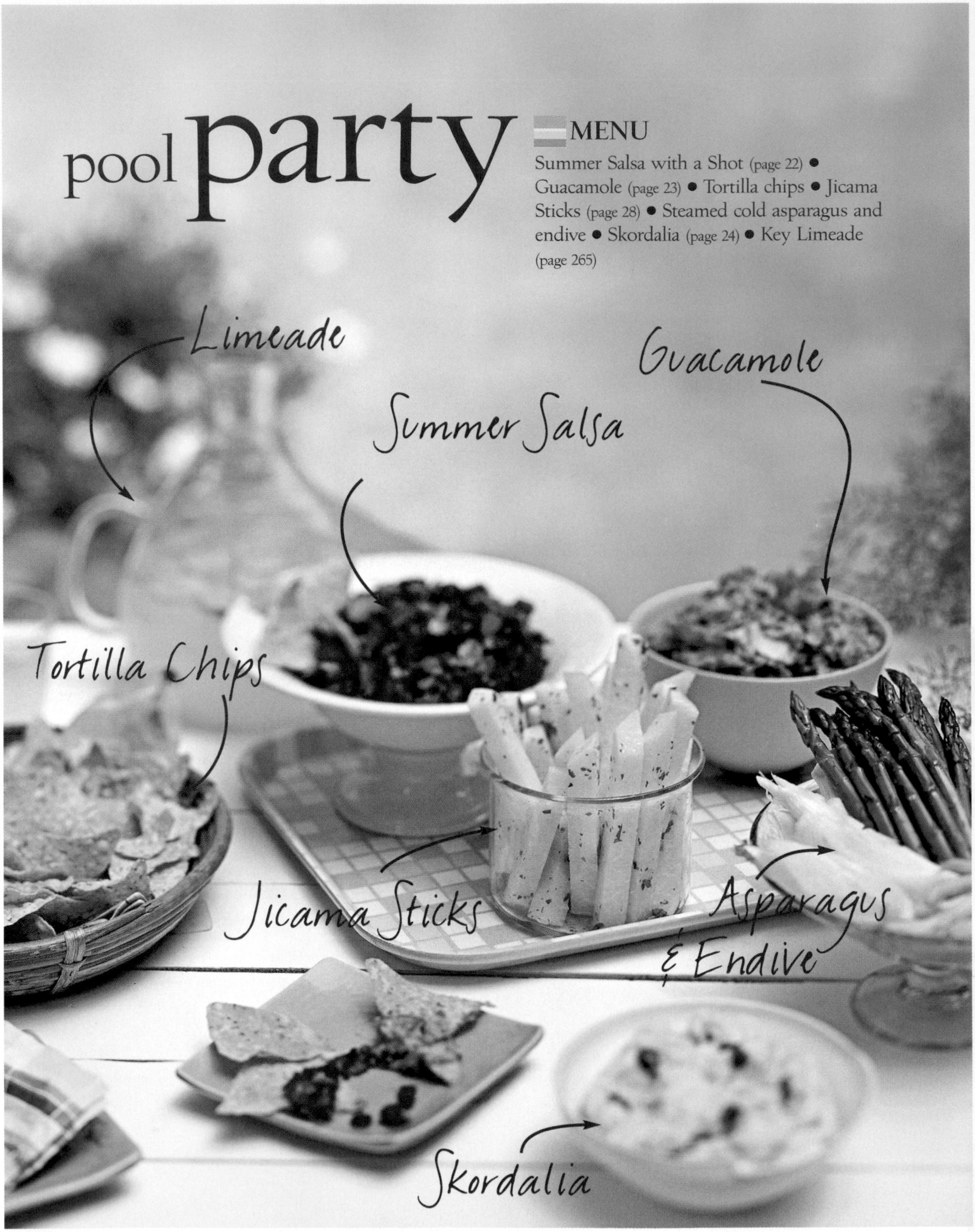

Summertime and the living is easy.
What's better than hanging poolside
and snacking on chips and salsa?

# summer salsa
## WITH A SHOT

4 to 6 servings

- 1 clove garlic
- 2 teaspoons kosher salt, plus additional for seasoning
- 4 medium ripe tomatoes, cored and diced
- 1/4 medium red onion, finely diced
- 1 jalapeño, stemmed and minced (with seeds for more heat)
- 1/4 cup chopped fresh cilantro
- 1 to 2 tablespoons silver tequila (optional)

  White corn tortilla chips, for dipping

**1.** Smash the garlic clove, sprinkle with 1 teaspoon of the salt, and, with the flat side of a large knife, mash and smear the mixture to a coarse paste. Mix the garlic, tomatoes, onion, jalapeño, and cilantro in a serving bowl. Add the tequila, if desired, and season with the remaining salt, adding more to taste if necessary.

**2.** Serve immediately or cover with plastic wrap and set aside for 1 hour at room temperature. Serve with the tortilla chips.

## KNOW-HOW

Why mash instead of mince garlic? For raw dips and sauces, when the garlic is reduced to a smooth paste, it flavors a dish more evenly and less harshly than if added in pieces. Another reason to love this "smushing": It's quicker than mincing.

## SHOPSMART

The best tomatoes—juicy with a bright, summer-sweet taste—are vine-ripened. A cue for great taste is a deep, rich color all the way up to the stem, but a full tomato aroma counts too. Don't be shy: It's OK to sniff a tomato. Store your tomatoes at room temperature, not in the refrigerator; chilling deadens their taste and mars their texture.

When summer tomatoes are at their peak, nothing is better than fresh salsa. We love the unexpected shot of tequila in this one. Salsa is so versatile; besides its starring role with chips, it's fabulous on grilled chicken or fish, or even burgers.

# guacamole

4 to 6 servings

2 cloves garlic, peeled

2 teaspoons kosher salt

$1/4$ medium red onion, minced

3 ripe Hass avocados

$1/2$ cup grape or cherry tomatoes, diced

$1/4$ cup roughly chopped fresh cilantro

1 to 2 jalapeño or serrano chiles (with seeds for more heat, without seeds for less), stemmed and minced

Juice of 1 lime (about 2 tablespoons)

White corn tortilla chips, for dipping

**1.** Smash the garlic cloves, sprinkle with 1 teaspoon of the salt, and, with the side of a large knife, mash and smear the mixture to a coarse paste. Put in a bowl with onion.

**2.** Halve the avocados lengthwise; carefully tap your knife into the pits, twist, and lift them out. Knock the knife on the edge of the counter and the pit will drop off. Score the flesh with the tip of a knife and use a spoon to scoop the avocado from the peel into the onion mixture.

**3.** Mix the tomatoes, cilantro, chiles, lime juice, and the remaining 1 teaspoon salt with the avocados with a rubber spatula or large fork just until combined, keeping the guacamole chunky. Serve immediately with tortilla chips. (Guacamole's more than just a dip. Use it as a spread for sandwiches and wraps or as a topping for grilled fish or vegetables.)

## SHOPSMART

A ripe avocado will yield to gentle pressure. Skin should be black, with almost no traces of green. Tuck hard avocados in a brown paper bag at room temperature with an apple or banana and they will ripen faster.

## KNOW-HOW

The heat level of jalapeños can vary widely. Some are fiery, others tame, so it's a good idea to add them according to your taste. A chile's seeds harbor a lot of the heat, so if the chile is a scorcher, hold them back—and if you want to raise the heat level, add more of them.

# skordalia
## (GREEK POTATO-GARLIC DIP)

Makes 3 cups

### Dip

1 pound russet potatoes, scrubbed (about 2 large potatoes)

8 cloves garlic

4 teaspoons kosher salt

3/4 cup whole blanched almonds

1/2 cup extra-virgin olive oil

1/2 cup water

1/3 cup freshly squeezed lemon juice (about 2 juicy lemons)

2 tablespoons white wine vinegar

Freshly ground black pepper

### Lemon-Herb Oil

1/4 cup extra-virgin olive oil

1/4 cup loosely packed fresh oregano leaves

2 strips lemon peel (about 2 1/2 inches long), roughly chopped

1/4 teaspoon crushed red pepper

Sliced fennel, red or yellow bell pepper strips, cucumbers, or pita chips, for dipping

**1.** Preheat the oven to 400°F. Bake the potatoes until fork tender, about 1 hour. Cool.
**2.** Meanwhile, make the Lemon-Herb Oil: Put the olive oil, oregano, lemon peel, and red pepper in a small saucepan. Cook over medium-low heat, swirling the pan occasionally, until fragrant and the oregano leaves are crisp, about 10 minutes. Set aside.
**3.** On a cutting board smash the garlic cloves, sprinkle with the salt, and, with the flat side of a large knife, mash and smear the mixture to a coarse paste. Process the garlic, almonds, and olive oil in a food processor into a paste. Peel potatoes and discard the skins and break the potatoes into pieces. Lightly pulse the potatoes into the nut mixture, adding the water, lemon juice, vinegar, and black pepper to taste until just incorporated into a thick dip. Don't overprocess or the dip will be gummy. Spread the dip on a large serving dish. Drizzle with the Lemon-Herb Oil and serve surrounded by dippers.

### KNOW-HOW
To strip fresh oregano from the stem, pull the leaves down while running the stem through your fingers.

Everyone loves this twist on classic chips and dip. The spuds are creamy and the chips are healthy. A familiar dish turned out in a whole new way is always a winner. Good food with a twist—we are all over that.

# spinach & artichoke dip

6 servings

1 large egg yolk

¹/₄ cup heavy cream

¹/₂ teaspoon kosher salt

Pinch freshly grated nutmeg

Dash hot sauce

2 tablespoons extra-virgin olive oil

4 scallions (white and green parts), thinly sliced

2 cloves garlic, peeled and minced

1 10-ounce bag fresh baby spinach, roughly chopped

2 6-ounce jars marinated artichokes, drained and chopped

6 ounces cream cheese, cut into small pieces

4 ounces feta cheese, crumbled (about ¹/₂ cup)

Tortilla chips, toasted bread, and/or red and yellow bell pepper strips, for dipping

**1.** Preheat the oven to 350°F. Lightly oil a 4-cup gratin dish. Whisk the egg yolk, cream, salt, nutmeg, and hot sauce in a small bowl. Set aside.

**2.** Heat the olive oil in a large skillet over medium heat. Add the scallions and garlic. Cook until the garlic is fragrant and the scallions begin to soften, about 2 minutes. Add the spinach and artichokes and cook, stirring, until the spinach wilts, about 3 minutes. Add the cream cheese and stir until melted, about 1 minute.

**3.** Remove the pan from the heat and stir in the cream mixture. Fold about three-fourths of the feta cheese into the dip and transfer it to the prepared gratin dish. Scatter the remaining cheese on top. Bake until the center of the dip is just set and the edges are golden brown, about 30 minutes. Serve warm or at room temperature with the tortilla chips, toasted bread, or pepper strips.

## SHOPSMART

On your trip down the spice aisle, opt for whole nutmeg over ground. Grate it just before using for maximum freshness.

## STYLE

Before serving, wrap the hot gratin dish in a pretty napkin or cloth to add a splash of color and to protect your guests' fingers from getting burned.

# EXTREME
# BBQ'd nachos

6 to 8 servings

1½ cups shredded North
Carolina-Style BBQ Pulled
Pork (see recipe, page 81) or
Pulled Turkey Legs (see recipe,
page 71) or leftover grilled
chicken

2 cups Kansas City-Style BBQ
Sauce (see recipe, page 218)
or store-bought sauce

1 12-ounce can pinto beans,
drained and rinsed

Juice of 1 lime (about
2 tablespoons)

1 tablespoon Cajun Rub
(see recipe, page 228)

Kosher salt

2 ripe medium tomatoes,
roughly chopped

2 pickled jalapeños, chopped

½ cup loosely packed fresh
cilantro, roughly chopped,
plus additional for garnish

Freshly ground black pepper

7 ounces white corn tortilla
chips (half of a large bag)

⅓ cup sour cream, plus
additional for garnish

12 ounces shredded cheddar
cheese (about 3 cups)

**1.** Position a rack about 6 inches
from the broiler and preheat to
high. Toss the meat with 1 cup of
the barbecue sauce and set aside.
Coarsely mash the beans in a
bowl with the lime juice, about
half the Cajun Rub, and salt to
taste. In another bowl, toss the
tomatoes with the jalapeños and
the ½ cup cilantro. Season with
additional salt and black pepper
to taste.
**2.** Scatter half the chips in an
ovenproof 13x9-inch baking dish.
Scatter the meat, beans, the
⅓ cup sour cream, and about
half the tomato mixture over the
chips. Cover with the remaining
chips, then scatter the remaining
tomatoes, sauce, and Cajun Rub
evenly over the chips. Sprinkle
the shredded cheese over all.
**3.** Broil the nachos until the
cheese melts and begins to
brown, about 7 minutes. Serve
warm, garnished with additional
sour cream and cilantro.

This decadent use
of the rewards of
good barbecue—
tangy sauce and
smoky, tender
meats—is a total
WOW! We keep
some sauce and
meat in the
freezer so we can
nosh on these
nachos anytime.

27

# jicama
## STICKS

4 to 6 servings

1 medium jicama (1 to 1¼ pounds)

Juice of 2 limes (about 4 tablespoons)

2 tablespoons extra-virgin olive oil

½ teaspoon kosher salt

½ to 1 serrano chile, with seeds, minced

1 tablespoon chopped fresh cilantro

**1.** Peel the jicama and slice into finger-size pieces. Put in a serving bowl and toss with the lime juice, olive oil, and salt. Add the serrano to taste, depending on the heat of your chiles. Cover and refrigerate until slightly chilled and lightly marinated, about 1 hour.

**2.** Stir the cilantro into the jicama and serve.

## SHOPSMART
Choose jicama that are heavy for their size. A light jicama will be woody and dry. Avoid those with any soft or moldy spots.

## STYLE
Serve with toothpicks if your party is formal; otherwise, these are finger food. Make sure you have napkins on hand—and margaritas too!

Supermarket produce sections have had a serious makeover in the decade Food Network has been on the air, which makes shopping so much more fun. Exotic fruits and veggies such as jicama, papaya, lemongrass, and fresh herbs—once a rarity—are now familiar. Can't find something? Do what we do: Make friends with your grocers. They're happy to get stuff for you.

NEW ORLEANS-STYLE
# BBQ shrimp

6 to 8 servings

- ½ cup extra-virgin olive oil
- 8 tablespoons unsalted butter
- 12 cloves garlic, peeled and smashed (about 1 head)
- 2 bay leaves
- 4 sprigs fresh thyme
- 1 pound large shrimp, shell on and deveined (see page 270)
- 1 teaspoon Worcestershire sauce
- 1 tablespoon kosher salt
- 1 tablespoon sweet paprika
- ½ to ¾ teaspoon cayenne pepper
- 2 tablespoons dry sherry
- 3 lemons, cut into wedges

  Loaf of crusty bread

**1.** Preheat the oven to 350°F. Heat the olive oil, butter, garlic, bay leaves, and thyme in a large ovenproof skillet over medium heat until the butter melts and the garlic and herbs are fragrant, about 5 minutes.

**2.** Toss shrimp, Worcestershire sauce, salt, paprika, and cayenne together in a bowl. Add to skillet along with the sherry and transfer to the oven. Bake until shrimp turn pink and curl, about 10 minutes. Transfer to a serving dish and serve with lemon wedges and lots of bread for sopping up the sauce.

## SHOPSMART

Shrimp come in a multitude of sizes, and it can be confusing, since one fishmonger's large may be another's medium. The best way to purchase them is by the number per pound—for example, 16 to 20 per pound for large. Most shrimp are frozen and thawed before selling. It often pays off to buy frozen and defrost them yourself.

## STYLE

Serve in a rimmed platter or shallow bowl to keep the shrimp bathed in the tasty sauce. Give your guests small plates or bowls to discard the shells (though the adventurous may want to eat them shells and all). Be sure to offer lots of napkins.

## COOK'S NOTE

BBQ shrimp is a Big Easy classic. Although it's not cooked over a live fire, it's the spicy, finger-licking sauce that gives it its BBQ pedigree. Whatever you call it, it's amazing.

# oysters on the half shell
## WITH TWO SAUCES

4 to 6 servings

1 to 2 dozen medium oysters such as Bluepoint, Chesapeake, Hood Island, or Wellfleet, shucked

### MIGNONETTE

1 tablespoon coarsely ground white pepper

1 medium shallot, very finely minced

1/4 cup white wine vinegar

### SOY-LIME SAUCE

1/4 cup soy sauce

Juice of 1 lime (about 2 tablespoons)

2 tablespoons finely sliced scallion (white and green parts)

1 teaspoon finely grated fresh ginger

1 clove garlic, peeled and finely minced

1/4 teaspoon chile paste, such as *sambal oelek*

### WHITE MIGNONETTE

Whisk the sauce ingredients in a small bowl. Serve with chilled oysters.

### SPICY SOY-LIME SAUCE

Whisk the sauce ingredients in a small bowl. Serve with chilled oysters.

## ▆ SHOPSMART

Oysters are always sold by place name, since the waters in which they grow contribute to their unique taste. East Coast oysters tend to be brinier than their Pacific cousins, but both are equally tasty. Serve different kinds together for a fun tasting experience.

## ▆ KNOW-HOW

Rinse the oysters before you open them, but never wash them once they're opened—you'll wash all the flavor off. There may be a little grit in the shell once they're opened, but just scoop it out with the tip of your oyster knife.

## ▆ COOK'S NOTE

Freshly ground pepper is the essential ingredient in a classic mignonette sauce. It's best to grind your own so the flavor's fresh and bright. Adjust your pepper mill to a coarse grind or use a spice mill to get just the right consistency.

1. Lay an oyster rounded side down on a towel on the counter; angle the shell hinge toward you.
2. Pry an oyster knife or church key bottle opener into the hinge. Rock the knife gently up and down to pop open the shell.

3. Slip the knife along the shell to free the oyster, taking care not to lose the delicious liquor.
4. Serve immediately or refrigerate up to 4 hours.

# little dishes from the grill
# two

WARM GOAT CHEESE WRAPPED IN GRAPE LEAVES • BLT CROSTINI • BACON-WRAPPED DATES WITH MANCHEGO • CHICKEN LIVER, PANCETTA & LEMON KEBABS • INDIAN-SPICED CHICKEN WINGS • THAI CURRIED SCALLOPS IN BANANA LEAVES • BEEF SATAY • FIG & GOAT CHEESE SALAD • PORK PINCHOS • ONION, PEAR & BLUE CHEESE PIZZAS • ROASTED GARLIC & ARUGULA PIZZAS • BABY ARTICHOKE & POTATO SALAD WITH CHEESE • VEGETABLE NAPOLEONS WITH TOMATO & BASIL DRESSING

# warm goat cheese
### WRAPPED IN GRAPE LEAVES

6 to 8 servings

- 2 or 3 large jarred, brined grape leaves, stems trimmed
- 8 ounces Bûcheron cheese, rind on (see ShopSmart, right)

  Slightly heaping ½ teaspoon anise seeds or fennel seeds

  Slightly heaping ¼ teaspoon crushed red pepper

- 2 tablespoons sambuca or ouzo (optional)
- 2 tablespoons extra-virgin olive oil

  Baguette slices, for serving

**1.** Soak the grape leaves in water for 5 minutes, then drain. Sprinkle the cheese with the anise and crushed red pepper. Wrap a grape leaf around the bottom of the cheese. If using the sambuca, place the cheese on a rimmed plate and sprinkle with sambuca. Wrap the top of the cheese with another grape leaf or two, using just enough leaves to form a single layer, then refrigerate for at least 1 hour.
**2.** Prepare an outdoor grill with a medium-low fire. Brush the cheese bundle with the olive oil and grill, turning, until the cheese is a little oozy and the leaves are slightly charred, about 4 minutes. Transfer to a plate and serve with baguette slices.

## ▇ SHOPSMART
Bûcheron is a mild goat cheese sold in rounds. The rind is edible and can be left on for this recipe. If you can't find it, substitute any disk of soft, mild goat cheese.

## ▇ COOK'S NOTE
Brined grape leaves range in size, and you don't know what yours will be until you open the jar. If the leaves are really huge, you may need to trim out the thick stem from the middle of the leaf—it's too tough to eat.

1. Place seasoned cheese on top of a grape leaf.
2. Bring points of grape leaf up around the cheese and press gently to get leaf to stick to cheese.
3. Wrap top of cheese with another grape leaf or two, using just enough leaves to form a single layer.
4. Don't worry if leaves don't hold fast; they'll stick once cheese is grilled.

BLT
# crostini

4 servings

1 medium head escarole (about 12 ounces)

Kosher salt

Freshly ground black pepper

8 slices lean bacon

¼ cup extra-virgin olive oil, plus additional for grilling

4 ½-inch-thick slices sourdough bread

1 ripe medium tomato, halved

4 lemon wedges, for serving

**1.** Preheat an outdoor grill with a medium fire. Soak four 6-inch wooden skewers in water for 30 minutes before grilling.
**2.** Remove wilted or tough outer leaves from escarole, then quarter head lengthwise through the core so the leaves hold together in wedges. Lay 2 slices of bacon on a cutting board and place a wedge of escarole on top. Season with salt and black pepper to taste. Wrap bacon tightly around the escarole and secure with a skewer. Repeat with the remaining escarole and bacon.

**3.** Brush bundles with ¼ cup olive oil. Grill bundles seam side down and covered with a disposable aluminum pan, turning, until bacon is cooked and crisp, about 12 minutes.
**4.** Meanwhile, lightly brush bread with additional olive oil, season with salt and black pepper to taste, and grill until lightly charred, about 1 minute per side. Remove and immediately rub toasts with cut side of a tomato to saturate with all the tomato's juices. Discard skins. Top each crostini with an escarole bundle and serve with a lemon wedge.

# bacon-wrapped dates
WITH MANCHEGO

4 servings

12 whole dates

3 ounces Manchego cheese

12 slices lean bacon

Kosher salt

Freshly ground black pepper

**1.** Prepare an outdoor grill with an indirect medium fire.
**2.** Slice into the dates lengthwise, just deep enough so that you can pull out the pits with your fingers. Discard the pits. Cut cheese into sticks to fit into the dates. Tuck some cheese inside each date, pressing to enclose the cheese. Wrap a slice of bacon

around each date, trim all but an inch of overlap, and secure with a toothpick. Season with salt and black pepper to taste.
**3.** Grill, turning as needed, until the bacon is cooked through and crisp, about 10 minutes. Transfer to a platter. Serve warm or at room temperature.

CHICKEN LIVER, PANCETTA & LEMON
# kebabs

6 servings

1 pound whole chicken livers (about 6 livers)

½ cup dry Marsala

1 head garlic, halved crosswise

8 long sprigs fresh rosemary, to use as skewers (see Know-How, right)

8 ounces pancetta or slab bacon, cut into twelve 1-inch cubes

2 lemons, cut into 6 wedges each, seeds removed

Olive oil, for brushing

Kosher salt

Freshly ground black pepper

Grilled sliced sourdough bread (optional)

**1.** Rinse and pat the livers dry. Separate the two lobes of each liver, if connected, and trim any membrane or green bits. Put livers in a bowl and pour Marsala over them. Roughly chop 4 garlic cloves together with the stripped leaves of 2 of the rosemary sprigs, then toss with livers. Cover and refrigerate at least 1 hour or overnight.

**2.** Put the pancetta and remaining garlic into a saucepan with cold water to cover. Bring to a boil over high heat, then immediately drain, discarding the garlic.

**3.** Thread remaining 6 rosemary sprigs with lemon, pancetta, liver, lemon, pancetta, and liver. Refrigerate until ready to grill.

**4.** Preheat an outdoor grill with a medium-hot fire.

**5.** Brush the skewers with olive oil, season generously with salt and black pepper to taste, and grill, turning as needed, until the pancetta crisps and livers are cooked but not too firm, 6 to 8 minutes total. Serve immediately with grilled bread, if desired.

## ▬ KNOW-HOW

Using rosemary as skewers takes a bit of work, but the flavor it imparts is worth it. Make sure you buy rosemary with long, woody stems. It will be easier to thread the pieces of food on the stems if you make a hole through them with a skewer first. Once you've made the holes, just thread the pieces onto the rosemary, pulling the bottom end through first.

# INDIAN-SPICED
# chicken wings

4 servings

8 tablespoons unsalted butter

1 teaspoon crushed red pepper

2 slightly heaping tablespoons Madras curry powder

1 teaspoon ground cumin

1/4 teaspoon ground cinnamon

1/2 medium onion, grated

1 1-inch piece peeled fresh ginger, finely grated

3 tablespoons freshly squeezed lime juice (about 1 1/2 limes)

2 tablespoons plain whole-milk yogurt

1 tablespoon kosher salt

2 pounds chicken wings, wing tips removed (see Know-How, right)

Mango or other chutney, for dipping

**1.** In the morning or up to two days before grilling, melt 4 tablespoons butter in a small skillet over medium heat, add the crushed red pepper, and cook, stirring, until fragrant, about 10 seconds. Add the curry powder, cumin, and cinnamon and cook, stirring, until fragrant, about 1 minute more. Add the onion and grated ginger and cook, stirring, to make a smooth, fragrant paste, about 2 to 3 minutes. Put in a large bowl and cool completely.

**2.** Stir 1 tablespoon of the lime juice, the yogurt, and salt into the curry mixture. Pat chicken dry and toss with the curry mixture to coat evenly. Cover and refrigerate for at least 6 hours or up to 24 hours.

**3.** Prepare an outdoor grill with a medium-hot fire, with both direct and indirect heat sources.

**4.** Melt the remaining butter in a small saucepan and whisk in the remaining lime juice. Grill the wings over direct heat, basting with the lime butter, until golden brown and lightly charred, about 4 minutes per side. Move the chicken to indirect heat and continue cooking, turning occasionally, until skin is crisp and the chicken is cooked through, about 4 minutes more. Serve warm or at room temperature with chutney for dipping.

## ■ KNOW-HOW

To trim the wing tips, lay a chicken wing flat on your cutting board. Use your knife to find the joint between the tip and middle section of the wing and slice through to remove the tip. Repeat with remaining wings; discard tips.

*We love this recipe. It's made with easy-to-get ingredients blended just right for tender wings that taste and look amazing.*

# thai curried scallops
## IN BANANA LEAVES

6 servings

1½ ounces Vietnamese-style rice vermicelli (glass noodles)

2 teaspoons peanut oil

1 13½-ounce can unsweetened coconut milk (avoid shaking the can)

1 to 1½ teaspoons prepared Thai red curry paste

1 6-inch stalk fresh lemongrass, smashed

1 tablespoon fish sauce

2 teaspoons firmly packed light brown sugar

Juice of 1 lime (about 2 tablespoons)

1 to 2 large banana leaves, rinsed and patted dry (see ShopSmart, right)

12 large sea scallops, foot removed, if necessary, and patted dry (about 1 pound)

Kosher salt

1 lime, very thinly sliced

**1.** Soak the noodles in hot water until softened and pliable, about 5 minutes. Drain and toss with the peanut oil.

**2.** Skim 2 tablespoons of the thick coconut cream from the top of the canned coconut milk and add it to a medium skillet along with the curry paste. Cook and stir over medium-high heat until fragrant and bubbly, about 2 minutes. Stir in the remaining coconut milk, the lemongrass, fish sauce, and brown sugar and boil, stirring occasionally, until the sauce is thick, about 6 minutes. Remove the lemongrass and discard and stir in the lime juice.

**3.** Prepare an outdoor grill with a medium-hot fire.

**4.** Cut the banana leaves into 6x8-inch rectangles. Place a small mound of the noodles in the center of a leaf, top with 2 tablespoons sauce, then place 2 scallops on the noodles and season with salt. Drizzle with another tablespoon of sauce and top with a very thin slice of lime. Fold the ends of the leaf over to form a square package and secure with a toothpick. Repeat with the remaining leaves and ingredients to make 6 packages.

**5.** Grill without turning just until the scallops are cooked through, about 8 minutes—take care not to overcook. (If you poke an instant-read thermometer through the packet into a scallop, the temperature should be between 115°F and 120°F.)

## ▮▮SHOPSMART

Banana leaves are used in both Asian and Latin cuisines and can be found in markets with a focus on those ingredients. Look for dry packages of leaves in the freezer section. It's worth seeking them out—they add an exceptional flavor that works wonderfully with spicy foods. In a pinch, use foil instead.

## ▮▮COOK'S NOTE

Time your fire to be ready when the packages are ready. If you think you will need extra time forming the packages, don't start the fire yet. Avoid refrigerating the packages or the noodles become gummy.

# beef satay

Makes 12 skewers

SATAY

1 pound beef flank steak, very cold (see Cook's Note, right)

3/4 cup canned unsweetened coconut milk

2 to 3 tablespoons prepared Thai red or massaman curry paste (use the larger amount for a spicier sauce)

2 to 3 tablespoons firmly packed light brown sugar (use the larger amount if you are using all the curry paste)

1 tablespoon fish sauce

Vegetable oil

PEANUT SAUCE

Makes about 1 cup

2 tablespoons coconut cream, skimmed from the top of the canned coconut milk

1 to 2 tablespoons prepared Thai red curry or massaman curry paste (use the larger amount for a spicier sauce)

1 cup unsweetened canned coconut milk

1/4 cup chunky peanut butter

2 tablespoons firmly packed light brown sugar

1 tablespoon soy sauce

1 tablespoon freshly squeezed lemon juice

**1.** Slice the steak against the grain into very thin strips that are about 1 inch wide. Whisk the coconut milk, curry paste, brown sugar, and fish sauce in a large bowl. Add the steak and mix to coat evenly. Cover and set aside to marinate at room temperature for 1 hour or refrigerate for up to 24 hours.
**2.** If using wooden skewers, soak in water for 30 minutes before grilling. Prepare an outdoor grill with a hot fire.
**3.** Thread beef onto skewers and lightly brush with oil. Working in batches, grill the satays, turning as needed, until the steak chars and is just cooked through, 2 to 4 minutes total, taking care to not overcook. Transfer the skewers to a serving platter and serve with peanut sauce.

PEANUT SAUCE
Cook coconut cream in a small saucepan over medium heat until shiny and sizzling, about 2 minutes. Add curry paste and cook and stir until fragrant, about 1 minute. Whisk in the coconut milk, peanut butter, brown sugar, soy sauce, and lemon juice. Bring to a boil, then simmer, stirring, until thickened, about 10 minutes more. Transfer the sauce to a small serving bowl and cool to room temperature.

## ■COOK'S NOTE
Place the steak in the freezer about 30 minutes to get it very cold before slicing. It will be much easier to get the thin slices you need for satay.

## ■KNOW-HOW
Soaking wooden skewers in water keeps them from catching fire. Another trick for grilling wooden skewers is to lay a long strip of double-folded aluminum foil on the grill grate. Arrange the skewers on the grill so the exposed part of the wood rests on the foil; they stay cool and are easier to turn.

# fig & goat cheese
SALAD

4 servings

DRESSING

1 tablespoon red wine vinegar

2 teaspoons Dijon mustard

½ teaspoon kosher salt

Freshly ground black pepper

3 tablespoons extra-virgin olive oil

3 tablespoons walnut oil

1 tablespoon finely minced shallot (about ½ shallot)

1 teaspoon minced fresh thyme

SALAD

8 ripe black or green fresh figs, halved lengthwise

Olive oil for brushing

Kosher salt

Freshly ground black pepper

8 long, angled baguette slices

1 medium head frisée, washed, dried, leaves separated, and torn (about 8 cups)

1 bunch watercress, washed, dried, and stems trimmed (about 3 cups)

¼ cup walnuts, toasted and roughly chopped

4 ounces slightly aged goat cheese, such as Bûcheron, rind trimmed and cheese crumbled

**1.** Prepare an outdoor grill with a medium-hot fire.

**2.** For the walnut dressing: Whisk the vinegar, mustard, salt, and black pepper in a small bowl. Gradually whisk in the oils, starting with a few drops and then adding the rest in a steady stream, to make a smooth, slightly thick dressing. Stir in the shallot and thyme.

**3.** For the salad: Brush the figs lightly with the olive oil and grill, turning as needed, until soft and lightly charred, about 6 minutes. Season with salt and black pepper to taste. Brush the sliced bread with olive oil and grill until lightly toasted.

**4.** While the figs grill, toss the frisée, watercress, and walnuts with the dressing. Add the goat cheese and toss lightly to keep the cheese from breaking up. Divide the salad among 4 plates, top with the warm figs, and serve with toasted bread.

## ■COOK'S NOTE

Walnut oil is expensive, but it has an assertive flavor—so a little goes a long way. All nut oils are highly perishable, so once opened, keep them in the refrigerator and take a little taste before using to make sure they're still good.

## ■SHOPSMART

The window for fig lovers to savor this luscious fruit has grown from a couple of short weeks to a season that spans from spring through fall. Whether choosing pale green or purple-black, select figs that are plump and heavy, that yield slightly when squeezed. If there is a bit of nectar at the stem, all the better. Store figs in the refrigerator, loosely arranged on a paper towel-lined plate—and enjoy them within a couple days of buying them.

# tapas style

## MENU

Pork Pinchos (page 46) • Almonds • Mixed olives
• Warm Goat Cheese Wrapped in Grape Leaves (page 35)
• New Orleans-Style BBQ Shrimp (page 29)

Whether called tapas, mezze, dim sum, or grazing, meals of little dishes are a wonderful way to party. Bites can be simple or grand, served in concert or at a laid-back pace. Keep it relaxed. Set out plates and platters and let folks help themselves. Round out the party with our White Fall Sangria (page 257) and you will be a happy host.

# pork pinchos

4 to 6 servings

6 cloves garlic, peeled

1 tablespoon kosher salt

1 tablespoon hot Spanish smoked paprika

2 teaspoons ground coriander

2 teaspoons ground cumin

2 teaspoons *ras al hanout* (see recipe, page 229)

2 tablespoons extra-virgin olive oil, plus additional for brushing

1½ tablespoons sherry vinegar

Freshly ground black pepper

1 pound boneless pork shoulder (see ShopSmart, right)

**1.** In the morning or a day before grilling, smash the garlic cloves, sprinkle with the salt, and, with the flat side of a large knife, mash and smear the mixture to a coarse paste. Mix the garlic paste and the paprika, coriander, cumin, and *ras al hanout* in a medium bowl. Whisk in the 2 tablespoons olive oil, vinegar, and black pepper to taste.

**2.** Trim excess fat from the pork and cut into 1-inch cubes. Add the pork to the bowl, tossing until all the pieces are evenly coated with the spice paste. Cover and refrigerate for at least 6 hours or overnight.

**3.** If using wooden skewers, soak them in water for 30 minutes before Step 4. Prepare an outdoor grill with a hot fire.

**4.** Thread 3 to 4 pieces of pork onto each skewer. Lightly brush the pork with oil. Grill the skewers, turning once, until the meat chars but is still moist, about 5 minutes per side.

## ■ SHOPSMART

When making kebabs from pork shoulder, ask your butcher for "Boston butt." We love this economical yet rich cut for kebabs. It has more meat and less sinew and cartilage than the "picnic" cut from the shoulder, so you'll be able to get bigger, meatier chunks.

Essentially, "pinchos" is Spanish for finger foods that don't require a plate—just our style.

ONION, PEAR & BLUE CHEESE
# pizzas

Makes 4 10-inch pizzas

- 1 recipe pizza dough (see recipe, page 48)
- 4 tablespoons unsalted butter
- 3 large yellow onions, thinly sliced
- 2 teaspoons herbes de Provence
- 1½ teaspoons kosher salt, plus additional for seasoning
- 2 ripe pears
  Extra-virgin olive oil
- 8 ounces blue cheese, such as Roquefort, crumbled

**1.** Make pizza dough through Step 2 on page 48.

**2.** While dough is rising, melt butter in a large nonstick skillet over medium-high heat. Pour off about 1 tablespoon butter and set aside. Add onions, herbes de Provence, and 1½ teaspoons salt and cook, stirring occasionally, until onions are juicy, about 5 minutes. Reduce heat to medium and cook until onions are very soft, about 25 minutes. Reduce heat to medium-low and cook until onions are jamlike, about 25 minutes more.

**3.** To prepare a charcoal grill: Fill a chimney starter with briquettes and heat until lightly covered with ash. Scatter a layer of cold hardwood charcoal over one-quarter of the grill, carefully spread the hot briquettes on top, and heat to medium-high heat. Set the grill grate on top and cover, making sure that all the vents are open, and heat for 5 minutes. (Or preheat half of a gas grill, covered, for direct and indirect grilling.)

**4.** Dust your work surface lightly with flour. Divide dough evenly into 4 balls and press them into the flour, flipping to dust both sides. Working with 1 piece at a time, hold dough up like a steering wheel and rotate and stretch it to make an 8-inch disk. Put it on a piece of plastic wrap and cover with a kitchen towel. Repeat with remaining dough.

**5.** Core and thinly slice the pears and toss with the reserved butter. Brush 1 disk of dough very lightly with oil. Place the disk oil side down directly over the hot coals. Cook, rotating frequently, until golden, 1 to 2 minutes. Brush the top lightly with oil and flip with spatula. Cook 1 to 2 minutes, rotating, and then move to cool side of grill. Repeat with another disk. Top each pizza with a layer of onions, then some pear slices and blue cheese, and cook, covered, until cheese is melted and dough is crisp, 8 to 10 minutes, rotating halfway through. Repeat with remaining dough and toppings. Serve immediately.

*Grilled pizza parties are the best. Get creative with toppings. The first pizza is the chef's choice.*

ROASTED GARLIC & ARUGULA
# pizzas

Makes 4 10-inch pizzas

DOUGH

- 1 cup tepid water
- 3 tablespoons extra-virgin olive oil, plus additional as needed
- 2 teaspoons sugar
- 1½ teaspoons kosher salt
- 3 cups all-purpose flour, plus additional for kneading
- 2½ teaspoons active dry yeast (1 package)

TOPPINGS

- 2 heads garlic, tops trimmed
- 5 tablespoons extra-virgin olive oil, plus additional for drizzling
- ½ teaspoon kosher salt, plus additional for seasoning
- 2 teaspoons aged sherry vinegar

  Freshly ground black pepper
- 3 cups arugula, stems trimmed
- 4 thin slices prosciutto (about 3½ ounces), cut into ½-inch ribbons
- 4 ounces crumbled fresh goat cheese (about ½ cup)

**1.** To make dough: Stir water, oil, sugar, and salt in a liquid measuring cup until the sugar dissolves. Whisk flour and yeast in a large bowl, make a well in the center, and add liquid mixture. With a wooden spoon or your hand, gradually stir flour into liquid to make a rough dough. Pull dough together into a ball. Turn onto a work surface dusted with flour. Knead until dough is smooth and elastic, about 10 minutes, using a little flour if necessary to keep it from sticking.

**2.** Shape dough into a ball. Put in a large, lightly oiled bowl and turn it to coat with oil. Cover the bowl with plastic wrap and let rise until double in size, about 1 hour. Punch dough down, knead briefly, shape into a ball, cover, and let rise until soft and puffy, about 45 minutes.

**3.** While dough is rising, roast garlic: Preheat oven to 350°F. Put garlic on a double layer of aluminum foil, drizzle with olive oil, sprinkle with ¼ teaspoon of the salt, seal foil, and roast until soft, 45 minutes to 1 hour. Cool garlic and squish cloves from skins into a small bowl. Whisk in 3 tablespoons of the olive oil.

**4.** To prepare a charcoal grill: Fill a chimney starter with briquettes and heat until lightly covered with ash. Scatter a layer of cold hardwood charcoal over one-quarter of the grill. Spread hot briquettes on top and heat to medium-high. Set grill grate on top and cover, making sure vents are open, and heat 5 minutes. (Or preheat half of a gas grill for direct and indirect grilling.)

**5.** Meanwhile, dust your work surface lightly with flour. Divide dough evenly into 4 balls and press into flour, flipping to dust both sides. Hold one piece of dough up like a steering wheel and rotate and stretch it to make an 8-inch disk. Put it on a piece of plastic wrap and cover with a kitchen towel. Repeat with remaining dough.

**6.** Brush 1 disk of dough with oil. Place oil side down over hot coals. Cook, rotating frequently, until golden, 1 to 2 minutes. Brush top with oil and flip with spatula. Cook 1 to 2 minutes, rotating, then move to cool side of grill. Repeat with another disk. Season with salt and black pepper to taste, spread with a heaping tablespoon of garlic, and cook, covered, until brown and crisp, about 8 minutes, rotating halfway through.

**7.** While pizzas grill, whisk vinegar, remaining ¼ teaspoon salt, and black pepper to taste in a medium bowl. Whisk in remaining 2 tablespoons olive oil. Add arugula and prosciutto and toss. Remove pizzas from grill, dot with goat cheese, and pile salad on top.

# baby artichoke
## & POTATO SALAD

4 servings

### SALAD

- 1 cup extra-virgin olive oil
- 1 cup dry white wine
- 12 to 14 baby artichokes
- 1 lemon, halved
- 1½ tablespoons plus 1 teaspoon kosher salt, plus additional for seasoning
- 9 cloves garlic, peeled and smashed
- 1 sprig fresh rosemary
- 1 bay leaf
- ¾ teaspoon coriander seeds, cracked
- 12 small red-skinned waxy potatoes, halved (about 12 ounces)

### DRESSING

- 1 clove garlic, peeled
- 1 teaspoon kosher salt, plus additional for seasoning
- 2 tablespoons white wine vinegar
- 2 teaspoons Dijon mustard

  Freshly ground black pepper
- ⅓ cup extra-virgin olive oil

- 1 small shallot, minced (about 2 tablespoons)
- 2 tablespoons chopped flat-leaf parsley
- 2 ripe tomatoes, sliced
- 4 to 6 ounces cheese, such as Robiola, fresh goat, or Camembert (optional)

**1.** For the salad: Put 3 cups water, olive oil, and wine in a medium saucepan. Trim the artichokes, rubbing the cut surfaces with lemon as you trim, and add to pan. Add the 1½ tablespoons salt, garlic, rosemary, bay leaf, and coriander. Simmer over medium-low heat just until the artichokes are tender, about 15 minutes. Remove artichokes with a slotted spoon and transfer to a paper towel-lined plate. Add the potatoes to the cooking liquid and simmer just until tender, about 10 minutes. Remove potatoes and drain with the artichokes.

**2.** For the dressing: Smash the garlic clove, sprinkle with the 1 teaspoon salt, and, with the flat side of a large knife, mash and smear the mixture to a coarse paste. Whisk the vinegar with the garlic, mustard, and black pepper to taste in a small bowl. Gradually whisk in the olive oil, starting with a few drops and adding the rest in a steady stream to make a smooth, slightly thick vinaigrette. Stir in the shallot.

**3.** Prepare an outdoor grill with a medium fire.

**4.** Pat the artichokes and potatoes very dry and season with salt and black pepper to taste. Grill, turning occasionally, until lightly charred, 8 to 10 minutes for the potatoes and 3 to 4 minutes for the artichokes. Toss the artichokes and potatoes with most of the dressing and the parsley and season with salt and freshly ground pepper to taste. Divide the tomato slices among 4 plates, season with salt to taste and drizzle with any remaining dressing. Top with the artichoke salad and serve with a wedge of cheese, if desired.

1. Trim the pointy top half of the artichokes with a knife, preferably serrated.
2. Cut the artichokes in half, rubbing the cut surfaces with half of a cut lemon as you work to keep them from discoloring.
3. With your fingers, snap off the tough outer green leaves to get at the tender yellow ones.

# vegetable napoleons
## WITH TOMATO & BASIL DRESSING

6 servings

  6  large banana peppers

      Kosher salt

      Freshly ground black pepper

 1/4  cup extra-virgin olive oil

  4  cloves garlic, minced

  1  small shallot, minced

  1  tablespoon fresh thyme

24  medium shiitake mushrooms, stems removed (about 6 to 8 ounces)

  1  yellow squash or zucchini, sliced into 1/4-inch-thick rounds (about 8 ounces)

1 1/2  cups shredded Gouda cheese (about 6 ounces)

1 1/2  cups Tomato & Basil Dressing (see recipe, page 201)

**1.** Prepare an outdoor grill with a medium fire.

**2.** Put the peppers in a microwave-safe dish, cover with plastic wrap, and microwave on high just until tender, about 3 minutes. When cool enough to handle, slice in half lengthwise, remove the seeds and ribs, but leave the stem on. Season pepper halves with salt and black pepper to taste.

**3.** To assemble the napoleons: Set a pepper half, cut side up, across two pieces of clean cotton kitchen twine (see photos, below). Repeat with 5 additional pepper halves. Drizzle each with some of the olive oil and season with salt and black pepper to taste. Layer the napoleons as follows, scattering some of the garlic, shallot, thyme, salt, and black pepper to taste between each layer: half the shiitakes, all of the squash, all of the cheese, then the remaining shiitakes. Top with the remaining pepper halves and tie twine around napoleons to enclose.

**4.** Grill until peppers are charred and just tender and the cheese is melted, 4 to 5 minutes on each side. Drizzle plated napoleons with some of the Tomato & Basil Dressing. Pass remaining dressing at the table.

## ▪COOK'S NOTE
If you have a grill basket, you can sidestep tying the bundles. Simply layer the vegetables in the basket. The tight fit on the closed grill basket keeps the bundles together and makes flipping a breeze.

## ▪STYLE
Halve the veggie bundles crosswise and stack them in a pool of the Tomato & Basil Dressing for a dramatic presentation—and don't forget to discard the strings before serving!

1. Set each pepper half, cut side up, across two pieces of clean cotton twine. Drizzle with olive oil and season with salt and black pepper. Scatter with some garlic, shallot, thyme, salt, and black pepper. 2. Layer vegetables and cheese as instructed in Step 3 above. 3. Top with remaining pepper half. 4. Tie bundles with twine to enclose.

# burgers, dogs & sandwiches
# three

# classic burgers

6 servings

1¼ pounds ground beef sirloin

1¼ pounds ground beef chuck

2 teaspoons kosher salt, plus additional for seasoning

Freshly ground black pepper

Vegetable oil, for brushing

6 slices cheese, such as American or cheddar (optional)

6 soft hamburger buns or English muffins, split

Crisp-cooked bacon, lettuce, tomato, onion, and assorted condiments, for garnish

**1.** Prepare an outdoor grill with a medium-hot fire.

**2.** Break both meats by hand into small pieces onto a large piece of waxed paper or parchment paper. Sprinkle with 2 teaspoons of the salt and black pepper to taste. Bring the meat together by hand, avoid kneading it, and don't worry if it seems loosely knit. (This light touch keeps the meat from getting tough.) Divide meat mixture into 6 equal portions, then into balls by gently tossing from hand to hand. Gently form into 1-inch-thick patties. Press the center of each patty so it is slightly thinner than the edges. Brush burgers with oil and season with salt and black pepper to taste.

**3.** Grill the burgers, turning once, until nicely browned: 12 to 14 minutes for medium-rare, 14 to 16 minutes for medium, and 16 to 18 minutes for well-done. If making cheeseburgers, top the burgers during their last couple of minutes of cooking with cheese and cover with a disposable aluminum pan. Transfer the burgers to a plate to rest. Brush buns with oil and grill until lightly toasted. Serve the burgers on the buns with the garnishes and condiments of your choice.

## SHOPSMART

Why two meats? We love the taste of sirloin and the richness—OK, the fat—of chuck. If the burger is made from lean sirloin alone it will be dry; for a juicy burger, you need fat. This 50/50 blend gives you the best of both. For a supreme burger, buy your own chuck and sirloin steaks and grind the meat yourself. It's a labor of love but well worth it.

## KNOW-HOW

Burgers bulge when cooked; by forming the patties thinner in the center than around the edges, you end up with the model bun-ready shape after grilling.

# LATIN
# pork burgers

6 servings

- ⅓ cup lard or corn oil
- 6 cloves garlic, chopped
- 2 tablespoons dried oregano, preferably Mexican
- 2 tablespoons ground ancho chile powder
- 2 tablespoons sugar
- 1½ teaspoons ground coriander
- 1 teaspoon ground cumin
- ½ teaspoon ground allspice
- ¼ teaspoon ground cloves
- 1¾ pounds coarsely ground pork
- 2 teaspoons kosher salt, plus additional for seasoning
- Freshly ground black pepper
- 1 large red onion, sliced into ½-inch-thick rounds
- Olive oil, for brushing
- 6 thick slices Jack or cheddar cheese (about 8 ounces)
- 3 hero rolls, halved crosswise to make 6 buns

**1.** Heat the lard in a skillet over medium-low heat and add the garlic, oregano, ancho chile powder, sugar, coriander, cumin, allspice, and cloves. Cook and stir until fragrant and garlic is golden, about 3 minutes. Transfer to a small bowl to cool completely.

**2.** Prepare an outdoor grill with a medium-hot fire.

**3.** Using your hands, gently mix the spice mixture into the ground pork in a large bowl. Season with 2 teaspoons of the salt and black pepper to taste. Divide meat mixture into 6 equal portions, then into balls by gently tossing from hand to hand. Gently shape into ½-inch-thick loosely packed oval patties. Press the center of each patty so it is slightly thinner than the edges. Thread a long skewer through the sides of the onion slices (if you're using a wooden skewer, soak it in water 30 minutes before grilling).

**4.** Brush the burgers and onions with oil and season with salt and black pepper to taste. Grill the burgers on the first side until lightly charred, about 5 minutes. Flip and continue to cook just until cooked through, about 5 more minutes. Lay a slice of cheese on top of each burger, cover with a disposable aluminum pan, and cook until melted, about 2 minutes more. Grill the onions until charred and tender, about 12 minutes, turning once. Cool slightly and break apart. Let burgers rest off the heat while toasting the buns.

**5.** Brush the buns with oil and grill until lightly toasted. Serve the burgers on the buns with the grilled onions.

*Is there anything better than a burger? No matter how you dress it, it's always satisfying.*

# turkey burgers

## WITH WASABI MAYO

6 servings

MAYONNAISE

4 teaspoons water

4 teaspoons wasabi powder

1/2 cup mayonnaise

BURGERS

2¼ pounds ground turkey

6 scallions (white and green parts), finely chopped

3 tablespoons soy sauce

1 tablespoon mirin (See Cook's Note, right)

1½ teaspoons dark sesame oil

1 teaspoon kosher salt, plus additional for seasoning

Vegetable oil, for brushing

Freshly ground black pepper

6 sesame seed hamburger buns

1½ ripe Hass avocados, halved, pitted, and thinly sliced

6 slices ripe tomato

1½ cups alfalfa sprouts

1/3 cup pickled ginger (see ShopSmart, right)

**1.** Prepare an outdoor grill with a medium-hot fire.

**2.** For the mayonnaise: Stir the water into the wasabi powder in a small bowl and let stand for 5 minutes. Stir in mayonnaise.

**3.** For the burgers: Using your hands, gently mix the turkey with the scallions, soy sauce, mirin, sesame oil, and 1 teaspoon of the salt in a large bowl. Divide turkey mixture into 6 equal portions, then into balls by gently tossing from hand to hand. Shape into 6 loosely packed 1-inch-thick patties. Press the center of each patty so it is slightly thinner than the edges. Brush the burgers with oil and season the outside with salt and black pepper to taste.

**4.** Grill the burgers, turning once, until cooked through, about 14 minutes total. Set burgers aside to rest while grilling the buns until lightly toasted. Season the avocado and tomato with salt to taste. Serve the burgers on the buns with the wasabi mayonnaise, avocado, tomato, sprouts, and pickled ginger.

## COOK'S NOTE

Mirin is the "sweet" component in many Japanese dishes. If you can't find this mild rice wine, substitute a few pinches of sugar.

## SHOPSMART

Pickled ginger or *gari* is the thin pink slices of ginger served at the sushi bar. You can find it in some large grocery stores or a well-stocked seafood market.

# lamb burgers
## WITH FETA

6 servings

2 pounds ground lamb

½ cup plain whole-milk yogurt

1 tablespoon dried savory

3 cloves garlic, minced

Finely grated zest of 1 lemon

¼ to ½ teaspoon crushed red pepper

1½ teaspoons kosher salt, plus additional for seasoning

Freshly ground black pepper

7 ounces feta cheese, crumbled into chunky pieces

Extra-virgin olive oil, for brushing

6 small plain pita pocket breads (see ShopSmart, right)

Sliced onions, tomatoes, and cucumbers, for garnish

Arugula and fresh mint leaves, for garnish

Tzatziki (see recipe, page 73) (optional)

**1.** Prepare an outdoor grill with a medium-high fire.

**2.** Using your hands, mix the ground lamb, yogurt, savory, garlic, zest, red pepper, 1½ teaspoons salt, and black pepper to taste in a large bowl. Gently mix in the crumbled feta. Divide meat mixture into 6 equal portions, then into balls by gently tossing them from hand to hand. Shape into 1-inch-thick loosely packed oval patties. Press the center of each patty so it is slightly thinner than the edges.

**3.** Brush the burgers with olive oil and season with salt and black pepper to taste. Grill the burgers, turning once, until firm to the touch with a little bit of give, 8 to 10 minutes. Set aside while grilling pitas. Slit a burger-size opening in the pitas, brush with olive oil, and season with salt and black pepper to taste. Grill until lightly toasted. Serve the burgers in the pitas with the garnishes of your choice and Tzatziki, if desired.

## SHOPSMART

We found the small or "mini" pitas to be the perfect size. The burgers fit snugly in the pocket without a lot of excess bread.

## COOK'S NOTE

We love savory and know you'll be wild about it too. This familiar Mediterranean flavoring tastes like a blend of thyme, oregano, and a bit of rosemary. There are two varieties of this underutilized herb—summer and winter. Both are fantastic— very food-friendly with meat, fish, poultry, potatoes, eggs, or tomatoes.

# ode to
# sausages

Sausages are one of our favorite foods, and we aren't alone. There has been an awesome explosion in the world of sausages. For grilling season there seems to be no limit to the shapes, sizes, and flavors available. You can find Old-World classics such as kielbasa side by side with Cajun andouille, Midwestern brats, or Southwestern chorizo, as well as creative combinations such as turkey and tapenade, or lemongrass chicken. A well-made sausage grilled to a turn has everything going for it: ease, fantastic flavor, versatility, and virtually no cleanup. We know why links aren't just for breakfast anymore.

For cooked sausages: A simple sear and warming over a medium flame is all they need. Pinched for time? Split them lengthwise before warming.

For uncooked sausages: Don't poke holes in raw sausages—they dry up and are more likely to cause flare-ups. Mellow heat is best. Start on an indirect heat. Once the sausages have firmed up, move them to a higher heat to get them beautifully brown. Some folks advocate parboiling sausage in beer, broth, or cider before the final dance across the grill.

Coils of sausage are easier to manage if you slip two skewers crosswise through the ring. They stay intact and look great.

Sausage makes a great starter, either sliced and layered on grilled garlic bread; slipped on a skewer; paired with dried fruit, nuts, and olives; or freshened up with salad greens.

Simple sides: Try sausages with grilled onions, kebabs of apples and pears, prepared chutneys and salsas, spicy mustards, sliced fennel, zipped-up kraut, and interesting breads such as sweet raisin semolina or deeply flavored pumpernickel rye.

# the best of the wurst

Italian Sausage

Kielbasa

Brats

Breakfast Links

Chicken—Apple
Sausage

# chili
## FOR DOGS

Makes about 5 cups

3 tablespoons olive oil

1 medium onion, chopped

5 cloves garlic, chopped

1 tablespoon kosher salt

12 ounces ground beef chuck

1 tablespoon ancho chile powder

1 teaspoon dried oregano, preferably Mexican

1 teaspoon ground cumin

$1/2$ teaspoon ground coriander

2 whole cloves

Freshly ground black pepper

1 tablespoon tomato paste

1 chipotle chile in adobo sauce, coarsely chopped, plus 1 tablespoon adobo sauce

1 15-ounce can whole peeled tomatoes

1 $15^1/2$-ounce can kidney beans, rinsed and drained

1 12-ounce can beer

**1.** Heat the olive oil in a large saucepan over medium-high heat, then add the onion, garlic, and salt. Cook, stirring, until lightly browned and fragrant, about 3 minutes. Add the beef, breaking it up with a wooden spoon, and cook until evenly browned, about 3 minutes. Add the chile powder, oregano, cumin, coriander, cloves, and black pepper to taste and cook, stirring, until fragrant, about 45 seconds. Stir in the tomato paste and chipotle.

**2.** Use your hands to crush the tomatoes right into the pan, then pour in the juices from the can. Add the beans and beer and bring to a boil, adjust the heat to maintain a simmer, and cook, stirring occasionally, until thick and fragrant, about 30 minutes.

With all the amazing food we cook and eat, few things hit the spot more than dressed-up dogs. They bring out the kid in all of us.

# beet sauerkraut

Makes about 2½ cups

- ¼ teaspoon cumin seeds
- 2 whole allspice berries
- 1 tablespoon vegetable, soybean, or corn oil
- 1 small onion, halved and thinly sliced
- ½ fennel bulb, cored and thinly sliced lengthwise (about 1 cup)
- 1 large clove garlic, chopped
- ½ teaspoon kosher salt, plus additional for seasoning
- 1 pound bagged or jarred sauerkraut, rinsed and drained (about 1½ cups packed)
- ¾ cup water or beef broth
- 1 large beet (about 10 ounces), peeled and grated
- 2 tablespoons red wine vinegar
- 3 tablespoons sugar
- Freshly ground black pepper
- ½ cup sour cream
- 1 to 2 tablespoons drained horseradish
- 1 tablespoon lemon juice
- 1 teaspoon chopped fresh dill

**1.** Toast cumin and allspice in a small pan over medium heat until fragrant, about 1 minute. Crush with a mortar and pestle or the bottom of a pan.

**2.** Heat the oil in a medium saucepan over medium heat, then add onion, fennel, and garlic. Season with ½ teaspoon salt and cook, stirring occasionally, until softened, about 5 minutes. Add crushed spices, sauerkraut, water, beet, vinegar, sugar, and black pepper to taste. Adjust the heat to maintain a gentle simmer and cook the sauerkraut until tender and coated with a little liquid, about 30 minutes. Set aside to cool slightly.

**3.** Meanwhile, mix the sour cream, horseradish, lemon juice, and dill in a small bowl and season with salt and black pepper to taste. Top grilled hot dogs or grilled sausages with sauerkraut and the sour cream.

## CURRIED
# ketchup

Makes about 1 cup

- 1 tablespoon neutral oil, such as grapeseed or vegetable
- 2 tablespoons Madras-style curry powder
- ½ to 1 teaspoon cayenne pepper (use the larger amount for really spicy ketchup)
- 1 cup ketchup

Heat the oil, curry powder, and cayenne in a small skillet over medium heat, swirling the pan until fragrant, about 1 minute. Add the ketchup and simmer until slightly thickened. Cool and serve.

## SHOPSMART

Curried ketchup is a mainstay of German wurst stands. Curry powders vary—some are hot, others more aromatic. If we had to pick one curry powder for our pantry, it would be a versatile Madras-style curry because this variety is fragrant but not too hot.

# sauerkraut

FOR DOGS

Makes 2 cups

- 2 tablespoons vegetable or corn oil
- 2 medium onions, halved and thinly sliced
- 2 cloves garlic, thinly sliced
- 1/2 teaspoon kosher salt, plus additional for seasoning
- 1 bay leaf
- 1/2 teaspoon caraway, dill, or celery seeds
- 2 tablespoons cider vinegar
- 1 pound bagged or jarred sauerkraut, rinsed and drained (about 1 1/2 cups packed)

- 1/2 cup canned tomato puree
- 1/4 cup chicken broth
- 1/4 cup firmly packed light brown sugar
- 2 tablespoons gin
- 1 small sprig thyme
- 1/4 teaspoon freshly ground black pepper

**1.** Heat oil in a medium saucepan over medium-low heat. Add onions, garlic, and 1/2 teaspoon salt. Cook, stirring occasionally, until onions are soft and light brown, about 25 minutes.

**2.** Increase heat to medium, add bay leaf and caraway, dill, or celery seeds and stir until fragrant, about 2 minutes. Add the vinegar and stir, scraping the bottom of the pan with a wooden spoon. Add sauerkraut, tomato puree, broth, sugar, gin, thyme, and black pepper. Simmer, covered, until tender and juices have thickened, about 20 minutes. Season sauerkraut with salt to taste. Serve hot on hot dogs.

SWEET CORN
# relish

Makes about 2 cups

- 2 medium ears fresh corn, shucked
- 1 medium green tomato, diced (about 3/4 cup)
- 1/4 red onion, minced (about 1/4 cup)
- 1/2 rib celery, minced (about 2 tablespoons)
- 1/2 clove garlic, minced
- 1 tablespoon plus 2 teaspoons rice vinegar
- 1 tablespoon extra-virgin olive oil

- 1 1/2 teaspoons sugar
- 1 teaspoon kosher salt, plus additional for seasoning
- 1 small sprig thyme
  Pinch ground cloves
  Freshly ground black pepper

**1.** Cut the corn kernels from the cobs. Working over a large bowl, run a knife along the cobs to press out the milky liquid.

**2.** Put the corn, green tomato, onion, celery, garlic, 1 tablespoon vinegar, the olive oil, sugar, 1 teaspoon salt, thyme, and cloves in a saucepan. Season with black pepper to taste. Simmer, covered, until the corn and onion are crisp-tender, about 5 minutes. Stir in the remaining vinegar and season with salt and black pepper to taste. Remove the thyme sprig and discard.

# hot diggity

Chili for Dogs

Beet Sauerkraut

Sauerkraut for Dogs

Sweet Corn Relish

Hot Dogs, Franks, Wieners

# HOG-TIED
# cheese dogs

8 servings

1 4-ounce piece cheddar cheese

8 beef hot dogs

8 slices bacon

8 hot dog buns

Toppings of your choice such as pepperoncini, chili, onions, mustard, and sauerkraut

**1.** Prepare an outdoor grill with a medium fire.
**2.** Slice the cheese into eight ¼-inch-thick sticks. Slice into but not through the length of each hot dog and stuff with the cheese sticks. Trim bacon slices of some of the excess fat on the edges. Spiral wrap each hot dog with a slice of bacon and secure the ends with toothpicks.
**3.** Grill the hot dogs on all sides, starting cheese side down and finishing cheese side up, until the bacon crisps and cheese melts, about 5 minutes total. Toast buns on grill, if desired. Remove toothpicks and serve dogs in buns with toppings of your choice.

## SHOPSMART

These days all manner of meats—and tofu too—are turned into tasty dogs. Traditionally, hot dogs are meat—beef or pork—blended with spices and formed into a natural casing. The casing gives a characteristic snap to old-fashioned dogs. Many modern wieners are "skinless," with no casing. Packages note which style dogs are inside. Kosher dogs are a good bet for a delicious all-beef hot dog without a lot of fillers.

*If you lined up all the hot dogs eaten at ballparks in one season, they'd stretch from Dodger Stadium to Camden Yards.*

# pulled turkey leg
SANDWICHES

6 servings

- 2 turkey legs with thighs (about 4¼ pounds)
- ½ cup Cajun Rub (see recipe, page 228)
- 2 cups wood chips, such as hickory or mesquite, soaked in water for 30 minutes and drained
- 2 cups Cola Barbecue Sauce (see recipe, page 217)
- 6 soft hamburger buns

**1.** Rub the turkey legs all over with the spice rub. Cover and refrigerate for several hours or overnight.

**2.** Prepare an outdoor grill with a medium-hot fire for both direct and indirect grilling. Position a drip pan under the grate on the cool side. Toss 1 cup of soaked wood chips onto coals.

**3.** Lay the turkey legs skin side up over the drip pan. Cover the grill and position the lid's vent holes directly over the meat. When the fire dies down, after 1 hour or so, add about a dozen pieces of cold charcoal and the remaining wood chips to maintain a medium to medium-low smoky fire.

**4.** Set aside about half the sauce for serving. After about 1 hour, mop the turkey legs with some of the remaining sauce and turn. Mop and turn every 20 minutes or so until the legs are browned and glazed and an instant-read thermometer inserted into the thickest part of the thigh registers about 170°F, about 2 hours in all.

**5.** Remove the turkey meat and skin from the bones and shred meat by hand or with two forks. Mix the meat and the reserved barbecue sauce in a medium saucepan and warm over low heat. Spoon pulled turkey onto the untoasted buns and serve.

## ▦ COOK'S NOTE
Pulled sandwiches—whether pork, poultry, or beef—are legion in barbecue circles. We love the way dark turkey meat takes to our spicy-sweet BBQ sauce. When "pulling" the meat off the bone, make sure to shred it well enough so it absorbs lots of the delicious sauce.

## ▦ SHOPSMART
The buns used for this classic pulled sandwich should be soft as a pillow. No self-respecting pit master would ever serve tender, smoky meat on crusty bread or a toasted bun.

# vegetable souvlaki

4 servings

## SOUVLAKI

- 8 small red-skinned waxy potatoes, halved (about 10 ounces)

  Juice of 4 large lemons (about $^3/_4$ cup)

- $^2/_3$ cup extra-virgin olive oil
- 3 cloves garlic, minced
- $^1/_4$ cup chopped fresh oregano
- 3 tablespoons chopped fresh thyme
- 2 teaspoons kosher salt, plus additional for seasoning
- $^1/_4$ teaspoon crushed red pepper
- 1 medium zucchini (about 6 ounces)
- 1 Asian eggplant (about 6 ounces)
- 1 red bell pepper, seeded and cut into 1-inch squares
- 16 small button mushrooms, trimmed
- 16 grape or cherry tomatoes
- 1 bunch scallions (white and green parts), cut into $1^1/_2$-inch pieces
- 4 pocketless pita breads

  Tzatziki (see recipe, right)

## TZATZIKI

Makes about 1 cup

- 2 cups plain whole-milk yogurt, or 1 cup Middle Eastern-style plain yogurt
- 1 cucumber, peeled and seeded

- 2 teaspoons kosher salt, plus additional for seasoning
- $^1/_2$ clove garlic, peeled
- 1 tablespoon extra-virgin olive oil
- 1 teaspoon freshly squeezed lemon juice
- $^1/_2$ teaspoon dried mint, finely crumbled

## SOUVLAKI

**1.** Put potatoes in a small saucepan with cold water to cover and season with some salt. Bring to a boil and simmer just until tender, about 10 minutes.

**2.** Whisk lemon juice, olive oil, garlic, herbs, 2 teaspoons salt, and red pepper in a large bowl. Drain potatoes and toss into marinade while still hot.

**3.** Halve zucchini and eggplant lengthwise and cut into 1-inch-thick half-moon pieces. Add to potatoes and toss with marinade. Cover and marinate at room temperature 1 hour or in refrigerator up to 12 hours.

**4.** If you are using wooden skewers, soak in water for 30 minutes before grilling. Prepare an outdoor grill with a medium fire.

**5.** Thread vegetables on 8 skewers by alternating various vegetables or threading all one kind on a skewer. Reserve marinade. Grill vegetables,

turning skewers 2 or 3 times, until vegetables are tender and slightly charred, about 8 to 10 minutes. Transfer the skewers to a serving platter. Lightly drizzle some of the remaining marinade over skewers.

**6.** Grill pitas until warm. Serve vegetables with pita and tzatziki.

## TZATZIKI

**1.** Stir yogurt and put in a coffee filter-lined strainer over a bowl. Let drain in refrigerator for at least 12 hours or overnight. (If using thick Greek or Middle-Eastern yogurt, skip this step.) Discard watery liquid in bottom of bowl and put drained yogurt in a medium bowl.

**2.** Grate cucumber on wide-holed side of a box grater into another bowl. Sprinkle grated cucumber with 2 teaspoons salt and toss gently. Set aside 20 minutes, then squeeze cucumbers to express as much liquid as possible. Add the cucumber to the bowl of yogurt.

**3.** Smash garlic, sprinkle with a generous pinch of salt, and, with the flat side of a large knife, mash and smear to a coarse paste. Add garlic, oil, lemon juice, and mint to cucumber-yogurt mixture and stir to combine. Refrigerate for about an hour so flavors come together.

ZUCCHINI, POBLANO & RICOTTA
# quesadillas

4 servings

1 teaspoon coriander seeds

3 medium zucchini, sliced lengthwise about $\frac{1}{3}$ inch thick

3 poblano chiles, stemmed, halved and seeded

Extra-virgin olive oil, for brushing

2 teaspoons kosher salt

Freshly ground black pepper

1 cup fresh ricotta (see Cook's Note, right)

$\frac{1}{3}$ cup chopped fresh cilantro, plus a handful of leaves for garnish

2 scallions (white and green parts), sliced (about 3 tablespoons)

1 jalapeño, seeded and minced (or leave seeds in for more heat) (about 2 teaspoons)

1 teaspoon finely grated lime zest

4 12-inch flour tortillas

4 lime wedges

Tomato salsa and guacamole, if desired

**1.** Prepare an outdoor grill with a medium-hot fire.
**2.** Toast coriander seeds in a dry skillet over high heat until fragrant, about 30 seconds. Coarsely grind seeds with a mortar and pestle or crush with the bottom of a pan.
**3.** Lightly brush zucchini and poblanos with olive oil and grill, turning as needed, until tender and lightly charred, about 4 to 6 minutes. Season the zucchini with the crushed coriander, $1\frac{1}{2}$ teaspoons of the salt, and black pepper to taste. Cut into bite-size chunks and set aside to cool slightly. Peel skin from poblanos with a knife and thinly slice.
**4.** Mix the ricotta, chopped cilantro, scallions, jalapeño, lime zest, $\frac{1}{4}$ teaspoon of the salt, and black pepper to taste in a medium bowl. Lay out the tortillas and spread one-quarter of the cheese mixture over half of each tortilla, leaving about a $\frac{1}{2}$-inch border around the edge. Divide the grilled vegetables among the tortillas and fold the tortillas in half. Brush the quesadillas lightly with oil, sprinkle with remaining $\frac{1}{4}$ teaspoon salt, and grill on both sides until the cheese warms and the outside is golden brown, about 2 minutes.

**5.** Place each quesadilla on a plate, scatter the cilantro leaves over the top, and serve with lime wedges and, if desired, salsa and guacamole.

## COOK'S NOTE
Look for fresh ricotta in a good cheese shop or Italian grocery. It will be firmer and less watery than the ricotta sold in plastic tubs in the grocery store. If you can get only the grocery-store ricotta, put it in a cheesecloth- or coffee filter-lined strainer over a bowl and refrigerate at least a couple of hours or overnight to drain off excess moisture.

## KNOW-HOW
If you have a mandoline—a handheld tool much like a planer with a finely honed blade—use it to get long, uniform slices of zucchini that will grill evenly.

CHILI-RUBBED
# chicken tacos

4 servings

## PICKLE

1 medium red onion, halved and thinly sliced (about 2 cups)

$1/4$ cup cider vinegar

2 tablespoons firmly packed light brown sugar

2 teaspoons kosher salt

Freshly ground black pepper

## CHICKEN

3 tablespoons corn oil

2 tablespoons chili powder

$1^1/2$ teaspoons kosher salt

1 whole boneless, skinless chicken breast (about 1 pound)

## SALSA

8 ounces tomatillos, husked and well washed (about 3 large tomatillos)

$1/2$ medium yellow onion, sliced lengthwise into 3 wedges

1 large clove garlic, unpeeled

$1/4$ cup fresh cilantro leaves

1 chipotle chile in adobo sauce

$1/2$ teaspoon kosher salt

## TACOS

8 corn or flour tortillas

2 heaping cups finely shredded green cabbage (about $1/4$ head)

$1^1/2$ cups shredded cheddar cheese (about 4 ounces)

$1/2$ cup sour cream or Mexican *crema*

**1.** Prepare an outdoor grill with a medium fire.

**2.** For the pickle: Put the red onion in a medium bowl. In a small saucepan, simmer the vinegar, sugar, salt, and black pepper to taste just to dissolve the sugar, about 1 minute. Pour over the onion and cover.

**3.** For the chicken: Mix the oil, chili powder, and salt in a small bowl to make a paste. Pound the chicken to an even thickness of about $1/2$ inch with a meat mallet or the broad side of a cook's knife. Rub chicken all over with the chili paste.

**4.** For the salsa: Grill the tomatillos, onion, and garlic. (Put the garlic on a skewer to keep it from slipping through the grate. If you use a wooden skewer, soak it in water 30 minutes before grilling.) Remove garlic when just charred. Grill tomatillos, turning as needed, until soft but not bursting. Grill onion until tender, about 15 minutes. Peel the garlic. Pulse all the charred vegetables in a blender with the cilantro, chipotle, and salt to make a slightly chunky salsa.

**5.** Grill chicken until firm to the touch, turning once, 6 to 8 minutes. Set aside to rest for 5 minutes, then shred meat into bite-size pieces by hand or with two forks. Just before serving, warm the tortillas on the grill and wrap in a kitchen towel.

**6.** To assemble the tacos: Set out bowls containing cabbage, cheese, sour cream, pickled onions, salsa, and the stack of tortillas. Let your guests fold and stuff their own tacos as desired.

## STYLE

Taco bars are a relaxing way to dress up a table. Spread out the fixin's and let your friends help themselves. Keep the tortillas warm and pliable by wrapping them in a colorful towel. Show off the dramatic hues of the edible elements—purple onions, jade green salsa, brick red chicken—by arranging them side by side in pale-colored bowls.

# soft-shell crab
## POOR BOYS

4 servings

REMOULADE

1   clove garlic, peeled

1   teaspoon kosher salt

1   large egg yolk

2   tablespoons freshly squeezed lemon juice

1   cup grapeseed or other neutral-tasting oil

1   rib celery, finely minced

2   scallions (white and green parts), thinly sliced

2   tablespoons whole-grain mustard

2   tablespoons chopped fresh flat-leaf parsley

1   tablespoon chopped fresh tarragon

1   teaspoon Worcestershire sauce

    Pinch cayenne pepper

    Freshly ground black pepper

CRABS

4   large soft-shell crabs, cleaned (see page 270)

    Olive oil, for brushing

    Kosher salt

    Freshly ground black pepper

8   thick slices soft egg bread, such as brioche, or 4 poor boy rolls

2   ripe tomatoes, cored and sliced

    Arugula

**1.** For the remoulade: Smash the garlic clove, sprinkle with a generous pinch of the salt, and, with the flat side of a large knife, mash and smear mixture to a coarse paste. Set aside.
**2.** Put about 1 inch of water in a saucepan and bring to a simmer over medium heat. Choose a heatproof bowl that just fits in the saucepan without touching the water. Off the heat, whisk egg yolk, lemon juice, and 1 tablespoon water. Place the bowl over the simmering water, whisking constantly, until slightly thickened but not scrambled, about 1 minute. Remove the bowl from the heat and gradually whisk in the oil, starting with a few drops and then adding the rest in a steady stream to make a smooth mayonnaise. Add the garlic paste, celery, scallions, mustard, parsley, tarragon, Worcestershire, cayenne, the remaining salt, and black pepper to taste. Cover and refrigerate for an hour or so to let the flavors come together.
**3.** Prepare an outdoor grill with a hot fire.
**4.** For the crabs: Brush the crabs lightly with olive oil and season with salt and black pepper to taste. Begin grilling the crabs belly side up, turning once, until tops are bright orange-red, about 6 to 8 minutes. While the crabs cook, brush the bread or rolls lightly with olive oil and grill until lightly toasted. Tuck each crab between 2 slices of toast, along with a healthy bit of the remoulade, some sliced tomatoes, and arugula.

## ■ COOK'S NOTE
Heating the yolk is key to the remoulade. Don't be afraid to move the bowl off the hot water to avoid scrambling the egg. Don't be tempted to blend the oil into the egg in a food processor. The action is too swift and the sauce won't hold together.

## ■ SHOPSMART
The best-tasting soft-shell crabs are purchased live and cleaned right before cooking. (If you are squeamish about dispatching the crabs yourself, choose active ones and ask your fishmonger to do it for you.) To keep the crabs from drying out on the way home, transport them in moist paper towels, newspaper, or seaweed.

# fajitas

4 servings

### STEAK

- ½ cup lime juice (about 4 limes)
- ½ cup chopped fresh cilantro leaves, roots, and stems
- ½ cup sherry vinegar
- ¼ cup extra-virgin olive oil
- 1 small red onion, chopped
- 1 jalapeño, roughly chopped
- 1 teaspoon freshly ground black pepper
- 1¼ pounds beef skirt steak

### PICO DE GALLO

- 1 large ripe tomato, cored and chopped
- 1 to 2 serrano or jalapeño peppers, minced
- ¼ medium red onion, minced
- ½ teaspoon kosher salt, plus pinch for garlic
- 1 clove garlic, peeled
- ¼ cup chopped fresh cilantro
- 2 tablespoons extra-virgin olive oil

### PEPPERS AND ONIONS

- 2 poblano peppers, seeded and sliced
- 1 red bell pepper, seeded and sliced
- 1 medium red onion, sliced
- 1 tablespoon extra-virgin olive oil
- 1 tablespoon dried oregano
- 1 teaspoon kosher salt, plus additional for seasoning

  Freshly ground black pepper
- 1 tablespoon sherry vinegar

### FIXIN'S

- 8 large flour tortillas
- 1 Hass avocado, halved, seeded, peeled, and thinly sliced
- 2 cups shredded cheddar cheese (about 8 ounces)
- ½ cup sour cream

**1.** For steak: Whisk all marinade ingredients except steak in a large shallow dish. Add steak to marinade, turning to coat. Cover and refrigerate several hours.

**2.** Prepare an outdoor grill with a hot fire.

**3.** For the pico de gallo: Toss tomatoes, chiles, onion, and the ½ teaspoon salt in a bowl. Smash the garlic, sprinkle with the pinch of salt, and, with flat side of a large knife, mash and smear to a coarse paste. Stir garlic paste into salsa with cilantro and olive oil.

**4.** For peppers and onions: On a large sheet of heavy aluminum foil, toss peppers and onion with olive oil, oregano, 1 teaspoon salt, and black pepper to taste. Bring edges of foil up and crimp closed. Place package on edge of grill and cook until vegetables are tender, about 10 minutes. Season with vinegar and salt and black pepper to taste.

**5.** Meanwhile, remove steak from marinade, pat dry, and season with salt to taste. Grill, turning once, until slightly charred and crisp, 4 to 6 minutes total. Rest steak for about 5 minutes. Grill tortillas until lightly charred, 1 to 2 minutes. Cut meat into 4-inch-long segments, then cut against the grain on an angle. Transfer to a platter and serve with vegetables and fixin's.

# london broil
## WITH ONION MARMALADE

6 to 8 servings

MEAT

4 large cloves garlic, chopped

3 sprigs rosemary, leaves roughly chopped (about 1 tablespoon)

½ cup balsamic vinegar

½ cup red wine

½ cup extra-virgin olive oil

Freshly ground black pepper

1 2-inch-thick piece beef top round for London broil (about 3 pounds)

Kosher salt

MARMALADE

4 medium red onions, halved and thinly sliced

3 sprigs rosemary, leaves chopped (about 1 tablespoon)

½ cup balsamic vinegar

⅓ cup extra-virgin olive oil

3 tablespoons dark brown sugar

2 teaspoons kosher salt

½ teaspoon freshly ground black pepper

TOAST

4 cloves garlic, peeled

½ teaspoon salt

8 tablespoons butter, softened

8 ¾-inch-thick slices good quality white or sourdough bread

1 bunch arugula, washed and trimmed

Mustard and/or horseradish

**1.** For the meat: Mix garlic, rosemary, balsamic vinegar, wine, olive oil, and black pepper to taste in a self-sealing plastic bag or a shallow dish. Add the meat, turning to coat, and cover or seal. Refrigerate for several hours or overnight.

**2.** Prepare an outdoor grill with a hot fire for indirect grilling.

**3.** For the marmalade: On a large sheet of heavy-duty aluminum foil (or a doubled piece of regular), toss the onions with the rest of the marmalade ingredients. Bring edges of foil up and crimp closed. Place package on the edge of the grill (over medium-high heat). Cook, turning the sealed package every now and then so the onions cook evenly until meltingly tender, about 45 minutes.

**4.** Remove the meat from the marinade, pat it dry, and season generously with salt and black pepper to taste. Lightly oil the grill and sear the meat over high heat for 5 minutes. Then rotate it (don't turn it over yet) about 45 degrees from its original spot on the grill. Once you've made your grill mark, flip and repeat on the other side. Move the steak to the cooler side of the grill, cover with an aluminum pan, and cook, rotating (not flipping) periodically, until a meat thermometer inserted into the thickest part of the steak registers 125°F, about 15 to 20 minutes. Let steak rest on a cutting board about 10 minutes.

**5.** For the toast: Meanwhile, sprinkle garlic cloves with salt. With the flat side of a large knife, mash and smear garlic mixture into a paste. Mix with the butter. Lightly oil the grill, place bread over direct heat, and toast on both sides until golden brown, about 2 minutes total. Remove bread from grill and spread generously with the garlic butter. Thinly slice steak against the grain on an angle. Top toasts with onion marmalade, arugula, and sliced meat. Serve open-faced with mustard and/or horseradish.

Southern Greens with Whole Spices (page 189)

# BBQ pulled-pork sandwiches

8 to 10 servings, with leftovers

- 1 8-pound bone-in pork shoulder, with skin
- 1 head garlic, separated into cloves and peeled
- 3/4 cup Memphis Shake (see recipe, page 231) or Cajun Rub (see recipe, page 228)
- 5 cups apple or other wood chips, soaked in water for at least 30 minutes and drained
- 2 batches of North Carolina-Style Vinegar BBQ Sauce (see recipe, page 218)
- 8 to 10 soft hamburger rolls
  Dill pickles

**1.** Make small holes all over the pork shoulder with a thin sharp knife and stuff in garlic cloves. Rub the meat all over with the rub of your choice; cover and refrigerate overnight.
**2.** Prepare an outdoor grill with an indirect medium-hot fire with a mix of briquettes and hardwood charcoal in half of the grill. Set grate over coals. Place pork, skin side up, in an aluminum pan with about

1¹/₂ cups water on the cooler side of the grate. Toss 1 cup of the soaked and drained wood chips onto the coals and cover the grill, making sure the lid's vents are directly over pork.
**3.** When the coals cool to medium-low heat, preheat a chimney-full of hot briquettes and hardwood charcoal. Whenever smoke stops coming out of the vents, about every hour, add more hot coals and 1 cup of soaked and drained wood chips to the fire. The goal is to maintain a medium-heat, smoky fire (but don't worry if it is hotter when the coals are added and cooler while preheating the coals). Rotate the pork when you add coals so it cooks evenly. Cook the meat until an instant-read thermometer inserted into the thickest part of the pork registers 180°F, about 6 hours.
**4.** Set aside 1 quart of the North Carolina-Style Vinegar BBQ Sauce. Once the pork reaches 180°F, begin mopping the entire

surface of the meat every 20 minutes with some of the remaining sauce and the pan drippings. Continue to cook the pork, covering the grill between mopping, until an instant-read thermometer registers 200°F, about 1 to 2 hours more.
**5.** Transfer the pork to a cutting board and let rest for at least 15 minutes. Remove the outer skin and discard. Cut large chunks from the bone and shred, using two forks or your fingers, (when cool enough to touch) or chop. Toss with about 1 cup of the reserved barbecue sauce for every 3 cups of meat. Tuck the pork into the soft rolls and serve with pickles.

## ◼ COOK'S NOTE
Toss the extra sauce with shredded cabbage, or you can serve it on the side for those who want more spice. Use leftover pork for Extreme BBQ'd Nachos (see recipe, page 27)—you won't regret it!

HALLOUMI, SCALLION & MINT
# flatbread

6 servings

- 1/3 cup plus 2 tablespoons extra-virgin olive oil, plus additional for brushing
- 2 teaspoons crumbled dried mint
- 3/4 teaspoon crushed red pepper
- 1 pound halloumi cheese (see ShopSmart, right)
- 1/2 clove garlic, peeled

  Kosher salt

- 1 large ripe tomato (about 12 ounces), cored and roughly chopped
- 1 tablespoon capers

  Freshly ground black pepper

- 2 bunches scallions (white and green parts), trimmed
- 3 flatbreads or pocketless pita breads

**1.** Put 1/3 cup of the olive oil, the mint, and red pepper in a shallow dish. Slice the cheese into 1/2-inch-thick pieces (about 12 slices) and put in a single layer in the oil, turning to coat. Set aside at room temperature for 2 hours or cover and refrigerate for up to 24 hours.

**2.** Prepare an outdoor grill with a medium fire.

**3.** Smash the garlic clove, sprinkle with a pinch of salt, and, with the flat side of a large knife, mash and smear the mixture to a coarse paste. Toss tomato, capers, garlic, and remaining 2 tablespoons olive oil in a bowl and season with salt and black pepper to taste.

**4.** Place the cheese on the grill, reserving the marinade. Dip the scallions in the marinade, then grill them, turning as needed, until wilted and lightly charred,

about 3 minutes. Coarsely chop the scallions. Cook the cheese, turning as needed, until browned, about 5 minutes per side. Return the grilled cheese to the marinade, if desired—especially if it marinated for a short amount of time.

**5.** Brush the flatbreads with olive oil and grill to warm through. Cut the breads in half, tuck 2 pieces cheese and some scallions into each folded flatbread half, top with the tomato mixture, and serve.

## ▬ SHOPSMART

Halloumi, a brined sheep's or goat's milk cheese from Cyprus, is finding its way into supermarkets and good cheese stores. It is firm and doesn't melt like other cheeses but browns superbly. It's the ultimate grilling cheese. In a pinch, use a dry feta as a stand-in.

# SWEET & SOUR BBQ
# tofu wraps

4 servings

TOFU

1 14-ounce package extra-firm tofu

1¾ cups Sweet & Sour BBQ Sauce (see recipe, page 221)

SLAW

1 medium carrot, peeled

1 3-inch piece daikon radish, peeled

¼ head napa cabbage, quartered, cored, and thinly sliced, (about 3 cups)

2 ounces pea shoots (about 2 cups) (optional)

¼ cup pickled ginger, drained and roughly chopped

1½ teaspoons kosher salt

Freshly ground black pepper

¼ cup rice vinegar

2 tablespoons peanut oil

4 large flour tortillas, flavored if desired

2 teaspoons *gomashio* (see ShopSmart, right)

**1.** For the tofu: Cut tofu into eight ½-inch-thick slabs and pat dry on paper towels, pressing down lightly to squeeze out excess moisture. Pour the barbecue sauce in a shallow baking dish and add the tofu, turning to coat each piece. Cover and refrigerate several hours.

**2.** Prepare an outdoor grill with a medium fire.

**3.** Meanwhile make the slaw: With a box grater shred the carrot and daikon into long strips. Toss the cabbage, carrot, daikon, pea shoots (if desired), ginger, salt, and black pepper to taste in a large bowl. Add the vinegar and peanut oil and toss again to coat. Set aside.

**4.** Remove the tofu from the sauce, allowing excess sauce to slip back into the bowl; reserve. Brush the grill grate with oil and grill the tofu, covered, until it is lightly charred with grill marks, about 3 minutes per side. Brush tofu with more sauce after turning, if desired.

**5.** Warm the tortillas on the grill, turning, until pliable. Lay 2 pieces of tofu across a tortilla, mound some slaw on top, and sprinkle some *gomashio* over the top. Fold the bottom up and wrap the tortilla into a snug package around the filling. Repeat with remaining ingredients. Serve with extra barbecue sauce.

## ▉ COOK'S NOTE

We found the tofu got the darkest grill marks cooked on a grill with a cast-iron grate. With some other grills, you may not get grill marks, so just take the tofu off when it's lightly charred all over.

## ▉ SHOP SMART

*Gomashio*, a Japanese sesame-seed spice blend, supplies big effects with little effort. It can be found in most supermarkets' ethnic or organic food aisle. In a pinch, subsitute toasted sesame seeds.

85

# chicken & other BBQ'd birds

# four

# jerk chicken

4 to 6 servings

- ⅓ cup cider vinegar
- ¼ cup dark rum
- 3 tablespoons firmly packed dark brown sugar
- 1 bunch scallions (white and green parts), roughly chopped
- 4 cloves garlic, chopped
- 1 Scotch bonnet chile, stemmed, seeded, and minced
- 2 tablespoons Pickapeppa sauce (see ShopSmart, right)
- 1 tablespoon freshly grated peeled ginger
- 1 tablespoon ground allspice
- ¼ teaspoon pumpkin pie spice
- 3 tablespoons vegetable oil
- 4 chicken halves (about 6 pounds)

**1.** Pulse the vinegar, rum, brown sugar, scallions, garlic, chile, Pickapeppa sauce, ginger, allspice, and pumpkin pie spice in a food processor to make a slightly chunky sauce. Heat the oil in a medium skillet and cook the sauce over medium heat, stirring, until the oil is absorbed and the sauce thickens slightly, about 3 minutes. Cool.

**2.** Rub the jerk paste all over the chicken halves, cover, and refrigerate for 2 to 24 hours.

**3.** Prepare an outdoor grill with a medium-high fire for both direct and indirect grilling. Position a drip pan under the grate on indirect side. Place the chicken, skin side down, over direct heat and cook until skin crisps and has definite grill marks, about 4 minutes per side. Move to indirect heat over the drip pan and cook skin side up, covered, until an instant-read thermometer inserted into the thickest part of the thigh registers 165°F, about 35 to 40 minutes. Let the chicken rest about 5 minutes, then cut into pieces and serve.

## ▌ SHOPSMART

Pickapeppa—the celebrated Jamaican bottled sauce—is a blend of tomatoes, onions, sugar, cane vinegar, mangoes, raisins, tamarind, peppers, and spices. Fans use this "Jamaican ketchup" on all manner of grilled foods. It adds a distinct punch to this version of the island's spicy jerk marinade.

We love the way the spices, chiles, and smoke of the grill go together in jerked foods.

# HERB-MARINATED
# chicken

4 to 6 servings

- ½ cup extra-virgin olive oil, plus additional for brushing
- ¼ cup white wine vinegar
- 2 shallots, sliced
- 2 cloves garlic, roughly chopped
- ½ cup roughly chopped mixed fresh herbs, such as flat-leaf parsley, sage, oregano, thyme, and rosemary
- 2 teaspoons kosher salt, plus additional for seasoning
  
  Pinch crushed red pepper
  
  Freshly ground black pepper
- 1 3- to 4-pound chicken, cut into 8 pieces, excess fat trimmed

**1.** Whisk the olive oil, vinegar, shallots, garlic, herbs, 2 teaspoons salt, crushed red pepper, and black pepper to taste in a dish large enough to hold the chicken. (Alternatively, put all the ingredients in a large self-sealing plastic bag, seal, and give it a good shake.) Add the chicken pieces and turn to coat evenly. Marinate at room temperature for 1 hour, turning once, or refrigerate for up to 12 hours.

**2.** Prepare an outdoor grill with medium-high fire for both direct and indirect grilling. Position a drip pan under the grate on the indirect side of the grill.

**3.** Remove the chicken from the marinade and pat dry; discard marinade. Brush the chicken lightly with olive oil and season with salt and black pepper to taste. Place the chicken pieces bone side down on the indirect side over the drip pan, positioning the dark meat closer to the fire. Cover and cook until golden brown, about 15 minutes. Turn and cook, uncovered, until the skin crisps and an instant-read thermometer inserted in the thickest part of each piece registers 170°F, about 15 minutes more. Serve warm.

*Lots of fresh herbs, chicken, and a hot grill work like a charm for a spontaneous summer supper.*

# chicken spiedini

8 servings

- ½ cup extra-virgin olive oil
- ¼ cup roughly chopped fresh marjoram, oregano, or thyme
- 3 tablespoons white wine vinegar
- 1 shallot, finely minced (about 3 tablespoons)
- 2 cloves garlic, roughly chopped
- 4 teaspoons kosher salt

  Freshly ground black pepper

- 1¼ pounds boneless, skinless chicken breasts, cut into 1½-inch cubes
- ¾ pound pancetta or slab bacon, cut into 1-inch cubes
- 2 cups dried bread crumbs (store-bought is fine)

**1.** Whisk the olive oil, marjoram, vinegar, shallot, garlic, 2 teaspoons of the salt, and black pepper to taste in a large bowl. Add the chicken and turn to coat evenly. Cover and marinate at room temperature for 1 hour, stirring once, or refrigerate for up to 4 hours.

**2.** Prepare an outdoor grill with a medium-high fire for direct grilling. If you're using wooden skewers, soak them in water for at least 30 minutes before grilling. Put the pancetta into a saucepan with enough cold water to cover. Bring to a boil over high heat, then immediately drain. Set aside. Remove the chicken from the marinade; discard the marinade. Put the bread crumbs in a shallow bowl or pie plate, season with salt to taste, and roll the chicken pieces in the bread crumbs to coat.

**3.** Alternate threading the chicken and pancetta cubes on 8 skewers, starting and ending with the chicken. Leave a little space around the meat so the heat gets to all sides. Grill, turning as needed, until the chicken is cooked through and the bread crumbs are crispy and golden brown, 8 to 10 minutes.

## ◼ KNOW-HOW

Marinades are a grand way to impart flavor to chicken, meat, or fish. But to keep foods safe and free of cross-contamination, never put cooked proteins back into marinades that have had raw proteins in them. If you want to use the mixture as a finishing sauce, bring it to a boil and cook for a couple of minutes before pouring it on.

## ◼ COOK'S NOTE

Sweet marjoram has an earthiness that is right in step with the smoky flavor of grilling. But if you can't find it, don't stress. The beauty of cooking with herbs is that you can substitute one for another with ease. Oregano, thyme, or rosemary (it's potent, so use less) would be delicious in these crispy spiedini.

# chicken caesar
## SALAD

4 to 6 servings

CHICKEN

4 boneless, skinless chicken breast halves (about 1³/4 pounds)

Lemon-Pepper Slather (see recipe, page 220)

SALAD

1 to 3 anchovy fillets

1 large egg

1 clove garlic, peeled

³/4 teaspoon kosher salt, plus additional for seasoning

Juice of 1 lemon (about 3 tablespoons)

¹/2 teaspoon Worcestershire sauce

¹/4 cup extra-virgin olive oil

Freshly ground black pepper

3 romaine lettuce hearts (1 package), torn into pieces

¹/4 cup freshly grated Parmigiano-Reggiano cheese

1 1- to 2-ounce wedge Parmigiano-Reggiano cheese, for garnish

CROUTONS

4 ³/4-inch-thick slices sourdough bread

2 tablespoons extra-virgin olive oil

1 medium clove garlic, peeled and halved

Kosher salt

**I.** For the chicken: Put the chicken in a self-sealing plastic bag, add the Lemon-Pepper Slather, seal, and turn the bag over a couple times to coat the chicken well. Refrigerate for 2 to 24 hours.

**2.** Prepare an outdoor grill with a medium-high fire.

**3.** For the salad: Soak anchovy fillets in cold water 5 minutes. Pat dry, chop coarsely, and put in a large salad bowl. Put the egg in a small saucepan with water to cover. Bring just to a boil over medium-high heat and drain. Crack the egg into the salad bowl (don't worry if some of the egg white remains attached to the shell; just discard it with the shell). Smash the garlic clove, sprinkle with the ³/4 teaspoon salt, and, with the side of a large knife, mash and smear the mixture to a coarse paste. Add to the egg. Add lemon juice and Worcestershire, then slowly whisk in oil to make a creamy dressing. Season with salt and black pepper to taste and refrigerate.

**4.** Pat chicken dry and season with salt and black pepper to taste. Grill chicken, turning once, until cooked through, about 4 minutes per side. Remove the chicken to a cutting board.

**5.** For the croutons: Brush the bread with the olive oil and grill until toasted, turning as necessary. After grilling, rub each toast with garlic and season with salt to taste. Break toasts into bite-size croutons.

**6.** Slice the chicken. Add the lettuce to the dressing in the salad bowl and toss to combine. Sprinkle with the cheese and croutons and toss again. Divide the salad among plates and top each with a sliced chicken breast. Use a vegetable peeler to shave large, thin pieces of Parmigiano-Reggiano over each. Serve immediately.

## SHOPSMART

Extra-virgin olive oil—the most full-flavored of the olive oils—varies in flavor from peppery to aromatic to flowery to apple-sweet. It all depends on the type of olive used and how ripe it was when it was picked. Intensely green oils, from underripe fruit, tend to be more pungent; golden ones, from mature olives, more restrained. Buy small bottles of differently hued oils and contrast and compare to find the style of "evoo" that suits your taste.

# chicken paillards
## WITH HERB-TOMATO SALAD

4 servings

2  ripe medium tomatoes (1 red and 1 yellow), cored and roughly chopped (about 1½ cups)

1  clove garlic, peeled and smashed

1  scallion (white and green parts), thinly sliced

3  tablespoons extra-virgin olive oil, plus additional for brushing

2  teaspoons red wine vinegar

2  teaspoons kosher salt, plus additional for seasoning

   Freshly ground black pepper

⅓  cup torn fresh basil

3  tablespoons roughly chopped fresh tarragon

3  tablespoons roughly chopped fresh flat-leaf parsley

4  chicken paillards, about 6 ounces each (see Know-How, right)

**1.** Prepare an outdoor grill with a hot fire.

**2.** Toss the tomatoes, garlic, scallion, the 3 tablespoons olive oil, vinegar, the 2 teaspoons salt, and black pepper to taste in a medium bowl. Add all the herbs to the bowl but don't toss.

**3.** Brush the chicken paillards lightly with olive oil and season with salt and black pepper to taste. Grill the chicken, turning once, until cooked through, about 2 minutes per side. Stir the herbs into the tomatoes. Put a paillard on each of 4 plates, spoon some herb-tomato salad on top (watch out for the smashed garlic—you might want to remove it), and serve.

## ▌ KNOW-HOW

Paillards, a.k.a. scaloppini, are very thin pieces of meat or fish. They cook in a wink and are easy to make: Start with a boneless, skinless chicken breast. Place between two sheets of plastic wrap or waxed paper. Use a meat pounder or the bottom of a small, heavy skillet to pound to an even thickness of about ½ inch. You also can save yourself time by asking your butcher to do it for you.

This is our favorite August dinner. While the paillards grill, snip herbs from the garden, toss them with a gorgeous summer tomato salad, and voila—dinner is served.

94

# chicken

4 to 6 servings

- 3/4 cup soy sauce
- 1/2 cup sugar
- 1/4 cup mirin (see Cook's Note, page 59)
- 1/4 cup sake
- 10 coin-size pieces fresh ginger
- 12 boneless chicken thighs (about 2 1/2 pounds)

  Sansho pepper (optional) (see ShopSmart, right)

  Grilled scallions (see page 211)

**1.** Prepare an outdoor grill with medium-high fire for both direct and indirect grilling.

**2.** Combine the soy sauce, sugar, mirin, sake, and ginger in a small saucepan and simmer until sweet and syrupy, for 15 to 20 minutes.

**3.** Put the chicken skin side down on the direct heat side of the grill and brush with some glaze. Cook until the skin crisps, about 5 minutes, moving the chicken occasionally to keep it from charring. Turn chicken over and move it to the indirect heat side of the grill, brush the skin side with some glaze, and cover. Continue to cook the chicken, brushing occasionally with the glaze, until firm to the touch and an instant-read thermometer inserted into the thickest part registers 170°F, about 20 to 25 minutes.

**4.** Sprinkle the skin side with sansho pepper, if desired, and serve with grilled scallions.

## SHOPSMART

Sansho pepper, a Japanese spice that comes from the prickly ash, has a bright peppery taste similar to that of Szechwan peppercorn. It is a common Japanese condiment and adds just the right zing to this simple chicken dish. A shake on plain white rice is fabulous too. It comes in small jars and can be found in Asian and health food markets.

# BEER-CAN
# chickens

4 servings

- 6 cloves garlic, peeled
- 2 teaspoons kosher salt, plus additional for seasoning
- 1/3 cup Memphis Shake (see recipe, page 231) or Texas Rub (see recipe, page 228)
- 2 chickens, about 3½ pounds each, excess fat trimmed and giblets removed
- 2 12-ounce cans beer

**1.** One or two days before you grill, smash 2 of the garlic cloves, sprinkle with the 2 teaspoons salt, and, with the flat side of a large knife, mash and smear mixture to a coarse paste. Mix the garlic and spice rub in a small bowl.
**2.** Slip your finger between breast meat and skin of the chickens, then rub some of the garlic mixture under the skin. Spread remaining mixture inside cavity and over surface of both chickens. Cover and refrigerate overnight or up to 2 days.
**3.** For a charcoal grill, fill 2 chimney starters with briquettes and light. When the coals have just ashed over, empty the chimneys on opposite sides of the grill to make 2 banked high-heat fires. Set a drip pan

between the coal piles, where the birds will sit, to prevent flare-ups. (If you have only one chimney starter, bank the hot coals and then divide one chimney's worth of unlit charcoal between the two piles.)
**4.** Open the beer and pour out or drink about ¼ of each one. Drop remaining garlic into beer cans. Carefully stand each chicken on a beer can inserted in the larger opening (the can should be well inside the cavity of the bird) and carefully place them standing over the drip pan with drumsticks sticking straight down. Cover and cook chickens until an instant-read thermometer inserted in thickest part of the thigh registers 170°F, about 1 hour. Add coals as needed to maintain a cooking temperature of about 350°F throughout the cooking time.
**5.** Carefully remove the chickens from the grill with the cans still intact. Set the chickens aside, resting on the cans, for 15 minutes. Carefully remove the cans with a towel, twisting the can slightly while lifting the chicken straight up. Cut the chickens into quarters. Serve warm or at room temperature.

## KNOW-HOW

Many grills come with an attached thermometer to monitor the cooking temperature inside the grill, If yours doesn't, you can buy an inexpensive oven thermometer and place it on the grill grate next to your food. Take care to check the temperature quickly so you don't lose too much heat when you uncover the grill.

## COOK'S NOTE

In its irreverent glory, beer-can chicken has become a favorite on the BBQ cook-off circuit. This unique method produces crispy skin and amazingly moist meat. It is outrageous, all right— outrageously good! We loved the flavor we got from a charcoal fire. Two banked fires provided the right cooking environment to produce perfectly golden, luscious birds. You also can do the birds on a gas grill, but only if it has three or more burners to replicate the "banked coals" cooking method.

# spit-roasted chicken
## WITH CITRUS MOSTARDA

4 to 6 servings

1  6- to 8-pound roasting chicken, excess fat and giblets removed

4  tablespoons coarse sea salt

Freshly ground black pepper

1  head garlic, plus 8 peeled cloves

3/4  cup extra-virgin olive oil

1  tablespoon fennel seeds

1  tablespoon juniper berries (see ShopSmart, right)

1/2  teaspoon crushed red pepper

2  bulbs fennel, cut into 1/2-inch wedges, root end intact

2  bunches small carrots with a bit of green stem, peeled and halved lengthwise

2  bay leaves

1/2  cup water

Citrus Mostarda (see recipe, page 225)

**1.** Season cavity of chicken with 1 tablespoon of the salt and black pepper to taste. Halve garlic head crosswise and stuff into bird. Truss chicken (see page 268).
**2.** Prepare a gas grill with a rotisserie attachment with a medium-high fire.
**3.** Thread the bird on the spit through the cavity. Brush chicken all over with some of the olive oil and sprinkle with 2 tablespoons of salt and black pepper to taste.
**4.** Coarsely grind fennel seeds, juniper, and crushed red pepper in a mortar and pestle or a spice mill. Toss fennel, carrots, and remaining garlic cloves with spices, remaining tablespoon of salt, and bay leaves in a disposable pan that will fit under the chicken as it turns on the spit. Add the water to pan.
**5.** Attach spit to the rotisserie and slip the pan of vegetables under the chicken. Make sure chicken can rotate completely and is positioned directly in front of the heat source. Arrange vegetables to catch the drippings from the chicken.
**6.** Cover grill and cook, basting chicken with olive oil every 15 minutes and stirring vegetables as needed to cook evenly. Cook chicken until an instant-read thermometer

inserted into thickest part of thigh registers about 170°F, about 1 hour 20 minutes.
**7.** To serve, transfer the vegetables to a serving platter. Place the chicken on top of the vegetables and serve with Mostarda.

## ▮ SHOPSMART

You won't find juniper berries in the produce section. They're in the spice area and are the purplish spice that gives gin its distinctive flavor. Juniper berries are used in cuisines as disparate as northern Italian and American Southwestern. Juniper goes great with lamb (see Juniper & Jalapeño Jelly-Glazed Lamb Chops, page 147), chiles, and dried beans.

# ring-of-fire chicken

4 servings

- 4 cloves garlic, peeled
- 1 tablespoon kosher salt, plus additional for seasoning
- $^{1}/_{2}$ cup extra-virgin olive oil
- 2 teaspoons crushed red pepper
- 4 chicken halves, about 1$^{3}/_{4}$ pounds each
- $^{1}/_{2}$ cup balsamic vinegar
- 4 ripe peaches, halved lengthwise and pitted
- 1 medium red onion, quartered
- 3 to 4 sprigs fresh thyme

  Freshly ground black pepper
- 1 tablespoon chopped fresh flat-leaf parsley

**1.** Smash garlic cloves, sprinkle with 1 teaspoon of the salt, and, with the flat side of a large knife, mash and smear mixture to a coarse paste. Put in a small bowl and stir in olive oil, remaining 2 teaspoons salt, and red pepper. Brush chicken with some garlic oil. Set aside.

**2.** If using wooden skewers, soak them in water for at least 30 minutes before grilling. To prepare the "ring of fire," light 2 chimneys of charcoal in your grill. When the coals are ashed all over, distribute in a ring around the edge of the grill.

**3.** Simmer the balsamic vinegar in small saucepan over medium heat until syrupy and reduced by about half. Meanwhile, skewer a peach half lengthwise, followed by an onion wedge, then another piece of peach. Repeat to make 3 more skewers.

**4.** Toss the thyme sprigs on the coals and put the chicken on the grill bone side down over indirect heat inside the ring. Cover and cook until the skin is golden and the chicken is about three-quarters cooked, about 20 minutes. Brush the chicken with the garlic oil again, turn, and cook, uncovered, until the skin is very crisp and an instant-read thermometer inserted in the thigh registers 170°F, about

15 minutes more. Remove the chicken from the grill and let it rest for about 10 minutes.

**5.** Grill the fruit skewers over the direct heat of the ring until lightly charred, about 5 minutes. Turn and grill the other side until the fruit softens, about 5 minutes. Remove from the grill, brush with the balsamic glaze, season with salt and black pepper to taste, and sprinkle with parsley.

**6.** Serve each chicken half with a fruit skewer.

## ■ KNOW-HOW

A ring of fire is a variant on indirect heat grilling, with the heat completely surrounding the chicken as it cooks. If you have a gas grill, set it up as a hot indirect fire and rotate the birds toward the heat periodically as they cook.

# chicken kebabs
## WITH TOMATO-ONION CHUTNEY

4 to 6 servings

CHICKEN

2  to 3 heads garlic, peeled and
   smashed (about 6 ounces)

1  6-inch piece ginger, peeled and
   cut into chunks (about
   6 ounces)

1½ teaspoons kosher salt, plus
    additional for seasoning

¼  cup extra-virgin olive oil

1  tablespoon dark sesame oil

4  boneless chicken breast halves
   with skin (about 5 ounces
   each)

   Freshly ground black pepper

CHUTNEY

Makes about 1½ cups

6  medium ripe tomatoes (about
   6 to 8 ounces each)

2  tablespoons unsalted butter

1  tablespoon vegetable oil

1  1-inch piece cinnamon stick

1  green cardamom pod, cracked
   (optional)

1  whole clove

⅛  teaspoon coriander seeds,
   cracked

⅛  teaspoon cumin seeds, cracked

   Pinch ground mace

   Freshly ground black pepper

1  medium onion, thinly sliced

1½ teaspoons kosher salt, plus
    additional for seasoning

½  serrano chile with seeds

2 teaspoons sugar

   Juice of half a lemon (about
   1½ tablespoons)

¼  cup chopped fresh cilantro

1. For the chicken: Puree garlic and
ginger in a food processor with the
1½ teaspoons salt to make a very
fine paste. With the processor
running, drizzle in olive oil. Set
aside 2 tablespoons of the paste for
the chutney. Cook remaining paste
in a medium skillet in sesame oil,
stirring, over medium heat, until it
is fragrant and starts to stick to the
bottom of pan, about 10 minutes.
Spread the paste on the bottom of
an 8x8-inch glass baking dish; let
cool. Remove the tenderloins from
the chicken breasts and cut each
breast lengthwise into 3 long
pieces. Season the chicken with salt
and black pepper to taste and place
on the paste. Cover and refrigerate
4 to 12 hours, turning the chicken a
couple of times while it marinates.
2. For the chutney: Meanwhile,
preheat oven to 375°F. Core and
halve tomatoes crosswise.
Arrange tomatoes cut side down
on a rack on a baking sheet and
roast until the skins shrink away
from the flesh, about 30 minutes.
Cool just enough to be able to
touch them. Pinch off and
discard the skins.

3. Heat the butter and oil in a
medium skillet over medium-
high heat. Add spices and cook,
stirring with a wooden spoon,
until fragrant, about 1 minute.
Add reserved ginger paste and
cook, stirring and scraping the
bottom of the pan, until golden
brown, about 1 minute. Add
onion and 1 teaspoon of the salt,
reduce heat to medium-low, and
continue cooking until onion is
tender, about 10 minutes. Add
tomato halves, chile, sugar, and
remaining salt. Cook, covered,
stirring occasionally, until
tomatoes begin to break apart,
about 30 to 40 minutes. Increase
heat to medium and simmer
uncovered until juices thicken,
about 10 to 15 minutes. Add
lemon juice, cilantro, and salt to
taste. (This can be prepared up
to a day ahead and refrigerated.
Allow to come to room
temperature before serving.)
4. Prepare an outdoor grill with a
medium-high fire.
5. Thread chicken strips and
tenderloins onto 16 skewers (if
using wooden skewers, soak in
water at least 30 minutes before
grilling). Lightly oil the grill. Grill
kebabs, uncovered, turning, until
skin is crispy and meat is cooked
through, about 8 to 10 minutes.
Serve with the chutney.

102

K.C.-BBQ'D GLAZED

# chicken

4 to 6 servings

2 cups Kansas City-Style BBQ Sauce (see recipe, page 218)

Vegetable oil, for the grill

3½ pounds mixed chicken parts (breasts halved)

Kosher salt

Freshly ground black pepper

**1.** Prepare an outdoor grill with a hot fire for both direct and indirect grilling. Position a drip pan under the grate on the indirect side. Put the sauce in a large bowl next to the grill along with some tongs.

**2.** Brush the grill grate lightly with oil. Season the chicken with salt and black pepper to taste and place it skin side down on the grate on the direct side. Cook until skin is crisp, turning as needed, about 5 minutes. Dip each piece of chicken in the sauce, letting any excess sauce drip off, then return chicken to the grill on the indirect side, over the drip pan. Arrange the dark meat pieces closer to the fire than the white meat. Cook, covered, basting once more, until nicely glazed and an instant-read thermometer inserted in the thickest part of each piece of chicken registers 170°F, about 25 to 30 minutes.

## ▓ KNOW-HOW

The components of many BBQ sauces are well-guarded secrets. But most have some sort of sugar, be it molasses, brown sugar, honey, maple syrup—even cola, which caramelizes easily. If the meat is mopped too early in the grilling process or is too close to the flame, you end up with the dreaded (and unintentional) blackened bird.

*Can't go wrong with a classic like this. Finger-licking never tasted so good.*

# backyard party

A chorus of all–American cookout classics is just the way to celebrate summer. Everyone loves a menu that is familiar and friendly yet has just the right note of up–to–the–minute freshness.

Chile Cornbread

Macaroni Salad

K.C.–BBQ'd Glazed Chicken

BARKS · HERBS

REG. U.S. PAT. OFF.

'RESHING

Spicy Iced Tea

'50s French Dressing

Green Salad

Confetti Coleslaw

MENU
K.C.-BBQ'd Glazed Chicken (page 103) ●
Green salad with '50s French Dressing (page 200) ● Chile Cornbread (page 205) ●
Macaroni Salad with Dill & Ham (page 185) ● Confetti Coleslaw (page 183) ●
Pickled Peaches (page 209) ● Pickled Okra (page 208)

# butterflied turkey

## WITH YUCATAN RUB

6 to 8 servings

TURKEY

- 1 gallon water
- 2 cups kosher salt
- 1 cup firmly packed light brown sugar
- 1 8- to 10-pound turkey, butterflied (back and breast bone removed by your butcher)

RUB

- ½ cup annatto paste (see ShopSmart, right)
- 8 cloves garlic, peeled and smashed
- 3 tablespoons dried oregano, preferably Mexican
- 1½ teaspoons ground coriander
- 1½ teaspoons freshly ground black pepper
- ¾ teaspoon kosher salt
- ¼ teaspoon ground allspice

  Juice of 3 limes (a scant ½ cup)

  Juice of 1 orange (about ⅓ cup)

- 3 tablespoons extra-virgin olive oil

**1.** For the turkey: The day before serving, heat 3 quarts of the water with salt and sugar in a large pan, stirring to dissolve salt and sugar. Remove from heat, add remaining 1 quart cold water, and stir. Set brine aside to cool to room temperature.

**2.** Put turkey in a large container and cover with the brine. Cover and refrigerate for 4 to 5 hours. (If you want to brine the turkey overnight, use half the amount of salt and sugar.)

**3.** For rub: Crumble annatto paste into a food processor and blend with the garlic, oregano, coriander, black pepper, salt, and allspice. Add the fruit juices and the olive oil and process to make a pasty sauce. Drain and pat the turkey very dry. Smear the rub all over the bird. Cover and refrigerate overnight.

**4.** Prepare an outdoor grill with a large medium-heat fire for direct and indirect grilling. Position a drip pan under the grate on indirect side of the grill.

**5.** Place turkey, breast side up, over the drip pan and grill, covered, until meat is cooked about halfway through, about 50 minutes. Turn and cook until an instant-read thermometer inserted in the thigh registers 170°F, about 50 minutes more. Move turkey to direct heat and rotate to evenly brown the skin in the last 10 minutes of cooking. Transfer to a carving board, cover, and let rest 10 minutes before carving.

## ■ COOK'S NOTE

The turkey can be grilled as soon as it's rubbed with the spice paste, and it will be great. But if you have time, let it marinate—it will be awesome.

## ■ SHOPSMART

Annatto paste is a Mexican flavoring composed of ground annatto, or achiote, seeds mixed with herbs—usually oregano— and spices. The rust-color paste is then pressed into a compact brick. Look for it in the Hispanic section of your grocery.

# prairie-spiced turkey
## WITH QUICK CRANBERRY-APPLE RELISH

6 servings

TURKEY

2 gallons water

2 cups kosher salt

1 cup firmly packed light brown sugar

1 10- to 12-pound turkey, excess fat trimmed and giblets removed

Kosher salt

Freshly ground black pepper

1 medium onion, quartered

1 head garlic, halved

2 bay leaves

1/2 cup Prairie Rub (see recipe, page 227)

4 cups wood chips, such as hickory or mesquite, soaked in water for 30 minutes and drained

RELISH

Makes 4 cups

1 small navel orange

1 12-ounce bag fresh or frozen cranberries

1 Granny Smith apple, peeled, cored, and cut into large chunks

1/2 cup sugar

Pinch kosher salt

3 tablespoons walnuts, toasted and coarsely chopped

**1.** A day before serving, heat 3 quarts of the water, the salt, and sugar in a large pan, stirring to dissolve the sugar and salt. Remove from the heat, add the remaining water, and stir. Cool to room temperature.

**2.** Put the turkey in a large nonreactive container and cover with the brine. Cover and refrigerate 12 hours or overnight.

**3.** Drain and pat the turkey very dry, inside and out. Season the breast cavity with salt and black pepper to taste. Place the onion, garlic, and bay leaves inside the cavity. Spread the Prairie Rub over the entire bird.

**4.** Prepare an outdoor grill with a medium-high fire for both direct and indirect grilling. Position a drip pan under the grate on indirect side of the grill.

**5.** Place turkey breast side up over the drip pan. Toss 1 cup of the wood chips onto the coals. Cover the grill and rotate the lid so that the vent holes are directly over the meat. To maintain a medium-low smoky fire, add about a dozen pieces of charcoal and another cup of wood chips to the fire whenever the fire dies down. Rotate turkey about every 45 minutes to prevent the side near the coals from overcooking. Cook until an instant-read thermometer inserted in the thigh registers 170°F, 2 1/2 to 3 hours. Transfer to a cutting board and let rest 10 minutes before carving. Serve with Quick Cranberry-Apple Relish.

QUICK CRANBERRY-APPLE RELISH
Wash and dry the orange. Coarsely chop the orange, including the peel, and put in a food processor. Add the cranberries, apple, sugar, and salt and pulse until coarsely chopped. Transfer to a bowl, cover, and refrigerate for at least 2 hours and up to 2 days. Just before serving, stir in walnuts.

## ▮ KNOW-HOW

Brines work culinary magic, transforming the meat of the turkey—particularly the breast—into a flavorful, succulent treat. If you plan on brining your bird, choose one that isn't kosher or injected with solutions.

# duck salad
## WITH SHERRY DRESSING

4 servings

1 4- to 5-pound whole duck, breasts boned with skin left on and legs removed with skin left on (ask your butcher to do this)

2 teaspoons Spanish smoked paprika

4 teaspoons kosher salt

Freshly ground black pepper

1/2 cup whole almonds

5 tablespoons sherry vinegar

2 tablespoons honey

1 teaspoon minced fresh rosemary

1 medium red onion, sliced into 1/3-inch rounds

2 large navel oranges

1/4 cup extra-virgin olive oil

12 cups mesclun greens (about 10 ounces)

1/3 cup pitted green Spanish olives

**1.** Prepare an outdoor grill of your choice with a medium-high fire for both direct and indirect grilling. Position a drip pan under the grate on indirect side.
**2.** Trim and skin duck breasts, reserving skin from one. Rub all pieces with the smoked paprika, 2 teaspoons of the salt, and black pepper to taste.
**3.** Put legs skin side up on grill over drip pan and cook, covered, until skin crisps and meat is tender, about 45 minutes to 1 hour. (If using a charcoal grill, stoke the fire as needed with more coals to maintain a medium-high heat. )
**4.** Meanwhile, cook reserved duck skin in a skillet over medium heat to render 3 tablespoons of fat; discard remaining skin. Add almonds, 1/2 teaspoon salt, and black pepper to taste and cook until browned and toasted, about 2 minutes. Remove nuts with a slotted spoon; set aside. Off the heat, whisk in 3 tablespoons of the vinegar, 1 tablespoon of the honey, and rosemary. Lay onion rounds in pan, season with 1/2 teaspoon salt and black pepper to taste, and cook over low heat until soft and browned, turning once, about 6 minutes per side. Set aside.

**5.** Juice an orange half and whisk in a bowl with remaining 2 tablespoons vinegar, remaining 1 tablespoon honey, and 1 teaspoon salt. Gradually whisk in olive oil, starting with a few drops and adding the rest in a steady stream. Trim peel and pith from remaining half and whole orange and discard; slice oranges into thin half-moons.
**6.** Grill duck breast over a direct medium-high fire until lightly marked and meat is just firm to the touch, about 3 minutes per side. Cook legs over the fire to crisp their skins, about 1 minute. Cut leg meat from the bone into bite-size chunks. Thinly slice the breast meat against the grain.
**7.** Toss greens, orange slices, almonds, and olives with dressing. Divide salad evenly among 4 plates and top with both breast and leg meat and onion rounds.

# rotisserie duck
## WITH CHIPOTLE-TAMARIND BBQ SAUCE

4 servings

- 1 Pekin (Long Island) duckling (about 5 pounds)

  Kosher salt

  Freshly ground black pepper

- 1 orange, quartered
- 1 red onion, quartered
- 4 cloves garlic, peeled and smashed
- 1 cup Tamarind Barbecue Sauce (see recipe, page 224)

**1.** Prepare an outdoor grill with a rotisserie attachment with a medium fire. (Note: If you have a thermometer, it should register an internal temperature of about 300°F with lid closed.)

**2.** Remove the giblets and neck from the cavity of the bird and discard. Trim the neck flap and excess fat from around the cavity. Rinse the bird inside and out and pat dry. Pierce the skin all over with a small knife or skewer at 1/2-inch intervals, taking care not to poke into the meat. Season the cavity generously with salt and black pepper to taste and stuff it with the orange, onion, and garlic.

**3.** Thread the duck on the rotisserie spit through the cavity. Attach spit to the rotisserie. Set a drip pan under the duck. Cook the duck, covered, lifting the lid to pierce the skin every 10 minutes to drain the fat while it cooks. Once the duck has rendered most of its fat and is almost cooked, in about 50 minutes, baste it with about 1/2 cup of the barbecue sauce. Cook, uncovered, until the duck has a rich mahogany glaze and a meat thermometer inserted in the thigh reaches 180°F, about 20 to 25 minutes more.

**4.** When the duck is cooked, transfer it to a cutting board and let it rest for 10 minutes before carving—don't cover it or you will forfeit its lovely crisp skin. Carve the duck and arrange pieces on a warm serving platter. Drizzle a bit more of the sauce over the pieces and pass the rest at the table.

## ▇ COOK'S NOTE

It's important to keep piercing the skin of the duck as it cooks to keep the fat draining off.

## ▇ SHOPSMART

Tamarind has become one of our favorite ingredients. Familiar to both Latin and Asian cooks, this tart fruit adds a distinctive acidic taste to myriad dishes—curries, sauces, marinades, steak sauces, drinks, and BBQ sauces. The concentrate makes using it effortless, and it keeps for months in the refrigerator.

GREEK MOUNTAIN
# hens

4 servings

- 6 cups roughly chopped escarole, tough outer leaves removed (about 1½ heads)
- 16 sun-dried tomatoes packed in oil, drained and roughly chopped
- ½ cup pitted green olives, such as Picholine, roughly chopped
- ½ cup toasted walnut pieces, roughly chopped
- 5 cloves garlic, minced
- 2 tablespoons dried oregano, preferably Greek
- ½ teaspoon finely grated lemon zest
- ¼ teaspoon ground cinnamon
- ¼ cup extra-virgin olive oil
- ⅓ cup honey

  Freshly ground black pepper

- 10 ounces Greek feta cheese, crumbled (about 2½ cups)
- 4 Cornish game hens (about 1½ to 1¾ pounds each)

  Kosher salt

**1.** Prepare an outdoor grill with a medium-high fire for both direct and indirect grilling.

**2.** For the stuffing: Mix the escarole, tomatoes, olives, walnuts, garlic, oregano, lemon zest, and cinnamon in a large bowl. Add 2 tablespoons of the olive oil and 1 tablespoon of the honey and season with black pepper to taste. Mix in the feta, taking care not to break up the cheese too much.

**3.** Cut the backbones out of the hens and remove breast bones (see page 268). Slip a finger under the skin, from the neck end to loosen the skin over the breasts, thighs, and legs, making a pocket for the stuffing. Stuff ¼ of the stuffing under the skin of the breast and thighs of each hen. Brush with the remaining olive oil and season with salt and black pepper to taste.

**4.** Grill the hens skin side up over the direct heat until the underside is just browned, for 3 to 5 minutes. Transfer to indirect heat skin side up and cook, covered, until skin is golden brown (it does brown, although not directly on the heat) and an instant-read thermometer inserted in the thigh registers 155°F, about 15 to 25 minutes. Brush the skin generously with the remaining

honey and cook, covered, until glazed and thermometer registers 160°F, about 5 minutes. Transfer hens to a cutting board and let rest 10 minutes before serving.

## ■ SHOPSMART

You'll notice a variety of honey in stores. The color and flavor of a honey depends totally on the flowers the bee visits. Some honeys come from the nectar of just one flower and have distinct flavors, while the regular honey you buy at the grocery store is a blend from many flowers. Our favorite honey for this dish is a floral one such as clover, thyme, or orange.

# spice-rubbed quail
## WITH CRACKED WHEAT SALAD

4 servings

QUAIL

2 tablespoons ground sumac

1 tablespoon dried mint

1 teaspoon toasted sesame seeds

1 teaspoon kosher salt

Freshly ground black pepper

8 quail

Extra-virgin olive oil, for brushing

SALAD

1 tablespoon extra-virgin olive oil

1 cup medium-grain bulgur

2½ cups low-sodium canned chicken broth

1 teaspoon kosher salt

Freshly ground black pepper

2 cups cherry or grape tomatoes, halved

1 Kirby cucumber, seeded and diced

1 scallion (green and white parts), thinly sliced

2 tablespoons chopped fresh dill

2 tablespoons chopped fresh mint

2 tablespoons chopped fresh flat-leaf parsley

1 clove garlic, minced

Finely grated zest and freshly squeezed juice of ½ lemon (about 2 tablespoons juice)

½ teaspoon kosher salt

Hot pepper oil

**1.** For the quail: Mix the sumac, mint, sesame seeds, salt, and black pepper to taste in a small bowl and rub the mixture all over the quail.

**2.** Prepare an outdoor grill with a medium-high fire.

**3.** For the salad: Heat the olive oil in a medium skillet. Stir in the bulgur and cook until lightly toasted, about 3 minutes. Add chicken broth, salt, and black pepper to taste. Bring the mixture to a boil, then adjust heat to maintain a gentle simmer. Cover and cook until the bulgur is tender but not mushy, about 8 to 10 minutes. Drain any excess liquid and set aside to cool. Meanwhile, toss the remaining salad ingredients, except for the pepper oil, in another bowl.

**4.** Lightly oil the grill grate. Brush the birds with oil and grill them breast side down until golden and crisp, about 4 minutes. Turn and cook until an instant-read thermometer inserted into the thickest part of the thigh reads 120°F, about

1½ minutes more. Set aside to rest about 5 minutes.

**5.** Toss the cracked wheat with the salad mixture. Divide wheat salad among 4 plates, top with quail, and drizzle with hot pepper oil.

## SHOPSMART

Sumac (no, this is not the stuff that makes you scratch) is a crimson-color Middle Eastern spice that has a lemony taste.

## STYLE

The charm of cooking outdoors is its casual air. Even though this dish has its own savoir faire, encourage your guests to pick up the quail with their fingers so they don't miss a morsel.

115

# meat of the matter
## five

PORTERHOUSE WITH ROASTED SHALLOTS AND PORTOBELLOS • PEPPER-CRUSTED STRIP LOIN ROAST WITH CHIMICHURRI • MATAMBRE (HUNGER KILLER) • FIERY FLANK STEAK & PAPAYA SALAD • MEDALLIONS OF BEEF WITH CHILE-COFFEE BBQ SAUCE • STEAK & POTATOES WITH CHIVE-HORSERADISH SOUR CREAM • SHELL STEAKS WITH RED WINE BUTTER • TEXAS BBQ BRAISED BEEF BRISKET • KOREAN SHORT RIBS WITH CUCUMBER KIMCHEE • MIXED GRILL WITH CHIMICHURRI SAUCE • PORK TENDERLOINS WITH PINEAPPLE-MINT CHUTNEY • PORK RIBS & ROAST WITH MOJO • MAPLE-GLAZED PORK LOIN WITH APPLE-CRANBERRY CHUTNEY • PORK CHOPS WITH GREMOLATA • PEACH-MUSTARD PORK CHOPS WITH VIDALIA-PECAN SALAD • BACKYARD BBQ'D SPARERIBS • ITALIAN-STYLE COUNTRY-CUT RIBS • CHINESE LACQUERED BABY BACK RIBS • HERB-GARLIC LEG OF LAMB • JUNIPER & JALAPEÑO JELLY-GLAZED LAMB CHOPS • LAMB BROCHETTES WITH TAPENADE • VEAL CHOPS WITH ENDIVE & LEMON

# porterhouse

### WITH ROASTED SHALLOTS AND PORTOBELLOS

2 to 4 servings

STEAK

1   2-inch-thick porterhouse steak
    (about 3 pounds)

6   large shallots, unpeeled

2   tablespoons extra-virgin olive
    oil, plus additional for
    brushing

    Kosher salt

    Freshly ground black pepper

1   bunch fresh rosemary

MUSHROOMS

4   medium portobello
    mushrooms (about 1 pound
    total), stems discarded

3   tablespoons extra-virgin
    olive oil

2   tablespoons chopped fresh
    flat-leaf parsley

1   tablespoon balsamic vinegar

1   clove garlic, minced

**1.** Prepare an outdoor grill with a high fire for indirect grilling.
**2.** About 20 or 30 minutes before grilling, remove the steak from the refrigerator and set aside. On a large sheet of heavy-duty aluminum foil (or a doubled piece of regular), toss the shallots with the olive oil and some salt and black pepper to taste. Top with a generous sprig of rosemary and wrap and seal the foil into a tight package. Place package on the edge of the coals and roast, turning occasionally, until the shallots are very soft, about 25 minutes.
**3.** Season one side of steak generously with salt and black pepper to taste. Brush grill grate lightly with oil. If using charcoal, add the remaining rosemary sprigs to the fire. Grill the steak seasoned side down over the hottest part of the grill until seared, about 4 minutes. Rotate the meat 90 degrees to make clear grill marks, then continue to cook 2 minutes more. Season the top with salt and black pepper to taste, flip, and repeat on the other side. Once the steak is marked, move it to the cooler side of the grill with the eye (smaller end) away from heat and cover with a disposable aluminum pan. Cook until an instant-read thermometer inserted crosswise into the middle of the steak registers 120°F for rare. Transfer the steak to a cutting board and let rest for 5 minutes before slicing.
**4.** While the steak cooks, grill the mushrooms: Brush the mushroom caps with 2 tablespoons of the olive oil. Lightly oil the grill grate. Put the mushrooms cap side down on the edge of the charcoal, cover with a disposable aluminum pan, and cook until juices collect in the center of mushrooms, 6 to 7 minutes. Pour the juices into a bowl, flip the mushrooms, cover, and cook until soft and tender, about 6 minutes more. Slice mushrooms and toss with reserved juices, the remaining 1 tablespoon olive oil, the parsley, balsamic vinegar, garlic, and salt and black pepper to taste.
**5.** Slice the steak and serve with mushrooms and roasted shallots.

## ▬ SHOPSMART

Porterhouse and T-bone are similar cuts and have the best of all worlds—a tasty shell and a tender tenderloin, linked by the bone. The porterhouse has a larger eye of the tenderloin.

## ▬ KNOW-HOW

Always pull your steak or whatever meat you are cooking from the refrigerator about 20 minutes before you cook it. If grilled cold straight from the refrigerator, it won't cook as evenly as it will if it's just cool.

# pepper-crusted strip loin roast
## WITH CHIMICHURRI

10 servings

- ³/₄ cup mixed black, white, pink, and green peppercorns
- 3 tablespoons coriander seeds
- 2 tablespoons cumin seeds
- 1 6-pound beef shell roast (a roast cut from the short loin)

Vegetable oil for grill

Coarse sea salt

Chimichurri Sauce (see recipe, page 225)

**1.** Very coarsely grind the peppercorns, coriander, and cumin seeds in a spice grinder or with a mortar and pestle in several batches. Pat the roast dry and coat with peppercorn mixture. (This can be done several hours or 1 day ahead—cover and refrigerate the roast.)

**2.** Prepare an outdoor grill with a high fire for indirect grilling. Position a drip pan under the grate on the cooler side of the grill.

**3.** Brush grill lightly with oil. Place roast on cool side of grill. Cover with lid and cook, rotating meat every 15 minutes to crisp all sides, until an instant-read thermometer reads 118°F for medium-rare or 125°F for medium, about 1 to 1¹/₄ hours.

**4.** Transfer the roast to a cutting board, loosely tent with foil, and let rest for 30 minutes to finish cooking. Slice the roast across the grain and season the cut meat with coarse salt to taste. Serve drizzled with Chimichurri Sauce.

## SHOPSMART

You may need to give your butcher a heads-up on this one and order the roast a few days in advance. But be aware that he may want to finagle an invitation to your party when he sees what you're serving.

## MATAMBRE
# (hunger killer)

6 servings

- 1 2-pound flank steak, about ¹/₂ inch thick
- 8 cloves garlic, peeled
- ²/₃ cup red wine vinegar, plus additional for drizzling
- 2 teaspoons chopped fresh thyme
- Freshly ground black pepper
- ¹/₃ cup freshly grated Pecorino Romano cheese
- 3 to 4 anchovy fillets, minced
- 2 tablespoons extra-virgin olive oil, plus additional for drizzling
- 1¹/₂ teaspoons finely grated lemon zest
- 6 ounces fresh spinach, stemmed and chopped
- 3 hard-cooked eggs, chopped
- ¹/₂ teaspoon kosher salt, plus additional for seasoning
- ³/₄ pound sliced bacon
- Vegetable oil for grill
- Tomato & Basil Dressing (see recipe, page 201) (optional)

**1.** Butterfly the steak by slicing it parallel to the work surface, starting on a long side and leaving it attached at the opposite side so that it opens like a book. (The seam will run parallel to the grain.) Open the steak and pound it to an even thickness. Roughly chop 6 of the garlic cloves and mix with the ²/₃ cup vinegar, thyme, and black pepper to taste in a large nonreactive baking dish. Put the steak in the marinade, turn to coat, and set aside.
**2.** Mince remaining 2 cloves of garlic and mix with Pecorino, anchovies, the 2 tablespoons olive oil, and lemon zest in a large bowl. Add spinach, eggs, the ¹/₂ teaspoon salt, and black pepper to taste and toss gently.
**3.** Remove the steak from the marinade, pat dry, and season all over with salt and black pepper to taste. Spread the spinach-egg mixture over the meat, leaving a 1-inch border around edge. Roll steak up from a short end. Lay bacon strips next to one another

so they overlap slightly. Place the steak seam down on one short end of the bacon strips and roll the steak with the bacon. (Don't worry if the bacon does not completely enclose the meat.) Tie a piece of butcher's twine around each strip of bacon and a piece lengthwise around the roll. (This can be done a day ahead, covered, and refrigerated.) Prepare an outdoor grill with medium-high fire for indirect grilling. Position a drip pan under the grate on the cooler side of the grill.
**4.** Brush grill grate lightly with oil. Put steak on the grill so a long side is about two-thirds over the drip pan and the other about one-third over the heat and cook, uncovered, rotating every 8 to 10 minutes, until bacon crisps on all sides, about 40 minutes. Transfer to a cutting board and rest for 5 minutes before slicing. Slice, sprinkle with salt, and drizzle with olive oil and vinegar or Tomato & Basil Dressing, if desired.

1. Slice steak parallel to work surface. Leave attached so it opens like a book. 2. Spread filling over meat, leaving a 1-inch border around edge. Roll up steak. 3. Lay bacon strips next to one another so they overlap slightly. Place steak seam side down on bacon and roll. 4. Tie a piece of twine around each bacon strip and lengthwise around roll.

# fiery flank steak
## & PAPAYA SALAD

4 servings

MARINADE

1 ripe Hawaiian papaya (about 12 ounces), peeled, seeded, and coarsely chopped

Juice of 2 limes

2 cloves garlic, minced

1/2 medium red onion, grated

1 fresh habañero chile, stemmed and minced

1 teaspoon kosher salt, plus additional for seasoning meat

1 1 1/2-pound flank steak

Freshly ground black pepper

CITRUS-HABAÑERO DRESSING

1 clove garlic, peeled

2 teaspoons kosher salt

Juice of 1 lime

Juice of 1/2 orange

1/3 cup extra-virgin olive oil

1/4 medium red onion, minced

1/2 to 1 fresh habañero chile, stemmed, finely chopped with seeds

1/4 cup coarsely chopped fresh cilantro

SALAD

1 small head green or red leaf lettuce, torn

1 small jicama (about 3/4 pound), peeled and diced

1 Hawaiian papaya, peeled, seeded, and diced

Kosher salt

Freshly ground black pepper

**1.** For the marinade: Puree the papaya with the lime juice in a food processor and pour into a nonreactive dish. Stir in the garlic, onion, chile, and the 1 teaspoon salt. Put the beef in the marinade and turn to coat well. Cover with plastic wrap and refrigerate for 1 to 4 hours, turning occasionally.
**2.** Prepare an outdoor grill with a high-heat fire.
**3.** For the dressing: Smash the garlic clove, sprinkle with the salt, and, with the side of a large knife, mash and smear the mixture to a coarse paste. Put the garlic paste in a medium bowl and whisk in the citrus juices. Gradually whisk in the olive oil, starting with a few drops, then adding the rest in a steady stream to make a smooth, slightly thick dressing. Stir in the onion, chile, and cilantro.
**4.** Remove the steak from marinade, pat dry, and season with some salt and black pepper to taste. Grill until slightly charred and crisp and medium-rare, about 6 to 7 minutes. (An instant-read thermometer inserted crosswise into the side of the steak should register 130°F.) Set aside on a cutting board to rest for at least 5 minutes before slicing.

**5.** For the salad: Thinly slice the meat across the grain. Season the greens with salt and black pepper to taste and toss with about half the dressing. Divide the greens among 4 plates and top with some of the beef, jicama, and papaya. Season with some salt and black pepper to taste and drizzle the remaining dressing over the salads. Serve immediately.

## ■ KNOW-HOW

Tropical fruits such as papaya, kiwi, and pineapple have an enzyme that tenderizes meat. Be careful: It does its job well—if the meat is marinated for too long or the pieces of meat are very small, they can get mushy.

## ■ SHOPSMART

We prefer the smaller, sweeter Hawaiian papayas to the massive Mexican ones. The Hawaiian variety is what you are likely to find in your American supermarket.

# medallions of beef
## WITH CHILE-COFFEE BBQ SAUCE

4 to 6 servings

3 ounces Cotija cheese or queso blanco

¼ cup toasted pine nuts

¼ cup chopped fresh cilantro

3 tablespoons extra-virgin olive oil

Freshly ground black pepper

1 tablespoon chili powder

1 tablespoon kosher salt

4 beef tenderloin medallions (about 8 ounces each)

¾ cup Chile-Coffee BBQ Sauce (see recipe, page 223)

**1.** Prepare an outdoor grill with a medium-high heat fire.

**2.** Crumble cheese into marble-size chunks and toss with the pine nuts, cilantro, 1 tablespoon of the olive oil, and some black pepper to taste. Set aside.

**3.** Mix the chili powder, salt, and some black pepper to taste in a small bowl. Brush the steaks on both sides with the remaining 2 tablespoons olive oil and sprinkle with the chili powder mixture. Grill until brown and crisp on both sides and medium-rare, about 8 minutes, turning halfway through. (An instant-read thermometer inserted crosswise into the meat should register between 120°F and 125°F.) Transfer the steaks to a cutting board and let rest 5 minutes before serving.

**4.** Spoon about 3 tablespoons of Chile-Coffee BBQ Sauce into centers of 4 plates. Put medallions on top of the sauce and top each with some of the cheese mixture.

# steak & potatoes
## WITH CHIVE-HORSERADISH SOUR CREAM

4 to 6 servings

STEAK

1 cup red wine vinegar

1/3 cup cognac or other brandy

1/2 cup extra-virgin olive oil

1 small onion, diced

2 tablespoons roughly chopped fresh rosemary

4 cloves garlic, roughly chopped

2 tablespoons sugar

Freshly ground black pepper

2¼ pounds beef shell, tri-tip, or sirloin steak, trimmed and cut into 1½-inch cubes

POTATOES

24 small to medium new potatoes (about 2½ pounds)

1 head garlic, halved crosswise

1 sprig fresh rosemary

10 black peppercorns

Kosher salt

SAUCE

1 bunch fresh chives, coarsely chopped (about 3/4 cup)

1 cup sour cream

1/3 cup prepared horseradish, drained

1¼ teaspoons kosher salt

Freshly ground black pepper

**I.** For the steak: Mix the vinegar, cognac, olive oil, onion, rosemary, garlic, sugar, and black pepper to taste in a large nonreactive pan. Add the cubed steak and turn to coat. Cover and refrigerate for 4 hours or overnight.

**2.** For the potatoes: Trim potatoes into cubes about the same size as the beef, leaving some skin on. Put the potatoes, garlic, rosemary, and peppercorns with cold water to cover in a medium saucepan; salt the water generously and bring to a boil. Reduce the heat and simmer just until tender, about 8 to 10 minutes; drain.

**3.** For the sauce: Bring a small pot of salted water to a boil. Add chives and cook, uncovered, until tender but still bright green, about 3 minutes. Drain and rinse under very cold water. Gently squeeze out excess water from chives and put in a blender with sour cream, horseradish, and salt. Blend until smooth and vibrant green. Transfer to a couple of small serving bowls.

**4.** If using wooden skewers, soak them in water for at least 30 minutes before grilling. Prepare an outdoor grill with a high-heat fire.

**5.** Thread 3 cubes of meat and 3 potatoes alternately onto each of 8 skewers, leaving a little space between meat and potatoes. Season with salt and black pepper to taste and grill, turning once, until browned and nicely marked, about 6 to 8 minutes. Let rest 5 minutes and serve with the sauce.

## ▮ COOK'S NOTE

We tried each of the different cuts suggested for use in this skewered twist on steak and potatoes. There was something to recommend in all. Our favorite was the shell steak, but our wallets took a real hit. The more economical tri-tip was wonderfully beefy and took to the marinade well. Old reliable sirloin had good flavor but more of a chew. We advocate piercing the meat repeatedly with a fork before cutting it into cubes.

# shell steaks
## WITH RED WINE BUTTER

4 to 6 servings

8 tablespoons unsalted butter, softened

3 cloves garlic, minced

1 shallot, minced

1 teaspoon coriander seeds, cracked

1/2 teaspoon black peppercorns, cracked

1/2 cup ruby port

1/2 cup red wine

2 teaspoons red wine vinegar

2 tablespoons minced fresh flat-leaf parsley

1 1/2 teaspoons kosher salt, plus additional for seasoning

Vegetable oil for grill

4 10- to 12-ounce shell steaks (also called club steak or New York steak), about 1 1/4 inches thick

Freshly ground black pepper

**1.** Melt 1 tablespoon of butter in a small saucepan over medium-high heat. Add the garlic and shallot and cook, stirring, until golden brown, about 3 minutes. Add the coriander seeds and peppercorns and cook until fragrant, about 30 seconds. Pull the pan from the heat and add the port and wine. Return the pan to the heat and, if cooking over a gas burner, tip the pan to let the alcohol ignite. (If cooking over electric or halogen, just keep cooking the mixture.) Bring the mixture to a boil, reduce the heat, and simmer briskly until syrupy, 20 to 25 minutes. Set aside to cool.

**2.** Beat the remaining butter in a medium bowl with a handheld electric mixer or whisk until smooth and light. Add the reduced wine mixture, vinegar, parsley, and 1 1/2 teaspoons salt and beat until evenly mixed.

**3.** Spread a 12-inch-long piece of plastic wrap on a work surface. Mound the butter across the plastic wrap, about 2 inches from edge nearest you. Fold the bottom edge of the plastic wrap over the butter and roll it up to make a 1-inch-wide log. Twist the ends together in opposite directions (like a party favor) and refrigerate until firm.

**4.** Prepare an outdoor grill with a high fire.

**5.** Brush grill grate lightly with oil. Season the steaks on both sides with salt and black pepper to taste. Grill 3 to 5 minutes, turning once, until an instant-read thermometer inserted in the meat reads 120°F to 125°F for rare; 125°F to 130°F for medium-rare; or 130°F to 135°F for medium. Transfer the steaks to a cutting board and let rest for 5 minutes. Serve each steak topped with a 3/4-inch-thick slice of the wine butter.

## COOK'S NOTE

Any leftover butter can be frozen and used with lamb and pork.

127

TEXAS BBQ BRAISED
# beef brisket

6 to 8 servings

## RUB

1/4 cup sweet Hungarian paprika

1 tablespoon kosher salt, plus additional for seasoning

1 tablespoon freshly ground black pepper, plus additional for seasoning

1 tablespoon light brown sugar

1 teaspoon cayenne pepper

1 5- to 6-pound piece beef brisket, preferably point cut, fat trimmed

6 cups wood chips, preferably hickory or mesquite

## BRAISING SAUCE

1 28-ounce can tomato puree

12 ounces lager or amber beer

2 ribs celery, minced

1 medium onion, minced

3/4 cup cider vinegar

1/2 cup brown sugar

1/4 cup yellow mustard

5 thick slices bacon, coarsely chopped (about 6 ounces)

10 cloves garlic, minced

4 canned chipotle chiles in adobo sauce, minced

3 ancho chiles, stemmed, seeded, and chopped

2 bay leaves

2 tablespoons chili powder

1 tablespoon kosher salt, plus additional for seasoning

Freshly ground black pepper

4 cups water

**1.** For the rub: Mix the paprika, 1 tablespoon each of salt and black pepper, the brown sugar, and the cayenne. Rub spice mixture all over brisket, wrap tightly, and refrigerate overnight.
**2.** Soak the wood chips in water for at least 30 minutes before grilling. Prepare an outdoor grill with a medium to medium-low fire for indirect grilling.
**3.** For the sauce: Mix the tomato puree, beer, celery, onion, 1/2 cup of the vinegar, the brown sugar, mustard, bacon, garlic, chiles, bay leaves, chili powder, 1 tablespoon salt, and black pepper to taste in a large disposable aluminum pan. Put brisket in the sauce.
**4.** Throw a handful of drained wood chips on the hot coals, put the pan over the cooler side of the grill, and cover so the vent holes are directly over the brisket. Baste meat every 30 minutes, turning occasionally and adding water to the pan as necessary to keep meat partially submerged, until the meat is tender and an instant-read thermometer inserted in the thickest part registers 200°F, about 3 3/4 hours. Replenish the charcoal as needed to maintain a medium to medium-low fire.

**5.** Transfer the brisket to a cutting board, tent with foil, and let rest for 20 minutes. Skim the fat from the braising sauce and stir in the remaining 1/4 cup cider vinegar and salt to taste. Reheat if necessary. Thinly slice brisket across the grain and arrange on a serving platter. Spoon some sauce over the meat and pass the rest at the table.

## ■ KNOW-HOW

There are lots of wood chips to choose from. We like the stronger, traditional flavor that hickory or mesquite gives to this dish. Fruit woods such as apple and cherry are delicious with milder meats, such as pork, poultry, or fish. Chips also come in different sizes—either chunks or bits. The chunks don't require soaking and produce a big blast of fast-burning smoke. The bits, which do require soaking, produce smoldering smoke.

# korean short ribs
## WITH CUCUMBER KIMCHEE

4 to 6 servings

RIBS

6 pounds beef short ribs, cut crosswise into twelve 2½-inch squares (ask your butcher to cut the ribs for you)

Korean BBQ Marinade (see recipe, page 221)

Vegetable oil for grill

CUCUMBER KIMCHEE

4 Kirby cucumbers

4 scallions (white and green parts), thinly sliced

5 cloves garlic, chopped

3 tablespoons grated peeled fresh ginger

3 tablespoons sugar

1½ teaspoons kosher salt

1½ teaspoons crushed red pepper, ground

**1.** Prepare ribs according to photo below. Place the ribs in one layer in a large nonreactive baking dish, pour in the Korean BBQ Marinade, and turn the ribs to coat. Cover and refrigerate. Marinate for 2 to 8 hours (longer makes the ribs too salty).
**2.** Prepare an outdoor grill with a high-heat fire.
**3.** Remove the ribs from the marinade. Brush the grill grate lightly with oil. Place the ribs on the grill meaty side down and cook, turning as needed, until well browned but still pink inside, about 10 to 12 minutes. Set ribs aside to rest for 5 minutes. Serve with Cucumber Kimchee.

CUCUMBER KIMCHEE
A day before serving, halve the cucumbers crosswise, set them upright on the cut end, and slice lengthwise into quarters, stopping about ½ inch from the cut end. Mix the scallions, garlic, ginger, sugar, salt, and red pepper and stuff about a tablespoon of the mixture into each cucumber. Put the cucumbers in a small nonreactive baking dish, cover with plastic wrap, and refrigerate overnight.

Remove any silver skin from the top of the meat. Butterfly the short ribs so they open like books, with the meat about ⅓ to ½ inch thick and still attached to the bone.

# mixed grill
## WITH CHIMICHURRI SAUCE

6 to 8 servings

2  beef blade steaks, each about 6 ounces

1  lamb leg steak, 1¼ to 1½ pounds

1  pork tenderloin, about 1¾ pounds

1  pound fresh chorizo sausage

Chimichurri Sauce (see recipe, page 225)

Olive oil for brushing meats

Kosher salt

Freshly ground black pepper

**1.** Twenty minutes before grilling, bring meats to room temperature.

**2.** Prepare an outdoor grill with a medium-high fire. While the grill heats up, make the Chimichurri Sauce and set it aside.

**3.** Preheat the grill grate for 5 minutes; scrape it clean with a grill brush. Brush the beef, lamb, and pork with olive oil and season generously with salt and black pepper to taste. Grill all the meats, turning once, until an instant-read thermometer inserted into the sides of the steaks registers 125°F. For medium-rare, the beef takes about 2 minutes per side, the lamb about 4 minutes. Grill the pork tenderloin until the thermometer registers 145°F, about 15 minutes, and the sausage 160°F, about 10 minutes, turning both as needed to get nice grill marks on all sides. Transfer the meats to a cutting board and let them rest 5 minutes. Slice the beef and lamb steaks across the grain, slice the pork tenderloin, cut the sausage into chunks, and serve all the meats with the Chimichurri Sauce.

## STYLE

For the crosshatched marks of a master griller, lay your steaks at an angle across the grill grate and don't move them until they get a good sear. Then rotate them (don't turn them over yet) about 45 degrees from their original spot on the grill. Once you've made your mark, flip and repeat on the other side.

# pork tenderloins
## WITH PINEAPPLE-MINT CHUTNEY

6 servings

PORK AND BRINE

1 teaspoon coriander seeds

8 whole allspice berries

4 whole cloves

1 cup cold water

3 tablespoons kosher salt, plus additional for seasoning

2 tablespoons dark brown sugar

1/4 cup chopped fresh ginger with peel

4 cloves garlic

1 cup dark rum

3 pork tenderloins

Freshly ground black pepper

CHUTNEY

1/4 teaspoon coriander seeds

4 whole allspice berries

2 whole cloves

2 tablespoons unsalted butter

5 coins peeled fresh ginger

2 cloves garlic, peeled and smashed

1/2 fresh jalapeño (seeds optional), stemmed

1/4 cup rice vinegar

1 tablespoon light brown sugar

3 cups chopped fresh pineapple

2 teaspoons kosher salt

2 scallions (white and green parts), thinly sliced

2 tablespoons chopped fresh mint

Juice of half a lime

**1.** For the brine: Crush the spices with the bottom of a saucepan. Put spices in a saucepan and toast, swirling pan over medium heat for 3 minutes. Add water, 3 tablespoons salt, brown sugar, ginger, and garlic to the pan. Bring to a boil, remove from heat, and stir in the rum; cool to room temperature. Remove silver skin from tenderloins and place in a bowl or shallow container. Pour the brine over the tenderloins. Cover and refrigerate 1 to 4 hours.

**2.** For the chutney: Put the coriander, allspice, and cloves in a small skillet and toast, swirling pan, over medium-high heat until fragrant, about 30 seconds. Crush spices with a heavy pan or a mortar and pestle. Heat butter in a small saucepan over medium-high heat. Add ginger, garlic, and jalapeño and cook, stirring, until lightly browned and fragrant, about 3 minutes. Add toasted spices, vinegar, and sugar and stir until dissolved. Stir in pineapple and salt. Bring to a boil, reduce heat to low, and simmer until slightly thickened, about 20 minutes. Cool, then stir in scallions, mint, and lime juice.

**3.** Prepare an outdoor grill with a medium-high fire for direct and indirect grilling.

**4.** Remove the tenderloins from the brine and pat dry. Brush the grill grate lightly with vegetable oil. Season tenderloins with coarsely ground black pepper and salt to taste. Grill the tenderloins over direct heat until each side is golden brown, about 6 minutes per side. Move the meat over to the cool side of the grill, cover with a disposable aluminum pan, and cook until an instant-read thermometer inserted in the center reads at least 145°F for medium, about 6 to 8 minutes more. Let rest 5 minutes before slicing. Slice the tenderloins into medallions and serve with the chutney.

# pork ribs & roast
## WITH MOJO

6 servings

MARINADE

1 generous tablespoon cumin
    seeds

8 cloves garlic, chopped

1/2 cup freshly squeezed lime
    juice (about 4 limes)

1/4 cup extra-virgin olive oil

2 tablespoons kosher salt

1 generous tablespoon dried
    oregano, crumbled

1 tablespoon freshly ground
    black pepper

1 6-chop pork rib roast, chine
    bone attached and notched at
    each rib (about 5 pounds)

MOJO

Makes about 1²/3 cups

1/2 teaspoon cumin seeds

6 cloves garlic, minced

1/2 cup olive oil

1 cup fresh lime juice

2 teaspoons chopped fresh
    oregano or 1 teaspoon dried
    oregano, crumbled

2 teaspoons kosher salt

1/2 teaspoon freshly ground black
    pepper

2 habañero chiles, seeded and
    minced

**1.** Toast both the 1 tablespoon
and the 1/2 teaspoon cumin seeds
in a small saute pan over high
heat until fragrant, about
30 seconds. Grind the seeds in a
spice grinder or with a mortar
and pestle and reserve
1/2 teaspoon for the Mojo. Mix
remaining cumin with garlic,
lime juice, olive oil, salt, oregano,
and black pepper. Remove the
pork loin from the ribs and
chine bone by cutting between
the meat and the bones. Rub the
marinade all over loin and ribs.
Place the loin back onto the ribs
where it was removed and tie
together with butcher's twine.
Place in a nonreactive container,
cover, and refrigerate for 4 hours
or overnight.

**2.** Meanwhile, make the Mojo
and reserve 3/4 cup to serve with
the pork.

**3.** Prepare an outdoor grill with
a medium-high fire for indirect
grilling. Position a drip pan
under grate on the cooler side of
the grill. Set the roast rib side
down over the pan on the side
opposite from the heat. Cover,
with the vent holes over the
pork and cook, basting the meat
periodically with the sauce.
Rotate the roast 180 degrees after
30 minutes so it cooks evenly.
(Add coals to the fire as needed
to maintain an even heat.) After

an hour, begin to baste with
Mojo every 15 minutes and set
the roast on its chine (back)
bone, with the fat facing the
heat, so it browns evenly. Cook
until a meat thermometer
inserted into the center of the
loin registers 140°F, about
1 1/2 hours in all.

**4.** Remove the roast from grill,
cut the twine, and let the loin
rest for 10 minutes. Meanwhile,
place the ribs on the grill over
direct heat with the side where
the loin was attached facing
down. Grill, turning as needed,
until evenly browned, about
4 minutes. Let rest 5 minutes
and cut between the ribs. Serve
ribs with sliced loin and
reserved Mojo.

MOJO

Heat the reserved 1/2 teaspoon
cumin in a skillet along with the
garlic and olive oil. Cook over
medium-high heat until garlic
begins to sizzle, about
2 minutes. Remove from heat,
transfer to a nonreactive bowl,
and stir in remaining ingredients.

# maple-glazed pork loin
### WITH APPLE-CRANBERRY CHUTNEY

4 to 6 servings

BRINE & PORK

  2 quarts cold water

  1/3 cup kosher salt

  1/4 cup dark brown sugar

  1 cup chopped fresh ginger, with peel

  1 head garlic, halved crosswise

  1 cinnamon stick

  1 teaspoon fennel seeds

  2 whole cloves

  1 star anise

  1 2-pound pork loin roast


GRILLING

  3 tablespoons Chinese five-spice powder

  2 tablespoons kosher salt

    Vegetable oil for brushing

  1 cup pure maple syrup


APPLE-CRANBERRY CHUTNEY

Makes about 1½ cups

  1/4 red onion, chopped

  1/4 cup red currant jam

  3 tablespoons cider vinegar

  1 tablespoon unsalted butter

  2 teaspoons minced, peeled fresh ginger

  1/2 teaspoon kosher salt

  1 teaspoon Madras curry powder

  1 cinnamon stick

    Pinch crushed red pepper

  3 soft cooking apples, such as McIntosh, peeled, seeded, and cut into large chunks

  2 tablespoons dried cranberries

  3 tablespoons chopped fresh cilantro


**1.** Six hours before grilling: Heat half the water with the remaining brine ingredients, except the pork, stirring until the salt and sugar dissolve. Add the rest of the water; cool. Put the pork and brine in a large nonreactive bowl or plastic container, cover, and refrigerate for 6 hours.

**2.** About 30 minutes before grilling, remove the pork from the brine, pat dry, and bring to room temperature. Mix the five-spice powder and salt in a shallow bowl.

**3.** Prepare an outdoor grill with a medium-high fire for direct and indirect grilling.

**4.** Brush the grill grate lightly with oil. Brush the pork with oil and rub all over with the spice mixture. Grill over direct heat, turning occasionally, until nicely marked on all sides, about

15 minutes. Move the meat to the cooler side of the grill, cover, and cook until an instant-read thermometer inserted in the center registers 130°F, about 50 minutes; rotate the meat halfway through. Brush the meat with some maple syrup, cover, and cook, basting occasionally with syrup, until the pork reaches 145°F for medium, about 20 minutes more. Rest meat for 10 minutes before slicing. Serve with Apple-Cranberry Chutney.

APPLE-CRANBERRY CHUTNEY
In microwave-safe bowl stir together the onion, jam, vinegar, butter, ginger, salt, curry powder, cinnamon stick, and red pepper. Cover with plastic wrap and microwave on high for 1 minute. Stir in apples and cranberries, cover, and microwave on high for 10 minutes. Vent the plastic wrap and set aside for 10 minutes. Stir in the cilantro just before serving.

# pork chops
## WITH GREMOLATA

4 servings

BRINE & CHOPS

1 tablespoon pickling spice

2 cups water

¼ cup chopped fresh ginger, with peel

3 tablespoons kosher salt

2 tablespoons firmly packed dark brown sugar

2 cloves garlic, unpeeled

4 1½-inch-thick rib pork chops (about 4 pounds)

Vegetable oil for the grill

GREMOLATA

2 cloves garlic, peeled

¾ teaspoon kosher salt

1½ cups fresh flat-leaf parsley, coarsely chopped

¼ cup extra-virgin olive oil

2 teaspoons finely grated lemon zest

Juice of ½ lemon

Pinch crushed red pepper

Freshly ground black pepper

**1.** For the pork chops: Use the bottom of a saucepan to crush the pickling spice, then scoop into the saucepan. Toast over medium heat until fragrant, about 3 minutes, swirling the pan frequently. Add 1 cup of the water along with the ginger, salt, sugar, and garlic. Bring to a boil, remove from heat, and add the remaining 1 cup cold water. Cool brine to room temperature, then add the pork chops, cover, and refrigerate 4 to 12 hours.

**2.** Prepare an outdoor grill with a medium-high fire for both direct and indirect grilling.

**3.** Meanwhile, make the gremolata: Smash the garlic cloves, sprinkle with the salt, and, with the side of a large knife, mash and smear the mixture to a coarse paste. Put the garlic in a small bowl and stir in the parsley, olive oil, lemon zest and juice, and red pepper. Season with black pepper to taste.

**4.** Remove the chops from the brine and pat dry. Rub the grill grate lightly with oil. Grill the chops on the hottest spot on the grill, turning once, until each side is slightly charred, about 4 minutes per side. Move chops over to the cooler side of the grill and continue cooking, covered with a disposable aluminum pan, until medium, about 5 to 7 minutes more. (An instant-read thermometer inserted crosswise into the chops should register about 140°F.) Remove from grill and let rest 5 minutes before serving. Divide chops among 4 plates and serve topped with the gremolata.

## COOK'S NOTE

Gremolata is usually the final flourish of flavor added to tender braised osso buco. But the notion of chopped fresh herbs with citrus and extra-virgin olive oil just calls out to the smokiness of grilled foods. Expand the herbs: Add rosemary or thyme and substitute orange for the lemon when serving with chicken, fish, or lamb.

# peach-mustard pork chops
## WITH VIDALIA-PECAN SALAD

4 servings

PORK CHOPS

4  1½-inch-thick pork chops

   Safflower or corn oil, for brushing

   Kosher salt

   Freshly ground black pepper

2  medium Vidalia onions, peeled, root end attached, and quartered

   Peach-Mustard BBQ Sauce (see recipe, page 220)

SALAD

2  tablespoons white wine vinegar

¾  teaspoon kosher salt

   Freshly ground black pepper

⅓  cup extra-virgin olive oil

8  cups mixed salad greens

   Candied Pecans (see recipe, right)

PECANS

⅓  cup sugar

½  teaspoon cayenne pepper

½  teaspoon kosher salt

½  cup pecan halves

**1.** For the chops: Prepare an outdoor grill with a high heat for both direct and indirect grilling. Position a drip pan under the grate on the cooler side of the grill.

**2.** Brush the pork chops on both sides with oil and season with salt and black pepper to taste. Set aside for 15 minutes. Brush the onions with oil.

**3.** For the salad: Whisk the vinegar, salt, and black pepper to taste in a large bowl. Gradually whisk in oil, starting with a few drops and adding the rest in a steady stream to make a smooth dressing. Add the salad greens to the bowl, but don't toss.

**4.** Grill the chops over the heat until brown on both sides, about 4 minutes per side. Move them to the cool side of the grill and brush with some of the Peach-Mustard BBQ Sauce. Cook the chops, covered, turning and basting with sauce every 5 minutes, until an instant-read thermometer inserted crosswise into the chops registers 140°F, about 15 minutes more. Let rest for 10 minutes. Grill the onions over direct heat, turning as needed, until charred and tender, about 10 minutes.

**5.** To serve: Roughly chop the Candied Pecans and toss with greens and dressing. Divide the salad and onions among 4 plates and top with the chops. Drizzle the chops with more sauce.

CANDIED PECANS
Line a baking sheet with aluminum foil. Stir the sugar, cayenne, and salt together in a medium saucepan. Cook over medium-high heat, stirring, until all the sugar melts. Add the nuts and stir to coat evenly. Reduce the heat to medium and continue to cook until the sugar caramelizes, about 2 minutes more. Carefully turn hot nuts out onto the prepared pan; cool.

## COOK'S NOTE

To avoid a soggy salad, cross salad utensils over the dressing and then add greens; it keeps them out of the dressing while you grill the chops.

## KNOW-HOW

For easy cleanup, fill the sugar-coated pot with water and add your sugar-covered spoon. Return to the stove to heat up. The hot water will remove the sugar from the sides of the pot and your spoon.

# spareribs

4 to 6 servings

2 racks pork spareribs (about 3 pounds each)

½ cup Memphis Shake (see recipe, page 231) or Cajun Rub (see recipe, page 228)

3 cups wood chips, soaked in water for at least 30 minutes and drained

2 cups of one of the following:

Kansas City-Style BBQ Sauce (see recipe, page 218)

Cola Barbecue Sauce (see recipe, page 217)

Chile-Coffee BBQ Sauce (see recipe, page 223)

**1.** Trim the membrane off the back of the ribs (see page 272) and rub ribs all over with spice blend. Cover and refrigerate for 2 to 24 hours. Soak wood chips in water for at least 30 minutes before grilling.
**2.** Prepare an outdoor grill with a medium fire for indirect grilling. Place a drip pan, half-filled with water, under the cooler side of the grill grate. Open bottom vents of the grill.
**3.** Set the ribs over the drip pan. (If you have a rib rack, use it.) Toss 1 cup of the drained wood chips onto the coals and cover the grill. Rotate the lid so that the vent holes are directly over the ribs. Add about 1 cup of hardwood charcoals to the fire about every hour during the cooking time to maintain a medium to medium-low fire (a temperature of about 250°F to 275°F is ideal). After 3 hours the meat should pull back from the bones and will have turned a reddish brown. Baste the ribs with some of the barbecue sauce of your choice and cook over direct heat until lightly glazed. Cut the racks into ribs and serve with extra sauce on the side.

## SHOPSMART

Spareribs always mean pork from the belly. A rack of 11 rib bones ideally weighs between 2 and 3 pounds. Spareribs are often sold with a meaty section of the flank attached; when trimmed, they are known as "St. Louis style."

## COOK'S NOTE

If you like your ribs dry, skip the sauce or simply serve it on the side.

Ribs rule when it comes to barbecue—they're intensely meaty, moist, and kissed with smoke. Who can resist gnawing on a bone?

ITALIAN-STYLE
# country-cut ribs

4 to 6 servings

10 country-style bone-in pork ribs (about 6½ pounds total)

2 tablespoons kosher salt

Freshly ground black pepper

1 35-ounce can whole peeled tomatoes, with liquid

1 cup Italian red wine, such as Chianti or Valpolicella

½ cup red wine vinegar

1 large onion, sliced

12 cloves garlic, peeled and smashed

3 tablespoons dried basil

2 tablespoons dried oregano

2 tablespoons fennel seeds

1 tablespoon dried savory

1½ teaspoons crushed red pepper

2 bay leaves

½ cup honey

**1.** Preheat the oven to 350°F. Put the ribs in a single layer in a large roasting pan and season with the salt and black pepper to taste. Add the tomatoes, wine, vinegar, onion, garlic, basil, oregano, fennel seeds, savory, red pepper, and bay leaves. Cover with parchment paper and braise in the oven for about 1¾ to 2 hours, or until meat is tender all the way through but not falling off the bone.

**2.** Let the ribs cool in the braising liquid until cool enough to handle, about 30 minutes. Remove ribs from the sauce, scraping any tomato or onion clinging to the meat back into the sauce. Remove and discard bay leaves. Puree the braising liquid with the honey in a blender (or right in the pan with an immersion blender) and transfer the sauce to a saucepan. Briskly simmer the sauce, skimming both the fat and the foam from the surface as it cooks, until thick, about 20 minutes. (The dish can be prepared up to this point 1 or 2 days ahead, cooled, covered, and refrigerated.)

**3.** Preheat an outdoor grill with a medium fire. Dip each rib into the sauce to coat evenly. Grill until browned and glazed, about 3 to 5 minutes per side. Serve ribs on a platter and pass the remaining sauce at the table.

## SHOPSMART

Economical country-style ribs vary from butcher to butcher. Cut from either the sirloin or the blade end of the loin, they can be butterflied chops, well-marbled meaty portions with bones but no ribs, or boneless portions that require a knife and fork for eating. If you have a particular way you want them, be specific with your butcher.

CHINESE LACQUERED
# baby back ribs

4 to 6 servings

2 racks baby back ribs (about 5 pounds total)

1 cup rice vinegar

½ cup roughly chopped, unpeeled fresh ginger

¼ cup soy sauce

5 cloves garlic, chopped

1 tablespoon toasted sesame oil

¼ cup five-spice powder

Kosher salt

Freshly ground black pepper

¾ cup hoisin sauce

2 to 3 teaspoons Asian chili sauce, such as Sriracha

4 scallions (white and green parts), thinly sliced

2 teaspoons sesame seeds, for garnish (optional)

**1.** Remove the inside membrane from the ribs (see page 272). Whisk the vinegar, ginger, soy sauce, garlic, and sesame oil in a nonreactive dish. Add the ribs, turning to coat evenly. Cover and refrigerate for at least 4 hours or, preferably, overnight.
**2.** Prepare an outdoor grill with a medium-high fire for both direct and indirect grilling. Position a drip pan under the grate on the cooler side. Remove the ribs from the marinade and discard the marinade. Pat dry and season on all sides with the five-spice powder, and salt and black pepper to taste. Place bone side down over the drip pan and cover grill. Cook until tender and crisp, about 1 to 1¼ hours, rotating every 30 minutes or so for even cooking.
**3.** Whisk the hoisin sauce and the chili sauce in a small bowl. Grill the ribs, brushing with the mixture every 10 minutes or so, until nicely glazed, about 30 minutes. Transfer the ribs to cutting board and let rest 5 minutes. Cut between the ribs and place on a serving platter. Scatter the scallions and sesame seeds, if desired, over the top.

## SHOPSMART

Five-spice powder is a Chinese spice mix containing more or less equal parts of cinnamon, cloves, fennel seeds, star anise, and Szechwan peppercorn, ground together to a fine powder.

144

# HERB-GARLIC
# leg of lamb

8 servings

   Zest and juice of 1 lemon

1 cup fresh flat-leaf parsley

1 cup fresh mint

1/2 cup fresh oregano

1/2 cup fresh thyme

1/4 cup Worcestershire sauce

1 tablespoon kosher salt, plus additional for seasoning

1 teaspoon ground allspice

1 teaspoon crushed red pepper

16 cloves garlic (about 1 head), peeled

3/4 cup extra-virgin olive oil

1 6-pound butterflied leg of lamb

   Vegetable oil for grilling

   Grilled flatbread (optional)

**1.** For the marinade: Process the lemon zest and juice, parsley, mint, oregano, thyme, Worcestershire sauce, 1 tablespoon salt, allspice, red pepper, and garlic in a food processor until smooth. With the motor running, drizzle in the olive oil to make a smooth puree. Pour the marinade into a large nonreactive bowl.

**2.** Pierce the meat all over with a fork. Cut the lamb in half following the natural seam that runs across the center of the meat, put the pieces in the marinade, and turn to coat evenly. Cover with plastic wrap and refrigerate for at least 2 hours or overnight.

**3.** About 30 minutes before cooking, take lamb from refrigerator. Prepare an outdoor grill with a medium fire.

**4.** Lightly brush the grate with oil. Grill lamb until well-browned and crisp on one side, 10 to 15 minutes. Flip lamb and continue grilling until an instant-read thermometer inserted into the thickest part of the meat registers 130°F to 135°F for medium-rare, about 10 minutes more. Transfer lamb to a cutting board and let rest for 5 to 10 minutes before slicing. Slice lamb across the grain and serve with flatbread, if desired.

JUNIPER & JALAPEÑO JELLY-GLAZED

# lamb chops

4 servings

- 8 juniper berries
- 1 teaspoon coriander seeds
- 2 tablespoons unsalted butter
- 4 cloves garlic, minced
- 1 10-ounce jar red jalapeño jelly (about 1 heaping cup )
- 2 tablespoons apple cider vinegar
- ¼ cup water
  Vegetable oil for grilling
- 8 rack lamb chops (about 1½ to 2 pounds), frenched (see ShopSmart, right)
- 1 teaspoon kosher salt
  Freshly ground black pepper

**1.** Prepare an outdoor grill with a medium-high fire for both direct and indirect grilling. Position a drip pan under grate on the cooler side of the grill.

**2.** Crack the juniper berries and coriander seeds in a mortar and pestle or with a small heavy pan. Melt the butter in a small skillet and cook the juniper, coriander, and garlic over medium heat until fragrant, about 3 minutes. Whisk in the jelly, vinegar, and water until smooth and simmer until slightly thick, about 5 minutes.

**3.** Brush the grill lightly with oil and season the chops all over with salt and pepper to taste. Lay the chops on the grate and grill, turning until nicely marked, about 3 minutes on each side. Move chops to the cooler side of the grill, over the drip pan, and brush generously with some of the jalapeño glaze. Cover and cook, brushing occasionally, until nicely glazed and an instant-read thermometer inserted into the chops registers 120°F for

medium-rare. Set aside to rest for 5 minutes. Serve chops drizzled with more of the jalapeño glaze.

## ▬ SHOPSMART

Frenched rack of lamb chops are trimmed of the cap of fat that rides on the bones and over the meat. Your butcher will be happy to do it for you, and it pays off with fabulous taste and ease. The chops grill quickly and you look like a master chef.

*These aren't the lamb chops with mint jelly your granny used to serve. They're big and bold and surprising.*

147

# a day in
# provence

Baby Artichoke &
Potato Salad

Lamb Brochettes with
Tapenade

Fig & Goat
Cheese Salad

# MENU

Lamb Brochettes with Tapenade (page 150) • Baby Artichoke & Potato Salad (page 50) • Fig & Goat Cheese Salad (page 43) • Baguettes

Dress a picnic table in summer yellows and blues and let this menu transport you to the Mediterranean countryside.

# lamb brochettes
## WITH TAPENADE

4 to 6 servings

### LAMB

1/3 cup extra-virgin olive oil, plus additional for brushing

3 tablespoons red wine vinegar

3 cloves garlic, minced

3 tablespoons herbes de Provence, crumbled

1 tablespoon freshly ground black pepper

2 teaspoons finely grated orange zest

2 teaspoons kosher salt

2½ pounds leg of lamb, cut into 1-inch cubes

### TAPENADE

1 cup mixed green and black olives, pitted and roughly chopped

1/4 cup extra-virgin olive oil

3 tablespoons chopped fresh flat-leaf parsley

2 tablespoons capers, rinsed

1 tablespoon red wine vinegar

2 to 3 anchovy filets, soaked, drained, and minced

1 clove garlic, minced

2 teaspoons chopped fresh oregano

Pinch crushed red pepper

1 large roma tomato

Kosher salt

Freshly ground black pepper

**1.** For the lamb: Whisk the 1/3 cup olive oil with the vinegar, garlic, herbes de Provence, black pepper, orange zest, and salt in a large nonreactive bowl. Add the lamb, cover, and refrigerate for at least 4 hours or overnight.

**2.** If using wooden skewers, soak them in water for at least 30 minutes before grilling. Prepare an outdoor grill with a high-heat fire.

**3.** For the tapenade: Mix the olives, olive oil, parsley, capers, vinegar, anchovies, garlic, oregano, and red pepper. Grill the tomato just until the skin chars. Peel the tomato, chop it roughly, and add to the olive mixture with salt and black pepper to taste.

**4.** Pat dry and thread 5 pieces of lamb onto each of 8 skewers and season with salt and black pepper to taste. Brush the grill grate lightly with olive oil and sear the brochettes, rotating to make grill marks on all sides, 5 to 6 minutes. Set aside to rest for 5 minutes. Serve with tapenade.

# veal chops
## WITH ENDIVE & LEMON

4 servings

MARINADE

1½ cups dry vermouth

¼ cup extra-virgin olive oil

Juice of 2 lemons (about ¼ cup)

2 large shallots, chopped

3 tablespoons chopped fresh sage

½ to 1 teaspoon crushed red pepper

Kosher salt

Freshly ground black pepper

4 10- to 12-ounce veal rib chops, about 1 inch thick

ENDIVE AND LEMONS

4 large endives (about 1½ pounds)

8 fresh sage leaves

8 thin slices prosciutto

Extra-virgin olive oil, for drizzling

Freshly ground black pepper

2 lemons, quartered and seeded

Vegetable oil for grilling

**1.** Whisk all of the marinade ingredients (except the chops)—including salt and black pepper to taste—in a large, shallow nonreactive baking dish. Add the veal, turning to coat it evenly. Cover dish with plastic wrap and refrigerate for 3 hours, turning once.

**2.** Halve each endive lengthwise and trim the core but keep the leaves intact. Place a sage leaf on each cut side and wrap with the slices of prosciutto.

**3.** Prepare an outdoor grill with a medium-high fire.

**4.** Pat the chops very dry, season generously with salt and black pepper to taste, and set aside for 10 minutes. Brush the endive lightly all over with some olive oil, season with black pepper to taste, and grill until the prosciutto is crisp and the endive tender, 3 to 4 minutes per side. Grill the lemons just until they are soft and juicy, about 2 minutes per side. Transfer endive and lemons to a platter and drizzle both with olive oil.

**5.** Brush the grill grate lightly with oil. Grill chops, turning once, until nicely browned and an instant-read thermometer inserted crosswise into the meat registers 125°F, 4 to 5 minutes per side. Let rest 5 minutes. Serve with endive and lemons.

# fish & shellfish
# six

MISO SALMON MEDALLIONS WITH SESAME-CUCUMBER SALAD • PESTO-STUFFED SALMON WITH TOMATO-CORN SALAD • PLANKED SALMON WITH PINOT NOIR SAUCE • TUNA WITH MINT AND RAINBOW PEPPERS • SUMMER SALAD WITH TUNA • RED SNAPPER WITH GRILLED MANGO CHUTNEY • SWORDFISH WITH FENNEL-SAFFRON COMPOTE • GRILL-SMOKED TROUT WITH APPLE-BEET SALAD • SPICY SHRIMP AND AVOCADO SALAD WITH GRAPEFRUIT DRESSING • JUMBO SHRIMP STUFFED WITH CILANTRO & CHILES • SHRIMP TOSTADAS • SEA SCALLOPS WITH ZUCCHINI RIBBONS AND MINT-CHIVE OIL • LOBSTER WITH TARRAGON BUTTER AND FINGERLING POTATOES • SEAFOOD PAELLA

# miso salmon medallions
## WITH SESAME-CUCUMBER SALAD

4 servings

SALMON

½ cup white miso

½ cup sake

¼ cup firmly packed light brown sugar

2 tablespoons finely grated peeled fresh ginger

1 teaspoon dark sesame oil

2 bunches scallions, roots trimmed (about 18)

4 10-ounce salmon steaks, with skin

   Peanut oil for grilling

1 tablespoon toasted sesame seeds

SALAD

1 English cucumber (about 12 ounces)

½ fresh jalapeño, minced (leave seeds in for more heat)

1 tablespoon rice wine vinegar

1 tablespoon peanut oil

2 teaspoons mirin (see Cook's Note, page 59)

2 teaspoons toasted sesame seeds

1 teaspoon finely grated peeled fresh ginger

1 teaspoon kosher salt

¼ teaspoon dark sesame oil

**1.** For the salmon: Whisk the miso, sake, brown sugar, ginger, and sesame oil in a shallow nonreactive dish; set aside about ¼ cup of the mixture for grilling.
**2.** Put the scallions in a microwave-safe dish, cover, and microwave on high until crisp-tender, about 1 minute. (Alternatively, steam for 1 to 2 minutes.) Set 8 scallions aside for tying salmon medallions together. Roughly chop the remaining scallions.
**3.** Remove the pin bones from the salmon steaks with tweezers or needle-nose pliers, if necessary. Use a sharp knife to trim off the bones along the belly flaps. Cut along both sides of the central bones to remove the backbone. Trim off about 2 inches of the skin along one side of each of the salmon steaks' belly flaps.
**4.** For each steak, brush miso mixture along central cut and scatter the chopped scallions on top. Fold the skinless flap into the center and wrap the other side around it to form a round medallion. Tie 2 scallions together to make a long length of scallion "ribbon" and use it to tie a medallion around its perimeter. Trim scallions as needed. Repeat with the remaining fish and scallions. Put the salmon medallions in the miso mixture and turn to coat. Cover and refrigerate for 4 to 6 hours.
**5.** Meanwhile, make the cucumber salad: Quarter the cucumber lengthwise and trim seeds with a knife. Slice crosswise to make thin fanlike slices. Toss in a medium bowl with remaining salad ingredients.
**6.** Prepare an outdoor grill with a medium fire.
**7.** Remove the salmon from the marinade and pat dry; discard the marinade. Brush the medallions with peanut oil and grill until seared, about 3 minutes. Turn, brush fish with reserved ¼ cup miso mixture, and grill until an instant-read thermometer inserted into the side of a medallion registers 130°F, about 3 minutes more. Set fish aside to rest for 5 minutes before serving.
**8.** Divide medallions among 4 plates and lightly sprinkle with sesame seeds. Serve with salad.

## COOK'S NOTE
We use scallions as edible string to hold the medallions together. If you'd like to put this together faster, use kitchen twine—just remove it before serving.

# pesto-stuffed salmon
## WITH TOMATO-CORN SALAD

4 servings

SALMON

¹/₂ cup loosely packed fresh basil

¹/₂ cup loosely packed fresh parsley

2 tablespoons blanched whole almonds

¹/₄ teaspoon minced garlic

¹/₄ teaspoon kosher salt, plus additional for seasoning

Freshly ground black pepper

3 tablespoons extra-virgin olive oil, plus additional for brushing

1 1¹/₂-pound center-cut skinless salmon fillet

Vegetable oil for grilling

SALAD

1 pound ripe mixed small tomatoes, halved or diced

1 cup cooked fresh corn kernels (from 2 ears)

3 tablespoons extra-virgin olive oil

1 tablespoon white wine vinegar

2 teaspoons minced fresh marjoram or oregano

Kosher salt

Freshly ground black pepper

1. For the salmon: Pulse the basil, parsley, almonds, garlic, ¹/₄ teaspoon salt, and black pepper to taste in a food processor to make a coarse paste. With the motor running, drizzle in the olive oil until incorporated. Lay the salmon fillet on a work surface. With a cut side facing you, cut a wide pocket with a narrow-bladed knife, taking care not to cut through the top or bottom of the fish. Hold the pocket open, season the inside with salt and black pepper to taste, and spread the pesto evenly inside the fish with a flat metal spatula. (The fish can be prepared up to this point a day ahead of grilling, then covered and refrigerated.)

2. Prepare an outdoor grill with a medium-high fire.

3. For the salad: Toss the tomatoes with corn. Add the olive oil, vinegar, marjoram, and salt and black pepper to taste. Toss again, taking care not to break up the tomatoes.

4. Lightly brush the grill grate with oil. Brush the fillet on both sides with olive oil and season the flesh side with salt and black pepper to taste. Lay the fish flesh side down on the grill and cook until there are distinct grill marks and you can lift the fish without its sticking, about 3 to 5 minutes. (Test it by gently lifting a corner—if it sticks, let it cook a bit longer.) When it lifts cleanly, carefully turn it about 45 degrees from its original position (don't turn it over). Cook for another 3 minutes, until marked. Season the skin side with salt and black pepper to taste, turn the fillet over, and cook about 3 to 5 minutes more or until an instant-read thermometer inserted in the side registers about 125°F. Transfer the fish to a plate and let it rest for 5 minutes. Cut salmon into 4 equal pieces and transfer to serving plates. Serve salmon warm or at room temperature topped with the Tomato-Corn Salad. Drizzle with any extra juices from the salad.

## ■ COOK'S NOTE

We like to use the microwave to cook corn. Just cut the kernels from the ears into a bowl and scrape the cobs with a knife to get out the juices. Cover and microwave on high for 1 minute.

# planked salmon
## WITH PINOT NOIR SAUCE

4 servings

SAUCE

10 tablespoons cold unsalted butter, cut into pieces

2 medium shallots, peeled and sliced

3 thick slices bacon, diced

3 cloves garlic, peeled and smashed

1 bottle Pinot Noir

1/4 ounce dried porcini mushrooms (about 2 tablespoons)

3 sprigs fresh thyme

1 bay leaf

2 tablespoons demi-glace (see Know-How, right)

2 teaspoons red wine vinegar

1 1/2 teaspoons kosher salt

  Freshly ground black pepper

SALMON

2 tablespoons unsalted butter, melted

1 teaspoon dry English-style mustard

1 tablespoon finely ground porcini powder (dried porcini mushrooms ground in a spice mill or coffee grinder)

1 3-pound side salmon fillet, pin bones removed

  Kosher salt

  Freshly ground black pepper

**1.** Soak a cedar or alder plank in cold water for 2 to 4 hours (see ShopSmart, right). Pat dry.
**2.** Prepare an outdoor grill with medium-high heat for indirect grilling.
**3.** For the sauce: Melt 1 tablespoon of the butter in a medium skillet, then add shallots, bacon, and garlic and cook over medium heat until the bacon renders its fat and the vegetables turn golden-brown, about 8 minutes. Pour off the fat and discard. Add the wine, dried mushrooms, and herbs, bring to a brisk boil, and cook until reduced by about half. Whisk in the demi-glace and heat until combined. Pull the pan from the heat and whisk in the remaining butter 1 tablespoon at a time. Add the vinegar and season with the salt and black pepper to taste. Strain the sauce and keep warm in a double boiler until ready to serve.
**4.** For the salmon: Whisk the melted butter, mustard, and porcini powder together. Lay the salmon skin side down on the plank and brush with butter-mustard mixture. Season with salt and black pepper to taste. Place the plank on the cooler side of the grill and cover. Cook until an instant-read thermometer inserted crosswise

into the thickest part of the salmon registers 135°F, about 20 to 30 minutes.
**5.** Transfer fish, on the plank, to the table and let rest for 5 minutes. Serve each portion of the salmon drizzled with the warm Pinot Noir Sauce. Pass extra sauce at the table.

## ■ SHOPSMART

Pacific Northwest Native Americans were the first to cook salmon on planks of wood. This ingenious technique has caught on. Cedar and alder planks specifically for cooking (they shouldn't be treated) are sold in sporting goods stores, cooking equipment and home improvement stores, and online.

## ■ KNOW-HOW

Demi-glace is a finely concentrated meat broth. We found ours at the meat counter, but it also can be found in specialty markets and on the web. To make your own, simply boil a hearty homemade beef, veal, or chicken broth down until it is a syrupy glaze.

157

# moveable feast

Set a table up anywhere in your yard—near a scented rosebush or on a patch of lawn with a sunset view. Don't forget extension cords for your paper lanterns or you'll have to cut this beautiful evening short.

# tuna
## WITH MINT & RAINBOW PEPPERS

4 to 6 servings

- 1 yellow bell pepper
- 1 red bell pepper
- 1 orange bell pepper
- 1/3 cup extra-virgin olive oil, plus additional for grilling
- 2 tablespoons white wine vinegar
- 1 garlic clove, peeled and smashed
- 2 teaspoons capers
- 1 1/2 teaspoons kosher salt, plus additional for seasoning

  Freshly ground black pepper
- 1 large bunch mint
- 1 1 1/2-pound piece center-cut tuna, about 2-inches thick

**1.** Position an oven rack in the upper part of the oven and preheat the broiler. Line a broiler pan with foil. Halve the peppers through the stem and remove the seeds and stems. Lay the peppers cut side down on the prepared baking sheet. Broil the peppers, moving as needed so the skins char evenly, about 8 minutes. Put the peppers in a large bowl, cover, and set aside just until cool enough to handle, about 5 minutes. (Don't leave them for too long or the peppers will get muddy-looking from the charred skins.)

**2.** Rub skins off peppers with your fingers and lightly rinse with cool water, if necessary, to remove any remaining charred skin. Slice the peppers into 3/4-inch-thick strips. Toss them in a bowl along with the olive oil, vinegar, garlic, and capers. Season with the 1 1/2 teaspoons salt and black pepper to taste. Set aside for 1 hour to let the flavors come together.

**3.** Meanwhile, pluck 24 small sprigs of mint, each with about

4 leaves. If you can't get 24 sprigs, supplement with larger leaves from the bottom of the stem. Measure an additional 2 tablespoons mint leaves, tear into pieces, and add to the peppers. Pierce 24 holes in tuna with a paring knife and stuff each with one of the mint sprigs or leaves. Cover and refrigerate if not grilling right away.

**4.** Prepare an outdoor grill with a high fire.

**5.** Brush the tuna with olive oil and season with salt and black pepper to taste. Grill tuna until rare, turning once, about 2 minutes per side. Set aside to rest for 5 minutes. Slice the tuna and serve with the peppers.

## ■ COOK'S NOTE

Bring the tuna to room temperature about 30 minutes before grilling.

## ■ SHOPSMART

If you like to serve tuna rare, as we do, choose a really fresh and thick piece. Great tuna should be pristine, rich red, and very firm. A good tip is to ask your fishmonger for a piece that is "sushi grade" and to cut it fresh just for you.

With the tip of a paring knife, pierce the flesh of the tuna—on top and on the sides—with 24 small holes. Tuck mint sprigs or leaves into each hole.

# summer salad

## WITH TUNA

4 to 6 servings

### DRESSING

- 2 tablespoons white wine vinegar
- 2 teaspoons Dijon mustard
- 3/4 teaspoon kosher salt
- Freshly ground black pepper
- 1/3 cup extra-virgin olive oil
- 1 medium shallot, minced (about 2 tablespoons)
- 2 anchovy fillets, mashed (about 1/2 teaspoon)
- 1 tablespoon fresh thyme, preferably lemon thyme

### SALAD

- 12 ounces small red-skinned waxy potatoes, halved (about 8 potatoes)
- 6 ounces haricots verts, green beans, or yellow wax beans
- 1/2 medium fennel bulb (about 8 ounces)
- 2 medium ripe tomatoes, cored and cut into chunks (about 12 ounces)
- 1/2 cup roughly chopped black olives, preferably niçoise
- Kosher salt
- Freshly ground black pepper
- 1 pound tuna steaks (about 1 inch thick)
- 1 tablespoon extra-virgin olive oil
- 7 ounces mesclun salad greens (about 8 cups)

**1.** For the dressing: Whisk the vinegar, mustard, salt, and black pepper to taste in a small bowl. Gradually whisk in the olive oil, starting with a few drops and then adding the rest in a steady stream to make a smooth, slightly thick dressing. Stir in the shallot, anchovies, and thyme. Set aside.

**2.** For the salad: Put the potatoes in a small saucepan with cold water to cover and season generously with salt. Bring to a boil, then simmer just until tender, about 10 minutes. Drain, put in a large bowl, and toss with 1/4 cup of the dressing. Bring a medium pot of water to a boil and salt it generously. Fill a medium bowl with ice water and salt it as well. Add beans to the boiling water and cook until crisp-tender, about 3 minutes. Drain and plunge immediately into ice water. Drain, pat dry, and add to the potatoes.

**3.** Cut the fennel in half lengthwise, core, and thinly slice with a mandoline or a very sharp knife. Add fennel, tomatoes, and olives to the potatoes and season with salt and black pepper to taste. (The salad may be prepared to this point up to 2 hours ahead.)

**4.** Prepare an outdoor grill with a high fire.

**5.** Brush the tuna with olive oil and season with salt and black pepper to taste. Grill until there are distinct grill marks on both sides, turning once, about 2 minutes per side for medium-rare. Cut or flake the tuna into chunks and toss with the vegetables, salad greens, and remaining dressing. Season with salt and black pepper to taste.

## ◼ SHOPSMART

There are times when you need a perfect, thick slab of tuna, but this isn't one of them. Just buy thin tuna steaks from your local fish shop and sear them on the grill to your liking. Combine the tuna with the other ingredients for a fresh, casual summer meal.

# red snapper

## WITH GRILLED MANGO CHUTNEY

4 servings

**FISH**

10 cloves garlic, peeled

2 tablespoons kosher salt, plus additional for seasoning

8 allspice berries, cracked, plus 1 tablespoon for grilling (optional)

2 Scotch bonnet chiles, minced, with seeds

1 teaspoon sugar

1 cup lime juice (about 8 limes)

3/4 cup extra-virgin olive oil, plus additional for grilling

2 whole red snappers, cleaned (about 2½ pounds each)

6 scallions (white and green parts), coarsely chopped

Kosher salt

**CHUTNEY**

6 scallions (white and green parts), thinly sliced

2 cloves garlic, chopped

2 Scotch bonnet chiles, minced without seeds

2 teaspoons finely grated, peeled fresh ginger

½ teaspoon kosher salt

2 tablespoons distilled white vinegar

½ cup firmly packed light brown sugar

2 ripe mangoes

**1.** For fish: Smash garlic cloves, sprinkle with 2 tablespoons salt, and, with the flat side of a large knife, mash and smear to a coarse paste. Add allspice, chiles, and sugar and chop to a coarse paste. Transfer to a large shallow dish. Whisk in lime juice and olive oil. Reserve ½ cup for grilling fish. Slash each fish crosswise 4 times on each side. Put fish in marinade. Rub marinade over and inside fish. Stuff scallions into each fish. Cover and refrigerate at least 2 hours and up to 4 hours.

**2.** Prepare an outdoor grill with a medium fire.

**3.** For the chutney: Combine all ingredients except mangoes in a medium bowl. Cut mango flesh away from the seed in 2 halves, with skin. Brush flesh side of mangoes with oil and grill over direct heat until there are distinct grill marks and mangoes are warmed, about 4 to 5 minutes.

**4.** Remove fish from marinade; discard marinade. Rub skin with olive oil and season with salt to taste. Brush a large fish grill basket with oil and put fish in it. Toss remaining allspice berries on the coals, if desired, and put fish on grill. Cook for 3 minutes on one side, then turn and cook for another 3 minutes on the other side. From this point, baste fish with reserved marinade and turn every 3 minutes until an instant-read thermometer inserted into the thickest part of fish registers 135°F, about 16 to 20 minutes.

**5.** Meanwhile, scoop grilled mango flesh out of skin with a spoon; discard skin. Coarsely chop mangoes and stir into chutney ingredients.

**6.** To serve, see photos below. Serve fish with a spoonful of chutney. Pass remaining chutney at the table.

1. Place fish on a large platter. Cut through the skin down to the bone at the head and tail, leaving skin on fillets. 2. Divide into 2 fillets through the long line running lengthwise down the center. 3. Gently remove fillets to a serving plate (this is one serving). Pull out backbone and remove bottom fillets to another plate.

# swordfish
## WITH FENNEL-SAFFRON COMPOTE

4 servings

COMPOTE

¹/₃ cup pine nuts

¹/₃ cup extra-virgin olive oil

1 medium onion, halved and sliced

1 fennel bulb, cored and sliced

3 cloves garlic, peeled and smashed

2 large strips lemon peel

1¹/₄ teaspoons kosher salt, plus additional for seasoning

1 teaspoon fennel seeds

Pinch saffron threads

Freshly ground black pepper

¹/₂ cup golden raisins

3 tablespoons chopped fresh flat-leaf parsley

FISH

4 8-ounce swordfish steaks (about 1 inch thick)

Extra-virgin olive oil, for brushing

¹/₈ teaspoon cayenne pepper

Kosher salt

1 large ripe yellow or red tomato

Freshly ground black pepper

Lemon wedges, for serving

**1.** Prepare an outdoor grill with a high fire.

**2.** For the compote: Toast the pine nuts in the olive oil in a skillet over high heat, swirling the pan, until the nuts are golden, about 3 minutes. Transfer the nuts to a dish with a slotted spoon and set aside, leaving the oil behind in the pan. Add the onion, fennel, garlic, lemon peel, 1¹/₄ teaspoons salt, fennel seeds, saffron, and black pepper to taste and cook until the onion and fennel are slightly wilted, about 2 minutes. Add the raisins and cook, stirring occasionally, until the mixture browns and softens, about 5 minutes. Stir in ¹/₄ cup water, pine nuts, and parsley. Cook, stirring occasionally, until liquid reduces and compote thickens, about 1 minute more. Set aside.

**3.** For the fish: Brush fish with oil and sprinkle with the cayenne and salt to taste. Lay the fish on the grill and leave it until you can see distinct grill marks and can lift the fish without its sticking, about 2 minutes. (Test by gently lifting a corner; if it sticks, cook a bit longer.) When it lifts cleanly, rotate about 45 degrees from the original position (don't turn it over). Cook about another 2 minutes, until grill marks appear. Flip the

fish and repeat this process for marking the fish on the other side, another 3 to 4 minutes.

**4.** Cut the tomato into thick slices, season with salt and black pepper to taste, and divide among 4 plates. Place the fish on top of the tomato slices, spoon some compote over, and finish with a wedge of lemon.

We're crazy about this compote. It's the essence of all the best Mediterranean flavors. Try it with chicken and lamb too.

# grill-smoked trout
## WITH APPLE-BEET SALAD

4 servings

TROUT

¼ cup pickling spice

3 cups cold water

½ cup kosher salt, plus additional for seasoning

6 tablespoons firmly packed dark brown sugar

1 cup gin

4 whole boneless rainbow trout (each about 10 ounces)

3 or 4 large handfuls hickory wood chips, soaked in water for about 30 minutes

Freshly ground black pepper

Vegetable oil for grilling

4 tablespoons butter, melted

SALAD

1 tablespoon cider vinegar

1 tablespoon minced shallots

1 teaspoon Dijon mustard

1 teaspoon honey

1 teaspoon kosher salt

Freshly ground black pepper

3 tablespoons walnut oil

3 tablespoons prepared horseradish, drained

2 medium tart green apples, such as Granny Smith

1 medium beet, peeled

¼ cup fresh flat-leaf parsley

**1.** For the trout: Use the bottom of a medium saucepan to crush the pickling spice, then scoop into the saucepan. Toast over medium heat until fragrant, about 3 minutes, swirling the pan frequently to avoid burning. Add 2 cups of the water, along with the salt and brown sugar. Bring to a boil, remove from heat, and add the remaining 1 cup water and the gin. Cool to room temperature. Put trout and brine in a nonreactive container to submerge fish, then cover and refrigerate at least 2 hours and up to 4 hours.

**2.** For the salad: Whisk the vinegar, shallots, mustard, honey, salt, and black pepper to taste in a large bowl. Gradually whisk in the walnut oil, starting with a few drops and adding the rest in a steady stream, to make a smooth, slightly thick dressing. Stir in the horseradish and set aside. With a mandoline or the julienne blade of a food processor, cut the apples and beet into long thin matchsticks. Add to the dressing and toss. Cover and refrigerate until you are ready to serve.

**3.** Prepare an outdoor grill with a medium-high fire for both direct and indirect grilling. When the fire is ready, drain the chips and scatter over the coals or heating element. Close the cover but leave vent holes open.

**4.** Once the chips begin to smoke, remove the trout from the brine and pat dry. Season both sides with salt and black pepper to taste. Brush the grill grate lightly with oil. Lay the trout on the cooler side of the grill. Close the cover and grill/smoke the trout until cooked through, about 8 to 10 minutes. Baste the trout generously with the melted butter just before removing from the grill.

**5.** Just before serving, add parsley to salad. Divide fish and salad among 4 plates and serve.

# spicy shrimp
## AND AVOCADO SALAD WITH GRAPEFRUIT DRESSING

4 servings

SHRIMP

2 cups water

$1/4$ cup chopped fresh ginger, with peel

3 tablespoons kosher salt

2 tablespoons dark brown sugar

2 cloves garlic, peeled and smashed

1 tablespoon pickling spice

$1^1/2$ pounds medium shrimp, peeled and deveined (see page 270)

SALAD

2 medium grapefruit

8 thin slices fresh ginger

$1/4$ cup extra-virgin olive oil, plus additional for brushing

1 tablespoon white wine vinegar

$1^1/2$ teaspoons soy sauce

1 teaspoon honey

$1/2$ teaspoon salt, plus additional for seasoning

Freshly ground black pepper

2 heads Bibb or Boston lettuce, trimmed, leaves torn into pieces

12 large fresh basil leaves, torn

1 small serrano chile, minced (leave the seeds in for more heat)

2 Hass avocados, halved, pitted, peeled, and sliced

**1.** For the shrimp: Put 1 cup of water, chopped ginger, salt, sugar, garlic, and pickling spice in a small saucepan. Bring to a boil, then pour into a large bowl. Add 1 cup of cold water and set brine aside to cool completely. Add shrimp and refrigerate for 30 minutes.

**2.** For the salad: Strip the peel from half of 1 of the grapefruits with a vegetable peeler, taking care not to include the bitter white pith. Warm the grapefruit peel, sliced ginger, and olive oil in a small saucepan over medium heat. As soon as the oil starts to bubble, about 2 minutes, remove from heat. Set oil aside to steep 30 minutes. Strain and reserve the oil.

**3.** Prepare an outdoor grill with a medium fire.

**4.** Segment both grapefruit over a bowl, reserving the juice (see page 000). Whisk 3 tablespoons of the reserved grapefruit juice with the vinegar, soy sauce, honey, and $1/2$ teaspoon salt in a medium bowl. Gradually whisk in the infused grapefruit oil, starting with a few drops and then adding the rest of the oil in a steady stream to make a slightly thick dressing. Season with black pepper to taste.

**5.** Remove shrimp from brine and pat dry. Brush shrimp with olive oil and grill, turning once, until shrimp are pink and just cooked through, 3 to 4 minutes.

**6.** Gently toss the shrimp, grapefruit segments, lettuce, basil, and $1/2$ teaspoon serrano with $1/4$ cup of the dressing. Gently toss in avocados and divide the salad among 4 plates. Sprinkle with the remaining serrano, if desired, and drizzle with a little more of the dressing.

## ■ KNOW-HOW

Citrus-flavored oils marry well with grilled foods. Try this same technique with lemons or limes and use the oil with great effect on chicken and pork. Flavored oils are more perishable than unflavored oils and should be refrigerated.

# jumbo shrimp
## STUFFED WITH CILANTRO & CHILES

4 servings

- 8 jumbo shrimp, in the shell (about 1¼ pounds)
- 3 sprigs fresh thyme, leaves stripped
- Juice of 2 limes (about ¼ cup)
- 2 tablespoons extra-virgin olive oil
- 1 teaspoon kosher salt, plus additional for seasoning
- Freshly ground black pepper
- 1 clove garlic, chopped
- ½ large jalapeño, with seeds
- 2 scallions (white and green parts)
- 1 cup coarsely chopped fresh cilantro

**1.** Prepare an outdoor grill with a medium-high fire. Without removing the shells, slit the shrimp down the ridged back and remove the vein that runs down the center. (See page 270.) Rinse and pat the shrimp dry. Whisk thyme leaves, lime juice, 1 tablespoon of the olive oil, ½ teaspoon of the salt, and black pepper to taste in a shallow nonreactive bowl or dish. Lay the shrimp cut side down in the lime mixture and refrigerate for 30 minutes.

**2.** In a food processor, pulse the garlic, jalapeño, scallions, remaining 1 tablespoon olive oil, and remaining ½ teaspoon salt to make a coarse paste. Add the cilantro and pulse just enough to incorporate into the mixture. Spoon the mixture into the opening in the shrimp and close the shrimp. Grill the shrimp shell side down (to keep filling from falling out) for 3 minutes. Turn to the other shell side, cover, and grill another 2 minutes or until the shrimp turn pink and are slightly firm to the touch. Sprinkle with salt and serve.

## ▮ STYLE

Jumbo shrimp in the shell can be a knife and fork sort of deal unless you're outside and it's summer and you are feeling very relaxed. Serve these with lots of napkins if your crowd is the peel-and-eat type.

## ▮ KNOW-HOW

Shrimp cooked in the shells are more intensely flavorful. Leaving the shells on provides a buffer against overcooking, a misfortune many shrimp suffer. Shrimp, even these jumbos, continue to cook once removed from the grill. It's always best to cook them just until opaque and let the delicate shellfish finish cooking off the heat.

# shrimp tostadas

4 servings

### SALSA

2 medium chayotes (see ShopSmart, right)

2 tablespoons corn oil

1 teaspoon chili powder

2 teaspoons kosher salt, plus additional for seasoning

Freshly ground black pepper

1 pint cherry tomatoes, halved

1 small red onion, diced

8 radishes, cut into small matchsticks or diced

1/2 cup lightly packed fresh cilantro

Juice of 1 lime (about 2 tablespoons)

1 serrano chile, minced, with seeds

### TOSTADAS

1 pound medium shrimp, peeled and deveined (about 24) (see page 270)

2 tablespoons corn oil

1 teaspoon ground cumin

Kosher salt

Freshly ground black pepper

8 corn tostada shells, prepared or homemade (See Know-How, right)

1 ripe firm avocado, halved, pitted, peeled, and sliced

Mexican crema, crème fraîche, or sour cream, for serving

**1.** Prepare an outdoor grill with a high fire.

**2.** For the salsa: Slice each chayote in half through the crinkle and remove the seed with a spoon or melon baller. Slice each half into 4 slices and toss in a bowl with the oil, chili powder, 2 teaspoons salt, and black pepper to taste. Grill slices until charred and slightly tender, 10 to 12 minutes. Let cool.

**3.** Dice the grilled chayote and toss with the tomatoes, onion, radishes, cilantro, lime juice, and serrano chile in a medium bowl. Season with salt and black pepper to taste.

**4.** For the tostadas: Toss the shrimp with oil, cumin, and salt and black pepper to taste. Grill shrimp until pink, turning once, about 1 minute per side.

**5.** Place 2 tostada shells on each of 4 large plates. Divide the salsa among the shells and top each one with 3 shrimp, avocado, and some crema.

## ▮ SHOPSMART

Chayote, also called mirliton, is a green, pear-shaped vegetable in the squash family. It's a favorite in Southern and Latin cooking and can be eaten raw or cooked.

## ▮ KNOW-HOW

If you have the time, try making your own tostada shells. Heat 1 cup of corn oil in a medium skillet over medium-high heat. When the oil begins to ripple, add a corn tortilla and fry for about 1 minute, turning once. The tortilla will bubble and inflate. Remove when golden and crisp to a paper towel-lined plate and sprinkle with salt to taste. Repeat for a total of 8 tostada shells.

# sea scallops
### WITH ZUCCHINI RIBBONS AND MINT-CHIVE OIL

4 servings

- 1 large zucchini
- 1¼ pounds large sea scallops, foot removed if necessary (about 12 to 14)
- ¼ cup roughly chopped fresh mint
- ¼ cup sliced fresh chives
- 3 tablespoons freshly squeezed orange juice
- 2 tablespoons canola or grapeseed oil, plus additional for brushing
- 1 tablespoon lemoncello (see Cook's Note, right)
- 1 teaspoon kosher salt, plus additional for seasoning

  Pinch cayenne pepper
- 2 large ripe tomatoes, preferably 1 red and 1 yellow

  Freshly ground black pepper

**1.** Prepare an outdoor grill with a medium-high fire. If you're using wooden skewers, soak them in water for at least 30 minutes before grilling. (Or you can use wooden toothpicks.)

**2.** For the scallops: Slice the zucchini lengthwise on a mandoline into thin slices, about ⅛ inch thick. When you get to the seedy center, rotate the zucchini ⅓ turn and continue to shave slices until you hit seeds. Give the zucchini a final ⅓ turn and shave off the remaining slices. (You want to end up with the same number of zucchini slices as you have scallops.) Discard the seedy center. Wrap a zucchini ribbon around the circumference of each scallop. Thread 2 to 3 scallops per skewer or 1 per toothpick.

**3.** For the dressing: Whisk the mint, chives, orange juice, 2 tablespoons oil, lemoncello, salt, and cayenne in a small bowl. Set aside.

**4.** Cut up the tomatoes, season them with salt and black pepper to taste, and divide them among 4 plates.

**5.** Brush scallops with oil and season with salt and black pepper to taste. Grill, turning to cook both sides, until zucchini and scallops are cooked through and have distinct grill marks, about 8 minutes total. Divide the scallops evenly among the plates, drizzle scallops and tomatoes with the dressing, and serve hot or at room temperature.

## ■ COOK'S NOTE

Lemoncello, the highly fragrant liquor from southern Italy, has gained fans stateside recently. Traditionally it is enjoyed as a digestif, or after-dinner drink, but it is delightfully refreshing over ice as a summer cocktail.

1. Wrap a zucchini ribbon around the circumference of each scallop.
2. Push the skewer or toothpick into the scallop through the end of the zucchini ribbon to secure it in place.
3. Thread 2 to 3 scallops per skewer or 1 scallop per toothpick.

# lobster with tarragon butter
## AND FINGERLING POTATOES

4 servings

POTATOES

1 pound mixed fingerling or other baby potatoes

1 head garlic, halved crosswise

1 bay leaf

1 teaspoon black peppercorns

Kosher salt

2 to 4 tablespoons unsalted butter

Freshly ground black pepper

LOBSTER

4 1½-pound lobsters

1 cup unsalted butter (2 sticks)

1 medium red onion, finely diced

¼ cup chopped fresh tarragon

¼ cup chopped fresh flat-leaf parsley

Juice of 1 lime (about 2 tablespoons)

2 teaspoons kosher salt

¼ teaspoon cayenne pepper

**1.** For the potatoes: Put the potatoes, garlic, bay leaf, and peppercorns in a large saucepan. Add cold water to cover by about an inch and season generously with salt. Bring to a boil, lower the heat, and simmer until potatoes are fork-tender, about 5 to 8 minutes. Drain and cut any large potatoes in half. Discard bay leaf. Toss with 2 to 4 tablespoons butter and salt and black pepper to taste. Keep the potatoes warm.

**2.** Meanwhile, prepare an outdoor grill with a medium fire on just one side of the grill.

**3.** For the lobsters: Prepare the lobsters for grilling (see page 271).

**4.** Melt the 1 cup butter over medium-low heat in a small skillet. Stir in onion, tarragon, parsley, lime juice, salt, and cayenne. Generously spoon some of the herb butter into the tail of each lobster, the cracked claws, and the body. Keep remaining butter warm for serving.

**5.** Grill the lobsters shell side down with heads over the hottest part of the grill. Cover claws with disposable aluminum pans. Cook until shells turn red and the flesh is just opaque, about 10 to 12 minutes. Serve with the potatoes and the remaining butter for dunking the lobster meat.

# seafood paella

6 to 8 servings

- ½ cup extra-virgin olive oil, plus 2 tablespoons for drizzling
- 1 pound jumbo shrimp in the shell
- 2 teaspoons salt, plus additional for seasoning
- 1 pound cleaned squid, cut into ½-inch rings, tentacles left whole (about 16)
- 1 medium onion, chopped
- 4 cloves garlic, minced
- 4 medium ripe tomatoes, halved and grated, skins discarded
- 1 cup jarred piquillo peppers or pimientos, drained and cut into thick strips
- 1½ teaspoons sweet Spanish smoked paprika

  Freshly ground black pepper

  Large pinch saffron threads, crumbled

- 3 cups short-grain rice, such as Spanish paella or medium-grain rice
- 10 ounces frozen lima or peeled fava beans, thawed (about 2 cups)
- 6 cups boiling water
- 1 pound mussels, scrubbed and debearded (about 24) (see page 271)
- ¼ cup chopped fresh flat-leaf parsley

**1.** Spread a single layer of briquettes over the bottom of a charcoal grill. Light 2 chimneys of hardwood charcoal. Pour them over the briquettes and burn until the briquettes are covered with a white ash, about 15 minutes.
**2.** Place a paella pan, 14 or 16 inches across and 2 inches deep, on the grill. Pour the ½ cup olive oil into the pan and add the shrimp. Season with salt to taste and cook, turning once, until the shrimp are pink on both sides, about 1 minute. Transfer the shrimp to a plate using a slotted spoon. Add the squid to the hot pan, season with salt to taste, and cook until the tentacles and the edges of rings curl, about 1 minute. Transfer squid to another plate.
**3.** Add the onion and garlic to the paella pan and cook, stirring, just until soft, about 5 minutes. Add the tomatoes and cook until they are thick and brick red, about 15 minutes. Stir in half the peppers, the 2 teaspoons salt, the paprika, black pepper to taste, and saffron. Add the rice and stir to coat well. Stir in the beans, boiling water, and cooked squid. Bring the paella to a boil, close the grill, and cook—making sure vents are open—without stirring, until the rice is plump

but slightly firm, about 12 minutes.
**4.** Nestle the cooked shrimp and mussels in the rice, close the grill, and cook until the mussels open, about 3 minutes more. Remove the paella from the grill and scatter the remaining peppers on top. Tent with foil and let rest 10 minutes. Drizzle the paella with the 2 tablespoons olive oil and sprinkle with parsley.

## ■ COOK'S NOTE

Line up all the ingredients and utensils next to the grill before you begin to cook. While a crispy rice crust on the bottom of the pan is desirable, a burnt crust is not—watch carefully at the end of cooking.

# salads & sides
## seven

SPRING GARDEN POTATO SALAD • HOT GERMAN POTATO SALAD • CONFETTI COLESLAW • BLUE CHEESE COLESLAW • MACARONI SALAD WITH DILL & HAM • HEIRLOOM TOMATO & MINT SALAD • GRILLED POLENTA WITH CHARRED TOMATOES • SOUTHERN GREENS WITH WHOLE SPICES • FATTOUSH (MIDDLE EASTERN BREAD SALAD) • ANTIPASTI SALAD • WATERMELON & BABY ARUGULA SALAD • BLACK-EYED PEA SALAD • THOUSAND ISLAND DRESSING • GINGER-MISO DRESSING • '50S FRENCH DRESSING • TOMATO & BASIL DRESSING • CHIPOTLE RANCH DRESSING • HERB-STUFFED DEVILED EGGS • SPICY BAKED BEANS • CHILE CORNBREAD • PICCALILLI • PICKLED OKRA • PICKLED BEETS & CUCUMBERS • PICKLED PEACHES • GRILLED VEGGIES • GRILLED RATATOUILLE • CORN WITH GARLIC-HERB OIL

Spring Garden Potato Salad (page 181)

Confetti Coleslaw (page 183)

Hot German Potato Salad
(page 182)

Blue Cheese Coleslaw (page 184)

SPRING GARDEN
# potato salad

6 to 8 servings

### DRESSING

2 cloves garlic, peeled

2½ teaspoons kosher salt

½ cup mayonnaise

2½ tablespoons white wine vinegar

Freshly ground black pepper

### SALAD

8 cups water

⅔ cup dry white vermouth

3 cloves garlic, smashed

2 tablespoons kosher salt plus additional for seasoning

1 sprig fresh thyme

1 bay leaf

4 black peppercorns

2 pounds small red-skinned waxy potatoes, sliced into ⅛-inch-thick rounds

5 medium carrots, peeled and sliced into ⅛-inch-thick rounds

1 bunch radishes, sliced into ⅛-inch-thick rounds (about 8)

½ English cucumber or 1 large Kirby cucumber, sliced into ⅛-inch-thick rounds

1 cup grape or cherry tomatoes, halved

3 scallions (white and green parts), thinly sliced

Freshly ground black pepper

½ cup lightly packed chopped mixed fresh herbs, such as flat-leaf parsley, dill, or tarragon

6 lemon wedges

**1.** For the dressing: Smash the garlic cloves, sprinkle with the salt, and, with the flat side of a large knife, mash and smear the mixture to a coarse paste. Put in a bowl and whisk with the mayonnaise, vinegar, and black pepper to taste.

**2.** For the salad: Put the water, vermouth, garlic, salt, thyme, bay leaf, peppercorns, and potatoes in a large saucepan and bring to a boil. Add the carrots, lower the heat, and cook until the vegetables are tender but not mushy, about 5 minutes. Stir in the radishes, then immediately drain all the vegetables in a colander in the sink. Remove and discard the garlic, thyme, bay leaf, and peppercorns. Cool slightly and toss the vegetables with the dressing. Cover and refrigerate about 30 minutes. (The salad can be prepared up to this point a day ahead.)

**3.** About 10 minutes before serving, toss the cucumber, tomatoes, and scallions in a small bowl with salt and black pepper to taste. When ready to serve, fold the cucumber mixture and herbs into the potato salad. Serve with lemon wedges.

## ▬ COOK'S NOTE

If you have a mandoline, use it to make slicing the vegetables for this salad a breeze.

HOT GERMAN
# potato salad

6 servings

- 2 pounds white-skinned waxy potatoes (about 5 large), scrubbed
- 2 tablespoons plus 2 teaspoons kosher salt, plus additional for seasoning
- 6 slices bacon (about 4 ounces)
- 1 small yellow onion, diced
- 3/4 cup chicken broth
- 1/3 cup fruity white wine, such as Riesling
- 3 tablespoons white wine vinegar
- 2 tablespoons whole-grain mustard
- 2 teaspoons sugar
- 1/4 cup chopped fresh flat-leaf parsley
- Freshly ground black pepper

**1.** Put the potatoes in a large saucepan; add 2 tablespoons of the salt and enough cold water to cover by 1 inch. Bring to a boil, lower the heat, and simmer until fork-tender, about 30 minutes. Drain and cool slightly.

**2.** When the potatoes are almost done, cook the bacon in a skillet over medium-high heat until crisp, about 4 minutes. Drain the bacon on a paper towel-lined plate. Lower the heat to medium. Add the onion and the remaining 2 teaspoons salt and cook, stirring occasionally, until onion is translucent, about 8 minutes. Whisk in the broth, wine, vinegar, mustard, and sugar and boil until slightly thickened, about 5 minutes.

**3.** Crumble the bacon into a serving bowl. Using a paring knife, peel the skins off the warm potatoes and cut them into bite-size chunks. Add the potatoes to bowl along with the hot vinegar dressing and the parsley. Toss gently and adjust seasoning with salt and black pepper to taste. Serve immediately or while still warm.

## COOK'S NOTE

This salad is best served immediately or while still quite warm. The key is that the dressing and the potatoes need to be warm when the salad is assembled. It suffers when reheated. If you are juggling a couple of dishes, cook the potatoes and keep them in their skins. Make the dressing but don't assemble the salad. Just before serving, heat the potatoes in the microwave, peel them, and toss with the dressing.

# coleslaw

6 servings

SALAD

- 1 small head red cabbage (about 1³/₄ pounds)
- 1 bunch medium carrots, peeled (about 5)
- 2 tablespoons kosher salt
- 2 Granny Smith apples
- 6 scallions (white and green parts), sliced
- 1 bunch watercress

DRESSING

- 3 tablespoons cider vinegar
- 3 tablespoons honey
- 2 tablespoons Dijon mustard
- 1 tablespoon celery seeds or 2 teaspoons caraway seeds
- 1 tablespoon plus 1 teaspoon kosher salt
  Freshly ground black pepper
- ¹/₃ cup extra-virgin olive oil

**1.** For the salad: Quarter and core the cabbage. Set up a food processor with the slicing blade. Slice the cabbage and then transfer it to a colander. Switch to the grating blade and shred the carrots; add to cabbage. Toss the cabbage and carrots with the salt and set colander in the sink until the vegetables wilt, 1 to 4 hours. Rinse cabbage mixture thoroughly in cold water and spin it dry in a salad spinner.

**2.** Meanwhile, make the dressing: Whisk the vinegar with the honey, mustard, celery seeds, salt, and black pepper to taste in a small bowl. Gradually whisk in the olive oil, starting with a few drops and then adding the rest in a steady stream to make a smooth, slightly thick dressing.

**3.** Quarter, core, and shred the apples. Toss the cabbage mixture with the apples, scallions, and about ¹/₂ cup of the dressing. Refrigerate until chilled and the flavors come together, about 1 hour. When ready to serve, toss the watercress with the remaining dressing. Make a ring on a platter with the watercress, and mound the coleslaw in the middle of the ring.

## ▮ KNOW-HOW

Salting the cabbage gives the slaw its characteristic tender bite, as well as expressing excess liquid. If you skip this step, your salad will be soggy and bland.

# BLUE CHEESE
# coleslaw

4 to 6 servings

½ medium red onion

2 tablespoons plus ½ teaspoon kosher salt

1 head savoy cabbage (about 1 pound)

1 medium carrot, peeled

½ cup crumbled blue cheese (about 2 ounces)

⅓ cup mayonnaise

⅓ cup sour cream

1 tablespoon apple cider vinegar

¼ teaspoon celery seeds

⅛ teaspoon Worcestershire sauce

Dash hot sauce

Freshly ground black pepper

**1.** Set up a food processor with the slicing blade. Slice the onion and then transfer it to a colander. Toss the onion slices with 1 tablespoon of the salt and set colander in the sink. Quarter and core the cabbage and slice in the food processor. Add the cabbage to the onions. Switch to the grating blade and grate the carrot; add to the colander. Toss the vegetables with another 1 tablespoon salt. Set aside until the vegetables wilt, 1 to 4 hours.

**2.** Wipe out the food processor, then pulse the blue cheese, mayonnaise, sour cream, vinegar, the remaining ½ teaspoon salt, celery seeds, Worcestershire sauce, and hot sauce to make a creamy dressing. Cover and refrigerate until ready to dress the slaw.

**3.** Rinse the slaw mixture thoroughly in cold water and spin dry in a salad spinner. Toss the slaw with the dressing and season with black pepper to taste. Refrigerate to let the flavors come together, about 1 hour.

## COOK'S NOTE

Savoy cabbage looks like a crinkled version of regular green cabbage but has a sweeter, less "cabbagey" taste.

## KNOW-HOW

You won't get your fingers all gunked up with the soft blue cheese if you pop it into the freezer for a couple of minutes before crumbling.

*This surprising and creamy slaw screams to be served with beef. It's absolutely delicious with either a simple burger or a sublime steak.*

# macaroni salad

## WITH DILL & HAM

4 to 6 servings

- ¼ medium red onion, minced
- 2 teaspoons kosher salt, plus additional for salting water
- 8 ounces elbow macaroni (about 2 cups)
- 2 tablespoons milk
- 2 tablespoons white wine vinegar
- 1 tablespoon Dijon mustard

  Freshly ground black pepper
- ⅓ cup extra-virgin olive oil
- ⅓ cup sour cream
- 6 ounces cooked ham, cut into ⅓-inch cubes
- ¾ cup frozen baby peas, thawed (about 4 ounces)
- 2 ribs celery, with leaves, diced
- 2 tablespoons chopped fresh dill

**1.** To mellow the minced onion, soak it in cold water while you make the salad.

**2.** Bring a large pot of cold water to a boil over high heat and salt it generously. Add the macaroni and boil, stirring occasionally, until al dente, about 8 minutes. Drain the macaroni in a colander, put in a serving bowl, and toss with the milk. Allow the macaroni to cool slightly while you make the dressing.

**3.** For the dressing: Whisk the vinegar, mustard, the 2 teaspoons salt, and black pepper to taste in a large bowl. Gradually whisk in the olive oil, starting with a few drops and then adding the rest in a steady stream to make a smooth, slightly thick dressing. Whisk in the sour cream.

**4.** Drain the onions, pat dry, and add to the macaroni along with the ham, peas, celery, and dill. Add the dressing and fold to coat the pasta evenly. Serve immediately or cover and refrigerate until ready to serve.

## KNOW-HOW

Why the milk? When we left it out of the recipe, the macaroni absorbed too much of the dressing and the salad was overly acidic. Adding just a couple tablespoons mellowed the dressing and gave the salad a wonderful old-fashioned quality without being goopy or heavy.

# heirloom tomato
## & MINT SALAD

4 servings

- 2 pounds vine-ripened heirloom tomatoes, assorted varieties preferred
- 1 shallot, thinly sliced
- 1 teaspoon coarse sea salt

  Freshly ground black pepper
- ¼ cup fresh spearmint leaves, torn into pieces
- ¼ cup fruity extra-virgin olive oil
- 2 tablespoons champagne vinegar or white wine vinegar

Cut the tomatoes into a variety of sizes and shapes, some thick slabs, wedges, halves, or chunks. Arrange them on a large platter and scatter the shallot over the tomatoes. Season with the salt and black pepper to taste. Set aside until juicy, about 5 minutes. Sprinkle mint over the top and drizzle with the olive oil and vinegar.

## KNOW-HOW

When a tomato is ripe, juicy, and ready to go, a good hit of coarse salt and freshly ground black pepper is really all it needs. Salting brings out all the flavor notes—the sweetness of the fruit along with its natural acidity. It also draws out the juices, making its own sauce.

## COOK'S NOTE

Heirloom tomatoes—found in farmers' markets and in your backyard garden—come in many different shapes, sizes, and colors and often with whimsical names to match, such as Brandywine, Green Zebra, Hillbilly, and Moonglow. Choose by taste and aroma—and never store a tomato in the refrigerator.

*It just doesn't get more summery or seasonal than fresh vine-ripened tomatoes.*

187

# grilled polenta
## WITH CHARRED TOMATOES

6 to 8 servings

1½ cups water

1½ cups chicken broth

1 sprig fresh thyme

⅔ cup quick-cooking polenta

½ cup freshly grated Parmesan cheese, plus additional for serving (optional)

½ cup freshly grated Pecorino Romano cheese, plus additional for serving

2 tablespoons unsalted butter

½ teaspoon kosher salt, plus additional for seasoning

Freshly ground black pepper

2 medium ripe tomatoes

Instant-blending flour, such as Wondra

2 tablespoons extra-virgin olive oil, plus additional for brushing

**1.** Bring the water, broth, and thyme to a boil in a small saucepan. Slowly whisk in the polenta, reduce the heat to low, and cook, whisking occasionally, until polenta is thick and creamy, about 15 minutes.
**2.** Pull the saucepan from the heat and whisk in the ½ cup of both cheeses, butter, ½ teaspoon salt, and black pepper to taste. Pour the mixture into a lightly buttered 8x8-inch baking dish and smooth with a spatula to an even thickness. Cover the surface with plastic wrap and chill until very firm, 2 to 24 hours.
**3.** Prepare an outdoor grill with a medium fire.
**4.** Grill the tomatoes whole, turning as needed, until the skins blacken and split, about 8 to 10 minutes. Turn polenta out of the pan onto a cutting board. Cut in half, dust with flour, and brush grill and polenta with olive oil. Season with salt and black pepper to taste. Grill, covered, until crisp with distinct grill marks on each side, about 3 minutes per side. Return to the cutting board and cut into serving pieces.
**5.** Core and roughly chop the tomatoes with the skin. Toss the tomatoes and 2 tablespoons olive oil in a bowl and season with salt and black pepper to taste.

Arrange the polenta on a platter, spoon the charred tomatoes on top, and sprinkle with additional cheese, if desired.

## ▬ KNOW-HOW

Instant- or quick-mixing flour is processed to dissolve at once in hot or cold liquids, so it's often used to thicken sauces and gravies. It also makes a crispy coating for our polenta (or other delicate foods, such as fish fillets) and helps to keep it from sticking on the grill.

## ▬ STYLE

Bring a nice big wedge of Parmigiano-Reggiano to the table and let your guests shave big curls over their polenta. Leave the cheese on the table when you clear the dishes and serve it with nuts and fresh fruit for an effortless cheese course.

# southern greens
## WITH WHOLE SPICES

6 servings

- 6 slices bacon, cut into 2-inch pieces (about 4 ounces)
- 4 medium carrots, thinly sliced (about 2 cups)
- 1 medium red onion, thinly sliced
- 4 cloves garlic, peeled and smashed
- 2 teaspoons kosher salt
- 1 teaspoon coarsely ground black pepper
- 2 teaspoons pickling spice
- 1 bunch mustard greens, washed, stems trimmed (about 1 pound)
- 1 bunch collard greens, washed, stems trimmed (about 12 ounces)
- 1 bunch kale, washed, stems trimmed (about 9 ounces)
- 2 cups chicken broth
- ¼ cup balsamic vinegar

**1.** Cook the bacon in a large pot over medium-high heat until almost crisp, about 3 minutes. Add the carrots, onion, garlic, salt, black pepper, and pickling spice to the pot and cook over medium-low heat until vegetables are soft, about 10 minutes.

**2.** Tear the greens into pieces, adding to the pot as you go, then stir in the broth and vinegar. Cover, bring to a boil, reduce heat, and simmer until greens are tender but not mushy, about 25 minutes.

## ▬ COOK'S NOTE

Pickling spice is a blend sold in most supermarkets and contains some or all of the following: allspice, bay leaf, cloves, coriander, mustard seed, and peppercorns. The spices are usually left whole, but most will sink down to the bottom of the pot—so you won't be crunching away as you eat the greens.

# easy elegance

## MENU

Greek Mountain Hens (page 113)
● Smoky Eggplant Dip (page 17)
● Grilled pita ● Vegetable
Souvlaki (page 73) ● Pickled Beets
& Cucumbers (page 209) ● Mixed
olives ● White wine ● Fattoush
(Middle Eastern Bread Salad)
(page 192)

A collection of candles lights the way to our grilled Mediterranean buffet. A simple strip of gossamer fabric transforms a patio into a dreamy tent. This room-temperature menu allows guests to dine as they come and go.

# fattoush
### (MIDDLE EASTERN BREAD SALAD)

6 servings

DRESSING

  1 large clove garlic, peeled

  2 teaspoons kosher salt

    Juice of 1½ lemons (about 4 or 5 tablespoons)

  ½ cup extra-virgin olive oil

    Pinch ground allspice

    Freshly ground black pepper

SALAD

  2 plain medium pocket pita breads

  ⅓ cup extra-virgin olive oil

  1 tablespoon dried savory

    Kosher salt

    Freshly ground black pepper

  2 medium bunches arugula, stemmed and leaves torn, if large (about 5 cups)

  2 medium ripe tomatoes, diced (about 1 pound)

  4 scallions (white and green parts), cut into ½-inch pieces

  1 Kirby cucumber, diced

  1 bunch radishes, halved and sliced (about 5)

  ½ cup lightly packed whole fresh mint leaves

    Pepperoncini or other pickled peppers, for serving (optional)

**1.** Prepare an outdoor grill with a medium fire.

**2.** For the dressing: Smash the garlic clove, sprinkle with the salt, and, with the flat side of a large knife, mash and smear the mixture to a coarse paste. Whisk the lemon juice and garlic paste in a small bowl. Gradually whisk in the oil, starting with a few drops and adding the rest in a steady stream to make a smooth, slightly thick dressing. Season with the allspice and black pepper to taste.

**3.** For the salad: Use a fork or knife to split the pitas into 4 rounds. Brush both sides of the bread with the olive oil and season with the savory, salt, and black pepper to taste. Grill, turning occasionally, until crisp and browned, about 3 minutes.

**4.** Toss the arugula, tomatoes, scallions, cucumber, radishes, and mint in a serving bowl.

**5.** To serve: Break the pita chips into bite-size pieces, add to the salad, and toss with the dressing. Serve with the pepperoncini, if desired.

## COOK'S NOTE

This is the perfect salad to enjoy at the height of summer with big, juicy farmers' market tomatoes. If you're craving it during cooler months, use plum tomatoes, which are consistently good year-round. For this recipe, you'll need about 6 to 8 plum tomatoes to make a pound.

# antipasti
## SALAD

4 to 6 servings

SALAD

- ¼ medium red onion, minced
- ½ medium fennel bulb, trimmed and cored
- 1 15-ounce can chickpeas, rinsed and drained
- 4 jarred roasted sweet red peppers, chopped (about ¾ cup)
- 1 6-ounce jar marinated artichoke hearts, rinsed, drained, and quartered, if whole
- 2 cups baby arugula
- 1 cup fresh flat-leaf parsley leaves
- ¼ cup kalamata olives, pitted (about 2 ounces)
- ½ to 1 cup freshly shaved Parmigiano-Reggiano cheese

DRESSING

- 1 small garlic clove, peeled
- 1½ teaspoons kosher salt
- 1 teaspoon freshly grated orange zest
- 2 tablespoons white wine vinegar

  Freshly ground black pepper
- ⅓ cup extra-virgin olive oil

**1.** For the salad: To mellow the minced onion, soak it in cold water for 10 minutes, then drain well, pat dry, and put in a serving bowl.

**2.** Meanwhile, make the dressing: Smash the garlic clove, sprinkle with ½ teaspoon of the salt, and, with the side of a large knife, mash and smear the mixture to a coarse paste. Put the paste in a bowl and add the orange zest, vinegar, remaining 1 teaspoon salt, and black pepper to taste. Gradually whisk in the olive oil, starting with a few drops and then adding the rest in a steady stream to make a smooth, slightly thick dressing.

**3.** Using a handheld mandoline or a knife, cut the fennel lengthwise into long, thin slices. Add to the onion and toss with the chickpeas, peppers, artichoke hearts, arugula, parsley, and dressing. Scatter the olives and shave the Parmigiano-Reggiano over the top.

## KNOW-HOW

Parmigiano-Reggiano shavings are a simple way to add texture, taste, and eye appeal to salads. To make them, hold the cheese firmly in one hand and run a vegetable peeler firmly across the longest edge of the cheese to peel off long, thin strips.

## SHOPSMART

Baby arugula has smaller, more tender leaves and a slightly less peppery and assertive flavor than "grown-up" arugula.

WATERMELON & BABY
# arugula salad

4 to 6 servings

SALAD

½ red onion, thinly sliced

4 pounds watermelon, preferably seedless, rind removed, cut into ¾-inch cubes (about 8 cups)

2 teaspoons chopped fresh oregano leaves

8 cups baby arugula (about 4 ounces)

¾ cup crumbled ricotta salata or feta cheese (about 4 ounces)

½ cup pitted niçoise olives (optional)

Freshly ground black pepper

DRESSING

2 tablespoons white wine vinegar

1¼ teaspoons kosher salt

Freshly ground black pepper

⅓ cup extra-virgin olive oil

**1.** For the salad: To mellow the onion, soak it in cold water for 10 minutes, then drain well, pat dry, and put in a serving bowl.
**2.** Meanwhile, make the dressing: Whisk the vinegar, salt, and black pepper to taste in a bowl. Gradually whisk in the olive oil, starting with a few drops and then adding the rest of the oil in a steady stream to make a smooth dressing.
**3.** Toss the watermelon and oregano with the onions and the dressing, taking care not to break up the watermelon chunks. (The salad can be made to this point up to 30 minutes in advance.)
**4.** When ready to serve, toss the arugula with the dressed watermelon. Scatter the cheese, olives (if desired), and a generous grinding of black pepper over the top.

## ■ KNOW-HOW

To pit the olives you can use a special tool if you are into gadgets. But really all you need is a broad knife. Place the olive under the flat side of the knife and give it a good whack. It cracks the olive and frees the fruit from the pit.

## ■ COOK'S NOTE

Even though we don't eat the melon skin or rinds, it's a good idea to wash the watermelon before cutting it. If bacteria are present on the outside of the melon, the knife—in the process of cutting—can transport them to the flesh, which can cause food-borne illnesses.

# black-eyed pea
## SALAD

4 to 6 servings

DRESSING

 1  small clove garlic, peeled

    Juice of 1½ limes (about
    3 tablespoons)

 2  teaspoons kosher salt

    Pinch of cumin

 ¼  cup extra-virgin olive oil

 3  tablespoons chopped fresh
    cilantro


SALAD

 1  pound frozen black-eyed peas,
    cooked according to package
    directions

 1  medium tomato, diced

 ½  small red onion, finely
    chopped (about ¼ cup)

 ½  jalapeño or serrano chile,
    seeded and finely chopped
    (about 1½ teaspoons)

    Kosher salt

    Freshly ground black pepper

 1  small Hass avocado, halved,
    pitted, and diced

**1.** For the dressing: Smash the garlic clove, sprinkle with a pinch of the salt, and, with the flat side of a large knife, mash and smear the mixture to a coarse paste. Whisk the garlic paste, lime juice, remaining salt, and cumin in a bowl. Gradually whisk in the olive oil, starting with a few drops and then adding the rest in a steady stream to make a slightly thick dressing. Stir in the cilantro.

**2.** For the salad: Toss the black-eyed peas, tomato, onion, and jalapeño in a large bowl. Add the dressing and toss to coat evenly. Season with salt and black pepper to taste. Gently fold in the avocado and serve.

## COOK'S NOTE

This salad can be made ahead and refrigerated, but don't cut or add the avocado until just before serving to keep it from darkening.

Black-Eyed Pea Salad (page 196)

Southern Greens with Whole Spices
(page 189)

Tomato & Basil Dressing (page 201), Thousand Island Dressing (page 199), '50s French Dressing (page 200), Ginger-Miso Dressing (page 200), Chipotle Ranch Dressing (page 201)

# thousand island
## DRESSING

Makes 1½ cups

1 large egg

1 clove garlic, peeled

2 teaspoons kosher salt

½ cup mayonnaise

⅓ cup sweet pickle relish

½ medium yellow onion, minced

Finely grated zest of ½ lemon

Juice of 1 lemon (about 3 tablespoons)

2 tablespoons ketchup

1 teaspoon Asian chile paste, such as *sambal oelek*

Freshly ground black pepper

**1.** Put the egg in a small saucepan with enough cold water to cover. Bring to a boil, cover, and remove from the heat. Set aside for 10 minutes. Drain the egg and roll it between your palm and the counter to crack the shell, then peel under cool running water. Chop egg coarsely and put in a bowl.

**2.** Smash the garlic clove, sprinkle with the salt, and, with the flat side of a large knife, mash and smear the mixture to a coarse paste. Add to the bowl with the egg, and whisk in the mayonnaise, pickle relish, onion, lemon zest and juice, ketchup, chile paste, and black pepper to taste. Serve or refrigerate in a tightly sealed container for up to 3 days.

With the right dressing, you can toss almost anything into a salad. Simple greens, tomatoes, corn, zucchini, peaches, last night's grilled chicken—you name it.

# ginger-miso
## DRESSING

Makes about 2 cups

1 clove garlic, peeled

$^{1}/_{2}$ teaspoon kosher salt

$^{1}/_{3}$ cup yellow miso

$^{1}/_{4}$ cup water

Juice of $1^{1}/_{2}$ limes (about 3 tablespoons)

1 $^{1}/_{2}$-inch piece peeled fresh ginger, grated

1 large shallot, minced

$^{1}/_{2}$ to 1 Thai bird chile, minced with seeds

1 cup extra-virgin olive oil

Smash the garlic clove, sprinkle with the salt, and, with the flat side of a large knife, mash and smear the mixture to a coarse paste. Transfer to a bowl and whisk with the miso, water, lime juice, ginger, shallot, and chile to taste. Gradually whisk in the olive oil, starting with a few drops and then adding the rest in a steady stream to make a smooth, slightly thick dressing. Serve or refrigerate in a tightly sealed container for up to 3 days.


# '50s french
## DRESSING

Makes $1^{1}/_{2}$ cups

$^{1}/_{4}$ cup tomato paste

$^{1}/_{4}$ cup water

1 tablespoon Dijon mustard

$^{1}/_{4}$ cup red wine vinegar

3 tablespoons firmly packed brown sugar

2 teaspoons kosher salt

$1^{1}/_{4}$ teaspoons sweet paprika

Freshly ground black pepper

$^{3}/_{4}$ cup extra-virgin olive oil

$^{1}/_{4}$ cup fresh flat-leaf parsley, roughly chopped

Whisk the tomato paste, water, and mustard in a bowl until smooth. Whisk in the vinegar, brown sugar, salt, paprika, and black pepper to taste. Gradually whisk in the olive oil, starting with a few drops and then adding the rest in a steady stream to make a smooth, slightly thick dressing. Whisk in the parsley. Serve or refrigerate in a tightly sealed container for up to 3 days.

# tomato & basil
## DRESSING

Makes 1½ cups

- 3 medium ripe tomatoes, halved
- 1 tablespoon white wine vinegar
- 2 cloves garlic, peeled and smashed
- 2 teaspoons kosher salt
  Freshly ground black pepper
  Pinch crushed red pepper
- ½ cup extra-virgin olive oil
- 1 cup loosely packed fresh basil

Scoop the flesh and juices of the tomatoes out of their skins with a spoon and into a bowl; discard the skins. Whisk in the vinegar, garlic, salt, black pepper to taste, and crushed red pepper, breaking up the tomato as you do. Gradually whisk in the olive oil, starting with a few drops and then adding the rest in a steady stream to make a chunky, slightly thick dressing. Roughly chop the basil and stir into the dressing. Set aside for 15 minutes to let the flavors come together. Remove the garlic and serve.

## ▓ COOK'S NOTE

Make sure you use your sharpest knife to chop the basil and make quick work of it to prevent the basil from turning black. If you want to make the dressing ahead, wait to add the basil until just before you serve to capture its bright, fresh flavor.

# chipotle ranch
## DRESSING

Makes about 1½ cups

- 3 cloves garlic, peeled
- 1 teaspoon kosher salt
- ⅔ cup mayonnaise
- ⅔ cup buttermilk
- ⅓ cup minced fresh cilantro
- 2 scallions (white and green parts), very thinly sliced
- 1 to 2 tablespoons chipotle hot sauce
- 2 teaspoons finely grated orange zest

Smash the garlic cloves, sprinkle with the salt, and, with the flat side of a large knife, mash and smear the mixture to a coarse paste. Scrape the garlic paste into a small bowl, add the mayonnaise, buttermilk, cilantro, scallions, hot sauce, and orange zest and whisk well to make a creamy dressing.

HERB-STUFFED
# deviled eggs

Makes 12 halves

- 6 large eggs
- 3 tablespoons mayonnaise
- 2 teaspoons Dijon mustard
- 1 tablespoon extra-virgin olive oil
- 1½ teaspoons finely chopped cornichons (see Cook's Note, right)
- 1½ teaspoons finely chopped fresh chives
- 1½ teaspoons minced fresh flat-leaf parsley, plus small whole leaves for garnish
- 1½ teaspoons minced fresh tarragon
- ⅛ teaspoon kosher salt

**1.** Put the eggs in a saucepan with enough cold water to cover. Bring to a boil, cover, and remove from the heat. Set aside for 10 minutes. Drain the eggs and roll them between your palm and the counter to crack the shell, then peel under cool running water. Halve eggs lengthwise and carefully remove the yolks from the whites. Slice a thin sliver from the rounded bottom of each half so they sit without wobbling on a serving platter. Mash the yolks in a bowl with a fork.
**2.** Whisk the mayonnaise and mustard into the yolks. Gradually whisk in the olive oil, starting with a few drops and then adding the rest in a steady stream. Stir in cornichons, chives, parsley, tarragon, and salt.
**3.** Spoon the yolk mixture back into the whites. Garnish with parsley leaves. The eggs can be stuffed several hours in advance, covered, and refrigerated until ready to serve.

## COOK'S NOTE
Cornichons are French gherkins—small, tart pickles that often accompany pâtés and smoked fish. They add just the right crunch to our deviled eggs.

# baked beans

SPICY

8 servings

1 pound dry Great Northern
  beans

6 tablespoons unsalted butter

1 medium yellow onion, thinly
  sliced

4 garlic cloves, minced

2 dried ancho chiles, seeded and
  roughly chopped or crumbled

1 tablespoon dried oregano

1½ teaspoons ground coriander

1 teaspoon ground cumin

  Pinch ground cloves

2 bay leaves

2 smoked turkey wings (about
  1 pound each)

6 cups water

1½ cups ketchup

½ cup firmly packed light brown
  sugar

⅓ cup dark molasses

¼ cup tamarind concentrate

1 tablespoon Worcestershire
  sauce

1 to 2 tablespoons red wine
  vinegar or dark rum

**1.** Put the beans in a large
saucepan, add cold water to
cover by a few inches, bring to a
boil, and cook for 5 minutes.
Remove from the heat, cover,
and set aside for 1 hour.
**2.** Preheat the oven to 300°F.
Melt the butter in a 6-quart
Dutch oven over medium heat.
Add the onion, garlic, chiles,
oregano, coriander, cumin,
cloves, and bay leaves and cook,
stirring occasionally, until onion
begins to brown, about 15 to
20 minutes.
**3.** Drain the beans and add them
to onion mixture along with
turkey wings and the 6 cups
water. Bring to a boil, cover, and
place in the preheated oven to
bake for 2 hours.
**4.** Mix the ketchup, brown sugar,
molasses, tamarind, and
Worcestershire and add to the
beans. Cover and continue to
bake until the beans are tender
and creamy and the turkey meat
falls from the bones, about
2 hours more. (If the beans get
very thick, add a little water.)
Stir the vinegar or rum into the
beans before serving.

## COOK'S NOTE

We like to use smoked turkey
wings as a flavorful, lower-fat
alternative to ham and bacon in
slow-cooked dishes such as this
one. Look for wings that are
naturally smoked without a lot
of additives.

CHILE

# cornbread

6 to 8 servings

    Unsalted butter, at room temperature, for buttering pan

2 cups yellow cornmeal, preferably stone-ground

1 cup all-purpose flour

$1/4$ cup sugar

4 teaspoons baking powder

$1^1/4$ teaspoons fine salt

1 large ear fresh corn, shucked

1 cup milk

$1/2$ cup buttermilk

2 large eggs at room temperature

1 to 2 chopped roasted green chiles, such as Anaheim or poblano (fresh or canned), seeded

6 tablespoons unsalted butter, melted

**1.** Preheat the oven to 400°F. Butter a 9-inch cast-iron skillet or cake pan.

**2.** Whisk the cornmeal, flour, sugar, baking powder, and salt in a large bowl. Cut the corn kernels from the cob with a knife. Working over a medium bowl, run a knife along the cob to press out the milky liquid. Whisk in the milk, buttermilk, eggs, corn, and chiles.

**3.** Fold the milk mixture into the cornmeal mixture until almost completely incorporated, then fold in the melted butter. Take care not to overwork the batter or the bread will be tough. Transfer the batter into the prepared skillet or pan and bake until lightly browned and a toothpick inserted in the center comes out clean, about 30 to 35 minutes. Set aside to cool slightly before serving.

## SHOPSMART

Stone-ground cornmeal has a better texture and a "cornier" taste than most commercially available cornmeal. It's worth searching out, but once you buy it, keep it refrigerated as it will go rancid faster than other types.

## STYLE

Loosen the cornbread and serve it in wedges straight from the skillet. It'll add a "down-home" touch to your barbecue and keep the bread warm at the table.

Pickled Peaches (page 209)

Pickled Beets and Cucumbers (page 209)

Pickled Okra (page 208)

Piccalilli (page 207)

# piccalilli

Makes 2 quarts

- 2 medium green tomatoes, cut into wedges (about 10 ounces)
- ½ head cauliflower, cut into small florets
- 1 small red onion, cut into wedges, root end trimmed but intact
- 1 rib celery, sliced on an angle
- 1 bulb fennel, halved, thinly sliced lengthwise
- 3 tablespoons plus 1 teaspoon kosher salt
- ¼ cup extra-virgin olive oil
- ½ teaspoon ground turmeric
- 1 medium carrot, peeled and sliced on an angle
- 1 yellow bell pepper, stemmed, seeded, and sliced
- 2 tablespoons peeled, finely grated fresh ginger
- 5 cloves garlic, peeled and smashed
- 2 teaspoons yellow mustard seeds
- 1 teaspoon fennel seeds
- ½ teaspoon crushed red pepper
- 3 cups water
- 1 cup cider vinegar
- 1 cup white wine vinegar
- ½ cup firmly packed light brown sugar

**1.** Toss the tomatoes, cauliflower, onion, celery, and fennel with 2 tablespoons of the salt in a colander and set in the sink until they wilt, about 45 minutes. Rinse thoroughly.

**2.** Heat the olive oil in a large saucepan or Dutch oven over medium heat and add the turmeric, stirring until the oil is an even color, about 30 seconds. Add the carrot, bell pepper, ginger, garlic, mustard seeds, fennel seeds, and crushed red pepper. Cook, stirring, until fragrant and vegetables are just tender and wilted, about 2 minutes. Add the water, vinegars, brown sugar, and remaining salt to the saucepan and bring the mixture to a boil. Remove from the heat and add the tomato mixture. Cool to room temperature. Transfer to a sealed container and refrigerate for 24 hours. The piccalilli will keep for 1 week tightly sealed in the refrigerator.

## KNOW-HOW

Before you refrigerate the piccalilli, make sure all the vegetables are completely covered by the vinegar mixture so they marinate evenly.

## COOK'S NOTE

Piccalilli is a vegetable relish with British roots. It really is cook's choice; we love using what is freshest in the market. It's the ideal side during grilling season. You can make a big batch and use it to complement everything from pork to chicken to fish. Vibrant and colorful, it dresses a buffet beautifully.

*We love the way funky, old-fashioned pickle jars dress a table. These quick, no-process pickles look gorgeous tucked into them.*

PICKLED
# okra

Makes about 6 cups

- 2 tablespoons kosher salt, plus additional for salting water
- 1 pound fresh okra, trimmed
- 1⅓ cups distilled white vinegar
- 1 cup water
- ½ cup sugar
- Zest from 1 lemon, peeled in large strips
- Juice of 1 lemon (about 2 tablespoons)
- 1 bay leaf
- Freshly ground black pepper
- 3 serrano chiles, split lengthwise with seeds
- 1 medium red onion, thinly sliced
- 2 tablespoons extra-virgin olive oil

**1.** Bring a saucepan of water to a boil and salt it generously. Add the okra and cook until crisp-tender, about 2 minutes. Drain. **2.** Meanwhile, mix the vinegar, water, sugar, lemon zest and juice, bay leaf, 2 tablespoons salt, and black pepper to taste in a saucepan. Bring to a boil and cook for 5 minutes. Put the okra in a nonreactive bowl with the chiles, onion, and olive oil. Pour the hot brine over the vegetables and cool to room temperature. Cover and refrigerate for 5 hours or overnight. The okra will keep for 1 week tightly sealed in the refrigerator.

## STYLE

How would you serve delicious quick pickles? As a nibble with cocktails, as part of an antipasti-type platter, or as a side dish with Southwestern or Middle Eastern food.

# pickled beets
## & CUCUMBERS

Makes 4½ cups

3½ cups water

¾ cup sherry vinegar

2 tablespoons firmly packed light brown sugar

1 bay leaf

2 teaspoons kosher salt, plus additional for seasoning

2 teaspoons Worcestershire sauce

1 teaspoon coriander seeds

1 teaspoon cracked black peppercorns

1 pound medium red beets (about 4), peeled and cut into sixths

1 Kirby cucumber, with peel, sliced into ¼-inch-thick slices

2 shallots, thinly sliced

3 tablespoons drained horseradish

**1.** Mix water, vinegar, sugar, bay leaf, 2 teaspoons salt, Worcestershire, coriander, and peppercorns in a large saucepan and bring to a boil.

**2.** Add beets to mixture and reduce heat to a simmer. Cook until beets are tender, 25 to 35 minutes. Set aside to cool.

**3.** Meanwhile, salt and toss cucumbers and shallots in a colander set in the sink. Let stand until vegetables wilt. Rinse and add to warm beet brine along with horseradish. Cool to room temperature. Transfer to a sealed container and refrigerate 24 hours. Beets will keep 1 week tightly sealed in the refrigerator.

PICKLED
# peaches

Makes about 2 quarts

1 tablespoon pickling spice

¼ teaspoon crushed red pepper

5 cups water

2½ cups white wine vinegar

2 cups sugar

1 tablespoon kosher salt

6 firm but ripe peaches, quartered and pitted, with skins (about 2¼ pounds)

**1.** Toast pickling spice and crushed red pepper in a dry medium saucepan over high heat until fragrant, about 30 seconds. Add water, vinegar, sugar, and salt and bring to a simmer, stirring to dissolve sugar. Add peaches and simmer just until tender, about 20 minutes. Remove peaches from liquid with a slotted spoon, reserving liquid, and set aside just until fruit is cool enough to touch.

**2.** Pinch the skin from peaches—if the skin pulls off easily—and discard. (If the skins cling, don't fret—the peaches will be beautiful and tasty that way as well.) Transfer peaches to a sealed container, cover with the reserved liquid, and refrigerate for at least 24 hours. The peaches will keep for 1 week tightly sealed in the refrigerator.

## ▬ COOK'S NOTE

Pickled Peaches are a great sweet-and-sour accompaniment to grilled pork and poultry dishes. They'd also be great as part of a Southern-style brunch or lunch.

# grilled veggies

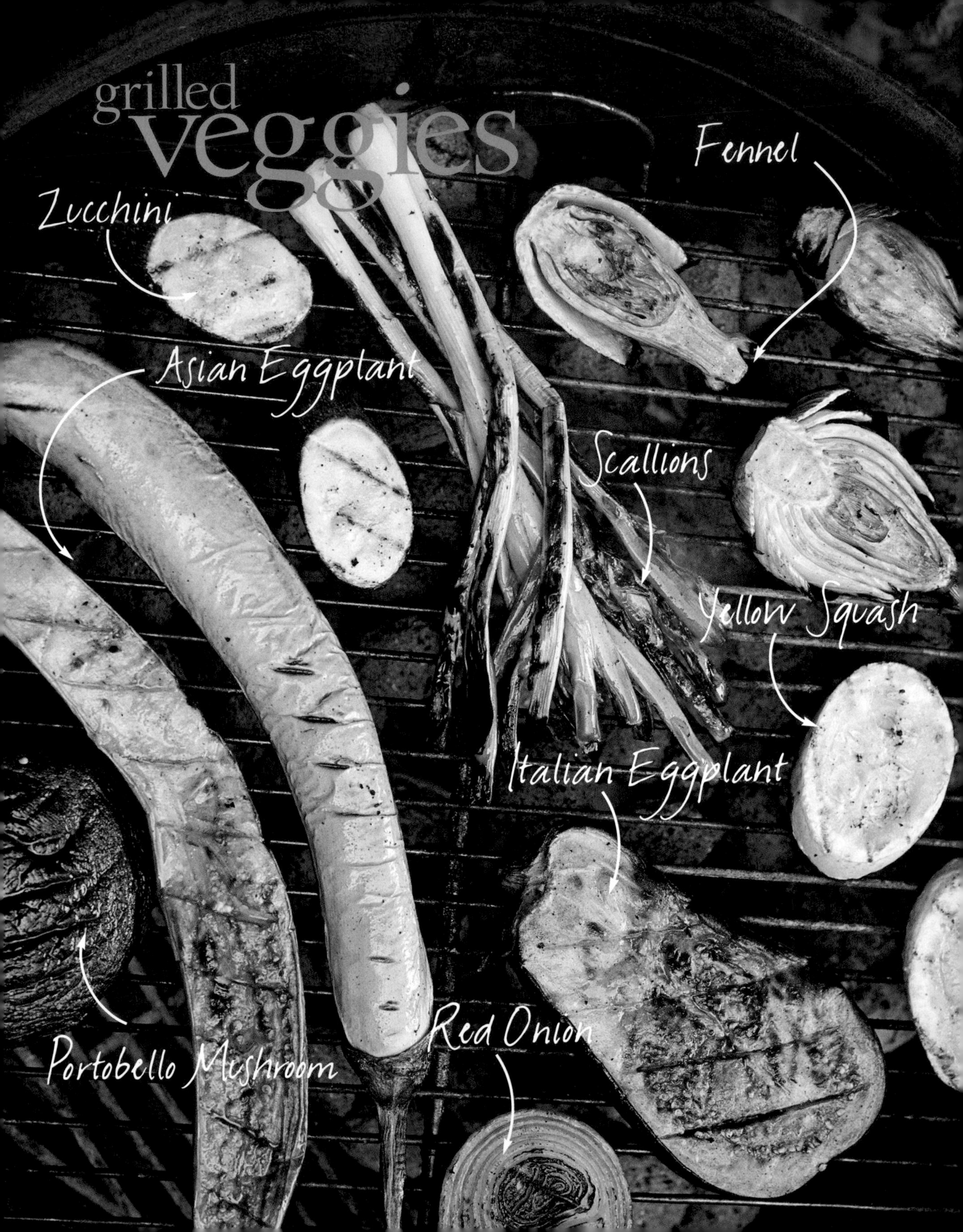

Zucchini

Fennel

Asian Eggplant

Scallions

Yellow Squash

Italian Eggplant

Portobello Mushroom

Red Onion

| Vegetable | Prep | Cooking Tip | Time | Finish |
|---|---|---|---|---|
| **Red, Vidalia, or White Onions** | Cut crosswise into ½-inch-thick disks with all the rings intact. Use a skewer to hold rings in place. | Lightly drizzle with olive oil and season with salt. Cook over medium-high direct heat, uncovered, turning occasionally, until softened and lightly charred. | 15 minutes | Wonderful as is, but chopped fresh herbs and a splash of balsamic vinegar are welcome finishing touches. |
| **Portobello Mushrooms** | Remove stem; trimming the dark gills is optional. | Brush the cap side with oil. Grill cap side down on medium direct heat, covered with a tin; cook until gills are juicy, about 5 minutes. Pour juices into a small bowl; reserve. Brush gill side with oil, turn, and finish by indirect heat, covered, until soft, about 5 more minutes. | 10 minutes | Salt and pepper. Serve whole or sliced into wide strips. Pour the juices back over the mushrooms or add to a sauce. Great basted with Chile-Coffee BBQ Sauce or Korean Marinade in second half of cooking time. |
| **Fennel** | Trim off fronds. Slice or quarter through the core. | Brush with olive oil and cook slowly over indirect heat. | 15 to 20 minutes | Season with salt and black pepper. Drizzle with lemon juice or balsamic vinegar and more olive oil. |
| **Scallions** | Trim the white roots and the ragged ends of the greens; otherwise, grill whole. | Drizzle with olive oil and season with salt. Cook uncovered, over medium-high direct heat, turning occasionally. | 2 to 3 minutes | Serve whole or sliced. |
| **Zucchini/ Yellow Squash** | Cut lengthwise or crosswise into ½-inch-thick slices. | Season with salt and pepper just before cooking. Lightly drizzle with olive oil. Cook, uncovered, over medium-high direct heat, turning once. | 2 to 3 minutes | Serve with salsa, Tomato & Basil Dressing, fresh herbs, or minced garlic and lemon juice. |
| **Peppers** | Cut off the sides in wide panels; discard seeds and skins. | Cook over medium-high direct heat skin side up, uncovered until soft. Flip, then cook until the skin chars. | 10 to 15 minutes | Either leave skin on or scrape off with a knife. Season with salt and pepper, white vinegar, and a drizzle of extra-virgin olive oil. |

GRILLED
# ratatouille

6 servings

1 large ripe tomato

1 head garlic, halved lengthwise

1 large zucchini, sliced lengthwise into ¹/₂-inch-thick strips

1 yellow squash, sliced lengthwise into ¹/₂-inch-thick strips

1 small eggplant, sliced lengthwise into ¹/₂-inch-thick strips

1 red bell pepper, seeded and sliced into wide strips

¹/₂ cup plus 1 tablespoon extra-virgin olive oil

1 tablespoon kosher salt, plus additional for seasoning

Freshly ground black pepper

2 tablespoons white wine vinegar

¹/₂ cup fresh basil, torn into pieces

1¹/₂ teaspoons roughly chopped fresh thyme

**1.** Prepare an outdoor grill with a hot fire.

**2.** Grill the tomato and garlic halves, turning as needed, until charred all over, about 6 minutes. Set garlic aside. Wrap tomato in foil and set aside.

**3.** Brush the zucchini, yellow squash, eggplant slices, and pepper strips generously with the ¹/₂ cup olive oil. Season with the 1 tablespoon salt and black pepper to taste. Grill the vegetables over direct heat until "kissed by the grill" and just tender, 2 to 3 minutes per side.

**4.** Chop the tomato and put it in a large bowl, along with the skin and juices. Squeeze the garlic from its skin, chop, and add to tomato. Dice the rest of the vegetables into large pieces and add to tomato. Drizzle with the remaining 1 tablespoon olive oil, vinegar, basil, and thyme. Season with salt and pepper to taste and toss gently, taking care not to overwork the vegetables. Serve warm or at room temperature.

## KNOW-HOW

The shot of white wine vinegar at the end brightens the flavor of the ratatouille and cuts through the smoky taste of the grill. Add it according to your taste to balance the char flavor from grilling.

# corn

## WITH GARLIC-HERB OIL

4 servings

²/₃ cup extra-virgin olive oil

8 cloves garlic, peeled and smashed

6 sprigs fresh sage

1 small bunch fresh thyme

6 sprigs fresh rosemary

8 large ears freshly picked corn, with husks (each about 8 ounces)

Kosher salt

Pinch crushed red pepper (optional)

**1.** Prepare an outdoor grill with a hot fire for both direct and indirect grilling.
**2.** Meanwhile, in a small saucepan over medium-low heat warm the olive oil with the garlic and two sprigs each of the sage, thyme, and rosemary until the garlic is golden and the herbs are aromatic, about 12 minutes. Remove from the heat and set aside. Tie the remaining herbs together with kitchen twine to use as a brush for basting.
**3.** Peel back the husks from the corn, leaving them attached at the ends and twisting to make handles. Remove the silk. Brush the corn with the oil and season with salt to taste. Arrange the corn on the cooler side of the grill, with the husks dangling over the side so they don't burn. Grill, brushing with the oil, and turning occasionally, until corn is glossy and the color deepens, about 5 minutes. Move to the hotter side and grill, turning as needed, until the kernels are lightly toasted and tender, about 8 to 10 minutes more.
**4.** Remove the corn from the grill, brush with additional oil, season with salt to taste and crushed red pepper, if desired.

## ▬SHOPSMART

Don't strip the husks off the corn—you need them to make handles! To find out how fresh the corn is, use the grip test our favorite corn grower taught us: Put the corn in your hand and feel its weight; it should feel heavy. (Old corn dries out and gets lighter.) Then use your hands to feel for the even distribution of the kernels.

sauces & rubs eight

# barbecue sauce

Makes 2 cups

- 4 cloves garlic, peeled
- 1/4 teaspoon kosher salt, plus a generous pinch for the garlic
- 3 cups cola
- 1 1/2 cups ketchup
- 1/4 cup cider vinegar
- 2 tablespoons Worcestershire sauce
- 1 slightly heaping tablespoon chili powder
- 1 teaspoon freshly ground black pepper, plus additional for seasoning
- 1/2 teaspoon hot sauce, plus additional for seasoning
- 1/4 teaspoon ground allspice
- 1 1/2 tablespoons freshly squeezed lime juice

**1.** Smash the garlic cloves, sprinkle with a generous pinch of salt, and, with the flat side of a large knife, mash and smear mixture to a coarse paste.

**2.** Stir garlic paste, the 1/4 teaspoon salt, cola, ketchup, vinegar, Worcestershire, chili powder, 1 teaspoon black pepper, 1/2 teaspoon hot sauce, and allspice together in a small saucepan. Bring to a boil, reduce heat, and simmer until thickened, about 45 minutes. Allow to cool slightly, stir in the lime juice, and season with black pepper and hot sauce to taste.

## ▰ KNOW-HOW

Barbecue sauces are all about balance: a sweet note offset by sour with a jolt of spice, all of which flourish in a cloud of smoke. There are lots of ways to work this magic—thick, thin, and in-between. Concocting a signature sauce is compulsory in some barbecue circles. Start with this basic riff and play with variations to suit your style.

## KANSAS CITY-STYLE
# BBQ sauce

Makes about 1 quart

- 2  tablespoons neutral-tasting oil, such as grapeseed or vegetable
- 6  cloves garlic, smashed
- 2  tablespoons tomato paste
- 1  slightly heaping tablespoon chili powder
- 1  tablespoon paprika
- 1  teaspoon crushed red pepper
- 1/4  teaspoon ground allspice

  Pinch ground cloves
- 2  cups ketchup
- 2  cups water

- 1/2  cup cider vinegar
- 1/4  cup dark molasses
- 1/4  cup firmly packed dark brown sugar
- 1  tablespoon kosher salt
- 1  tablespoon soy sauce
- 1  tablespoon Worcestershire sauce
- 2  teaspoons English-style dried mustard
- 1  teaspoon freshly ground black pepper
- 1  bay leaf

Heat the oil in a medium saucepan over medium heat. Stir in the garlic, tomato paste, chili powder, paprika, red pepper, allspice, and cloves and cook, stirring, until paste is dark brick red, about 3 minutes. Add the ketchup, water, vinegar, molasses, brown sugar, salt, soy sauce, Worcestershire, mustard, black pepper, and bay leaf. Adjust the heat to maintain a gentle simmer and cook until the flavors come together, about 30 minutes. Remove and discard bay leaf before using.

## NORTH CAROLINA-STYLE
# vinegar BBQ sauce

Makes about 1 quart

- 3  cups cider vinegar
- 3/4  cup sugar
- 1/3  cup ketchup
- 1/4  cup honey
- 1/4  cup kosher salt
- 2  tablespoons crushed red pepper
- 1 1/2  teaspoons freshly ground black pepper

Heat the vinegar and sugar in a medium saucepan over medium heat until the sugar dissolves. Off the heat, stir in the ketchup, honey, salt, red pepper, and black pepper.

## ■COOK'S NOTE

BBQ experts assert that the vinegary North Carolina sauces are the original American sauces. Within the state, you know which side of the Piedmonts you are on by what sauce douses your pulled pork. Along the coast, sauces are reduced to the basics—vinegar and red pepper. Up in the mountains, tomato makes an appearance, and the sauces are thicker.

218

CIDER

# mop

Makes 1½ cups

- 1 tablespoon unsalted butter
- 2 tablespoons finely grated peeled fresh ginger
- 2 shallots, peeled and sliced
- 6 cloves garlic, peeled and smashed
- 1½ cups bourbon
- 1 quart sweet apple cider
- 1 cup apple jelly
- ¼ cup dark molasses
- 1 bay leaf
- 2 teaspoons coriander seeds
- ½ teaspoon black peppercorns
- 2 sprigs fresh sage or 1 teaspoon dried sage
- 2 tablespoons lemon juice
- ½ teaspoon kosher salt
  Freshly ground black pepper

**1.** Melt the butter in a medium saucepan over medium heat. Add the ginger, shallots, and garlic. Cook, stirring frequently, until the vegetables are soft and brown, about 5 minutes. Remove the pan from the heat and carefully add the bourbon. Return the pan to the heat and with a wooden spoon scrape up any of the browned bits that cling to the bottom. Add the cider, jelly, molasses, bay leaf, coriander seeds, peppercorns, and sage. Bring to a boil and reduce until the mixture is syrupy and yields about 1½ cups, about 1 hour.
**2.** Strain and add lemon juice, salt, and black pepper to taste.

# jerk
SAUCE

Makes about 1½ cups

- ⅓ cup cider vinegar
- ¼ cup dark rum
- 3 tablespoons firmly packed dark brown sugar
- 1 bunch scallions (white and green parts), roughly chopped
- 4 cloves garlic, chopped
- 1 Scotch bonnet chile, stemmed, seeded, and minced
- 2 tablespoons Pickapeppa sauce
- 1 tablespoon freshly grated peeled ginger
- 1 tablespoon ground allspice
- ¼ teaspoon pumpkin pie spice
- 3 tablespoons vegetable oil

Pulse the vinegar, rum, brown sugar, scallions, garlic, chile, Pickapeppa sauce, ginger, allspice, and pumpkin pie spice in a food processor to make a slightly chunky sauce. Heat the oil in a medium skillet and cook the sauce, stirring, until the oil is absorbed and the sauce thickens slightly, about 3 minutes. Cool.

# peach-mustard
## BBQ SAUCE

Makes about 1¼ cups

- 3 tablespoons unsalted butter
- 2 tablespoons minced onion
- 2 cloves garlic, minced
- 3 tablespoons cider vinegar
- ½ cup whole-grain mustard
- ¼ cup Dijon mustard
- ¾ cup peach jam or preserves
- 1 tablespoon bourbon
- ½ teaspoon kosher salt

Melt the butter in a saucepan over medium heat. Add the onion and garlic and cook until translucent, about 3 minutes. Add the vinegar and boil until almost completely reduced and the mixture looks like wet sand, about 4 minutes. Whisk in both mustards and the jam or preserves. Simmer, whisking, until jam melts, about 1 minute. Remove the pan from the heat and stir in the bourbon and salt.

## COOK'S NOTE

The bourbon is stirred in at the end—uncooked—to give a genuine jolt to the sauce. This Southern blend goes great with pork but is also a good finisher for chicken, duck, or veal.

## LEMON-PEPPER
# slather

Makes ⅔ cup

- 1 teaspoon white peppercorns
- 1½ teaspoons coarse sea salt
- 1 teaspoon sugar
- ½ cup extra-virgin olive oil
- ¼ cup finely grated lemon zest (from 4 large lemons)
- 2 cloves garlic, smashed

Pulse the peppercorns in a spice grinder until coarsely ground. Add the salt and sugar and pulse a few more times. Transfer to a bowl and stir in the olive oil, lemon zest, and garlic. Microwave until hot but not boiling, about 45 seconds. Let cool.

## COOK'S NOTE

This rub—inspired by jarred lemon-pepper seasoning, but oh-so-much fresher—is incredibly versatile. We love the bright flavor it gives to fish, chicken, and vegetables. It will keep, covered and refrigerated, for a couple of weeks.

# korean

BBQ MARINADE

Makes about 1½ cups

1 cup soy sauce

4 large cloves garlic, peeled and chopped (about 2 tablespoons)

2 tablespoons finely grated peeled fresh ginger

4 scallions (white and green), thinly sliced

¼ cup sugar

2 tablespoons dark sesame oil

Freshly ground black pepper

Whisk soy sauce, garlic, ginger, scallions, sugar, sesame oil, and black pepper to taste in a medium bowl. Use marinade immediately or refrigerate for up to 2 days.

## SHOP SMART

Not all soy sauces are the same. Some are saltier, others sweet and thick. Light soy sauces are salty; the "light" refers to the body of the sauce. Dark soy sauces are sweeter and thicker. For the best results with this marinade, choose a dark Japanese or Korean soy sauce.

# sweet & sour

BBQ SAUCE

Makes about 1¾ cups

2 tablespoons peanut oil

2 cloves garlic, chopped

2 tablespoons finely grated peeled fresh ginger

½ cup dry sherry

½ cup hoisin sauce

½ cup ketchup

1½ teaspoons Vietnamese chili-garlic sauce

2 teaspoons soy sauce

2 teaspoons dark sesame oil

Heat the oil in a small saucepan over high heat. Add the garlic and ginger and cook over high heat until fragrant, about 2 minutes. Whisk in the sherry, hoisin sauce, ketchup, chile-garlic sauce, soy sauce, and sesame oil and bring to a boil. Remove from heat and let cool.

221

CHILE-COFFEE
# BBQ sauce

Makes 1 quart

- 3 guajillo chiles
- 3 mulato chiles
- ½ medium onion, cut into wedges
- 6 cloves garlic, unpeeled
- 2 tablespoons corn oil
- 1 cup tomato puree
- 1 cup strong black coffee
- ¼ cup turbinado sugar
- 1 tablespoon kosher salt, plus additional for seasoning
- 1 teaspoon dried oregano, preferably Mexican
- Pinch ground cloves
- Pinch cumin
- 2 teaspoons cider vinegar

**1.** Split, stem, and seed the chiles. Toast the chiles in a dry skillet over medium-high heat, turning and flattening with a spatula, until fragrant, about 3 minutes. Put the chiles in a heatproof bowl, cover with very hot water, and set aside until soft, about 30 minutes. Drain, reserve soaking liquid, chop chiles roughly, and set aside.

**2.** While the chiles soak, char the onion and garlic in the same dry skillet over medium heat until the onion blackens slightly and garlic softens in the skin, about 8 minutes. Cool, squeeze the garlic out of the skin, and put in a blender with chiles and onion. Puree to a paste, adding soaking liquid as needed (about ³/₄ cup) to help the mixture break down.

**3.** Heat the oil in the skillet over medium-high heat. Add the chile mixture and cook, stirring, until thick and fragrant, about 4 minutes. Add the tomato puree, coffee, sugar, 1 tablespoon salt, oregano, cloves, and cumin. Adjust the heat to maintain a gentle simmer and cook, stirring occasionally, until slightly thickened, about 15 minutes.

**4.** Stir in vinegar and season with salt to taste.

## COOK'S NOTE

For this recipe, we prefer Mexican oregano. It's stronger than Italian oregano, so it can hold its own with the other assertive flavors in this sauce.

# tamarind
## BARBECUE SAUCE

Makes 1½ cups

1 ripe medium tomato

½ cup tamarind concentrate

⅓ cup packed dark brown sugar

3 canned chipotle chiles in adobo sauce, chopped

2 tablespoons sherry vinegar

1 clove garlic, peeled and smashed

1 tablespoon kosher salt

**1.** Preheat a broiler. Line a small pan with aluminum foil and broil the tomato, turning as needed, until the skin chars and splits on all sides. Wrap the tomato in the foil and cool.
**2.** Core the tomato and chop it roughly, skin and all—it is going to be quite juicy, and you want to keep all of it. Puree the tomato with the juices in a food processor or blender with the tamarind concentrate, brown sugar, chipotles, vinegar, garlic, and salt until smooth. Use immediately or refrigerate for up to 1 week.

## ▬COOK'S NOTE

For safety's sake, always add liquor off the burner—even the fumes from alcohol can cause a flare-up. Try this brushed on pork and chicken.

# citrus mostarda
## WITH HONEY & CHERRIES

Makes 1 quart

- 1 grapefruit
- 1 Valencia orange
- 1½ cups sugar
- ½ cup water
- ½ cup semi-dry white wine (such as Sauvignon Blanc)
- ⅔ cup dried cherries
- 3 tablespoons powdered mustard
- 1 tablespoon mustard seeds
- ½ teaspoon crushed red pepper
- 1 small sprig fresh rosemary

**1.** Remove peel from grapefruit and orange with pith attached. Juice the citrus flesh, squeezing by hand, and strain the juice (you should have about 1 cup). Slice the peel with pith lengthwise into ¼-inch-thick strips. Place strips in a small saucepan, cover with cold water, and bring to a boil. Drain and repeat this process 2 more times. **2.** Whisk the fruit juice, sugar, water, and wine in a medium saucepan; bring to a boil to dissolve the sugar over medium heat. Stir in the blanched fruit peel, cherries, powdered mustard, mustard seeds, red pepper, and rosemary and bring to a simmer. Cook until fruit peel is tender and cherries are plumped, about 45 minutes. Transfer to a nonreactive container and remove rosemary. Refrigerate for at least 3 days and up to 1 week before using. Leftover mostarda will keep refrigerated for up to 1 month.

# chimichurri
## SAUCE

Makes about 2½ cups

- 6 cloves garlic, sliced
- 2 shallots, sliced
- 2 cups packed fresh flat-leaf parsley
- ¼ cup fresh oregano
- 1 heaping tablespoon kosher salt
- 1 teaspoon crushed red pepper
- 1 cup extra-virgin olive oil
- ½ cup red wine vinegar
- ¼ cup water

Pulse the garlic, shallots, parsley, oregano, salt, and red pepper in a food processor until roughly chopped. Add the oil, vinegar, and water and pulse to make a textured sauce. Transfer to a serving bowl.

## ■ COOK'S NOTE

Make sure to pluck the oregano leaves off the stems—hard stems make the sauce a little too textured. Toss the herb stems onto the fire to flavor whatever you are grilling.

225

# prairie rub

Makes about 1¼ cups

3 tablespoons firmly packed light brown sugar

3 tablespoons dried Italian seasoning

2 tablespoons English-style dry mustard

2 tablespoons granulated garlic

2 tablespoons sweet paprika

1 tablespoon ground ginger

1 tablespoon minced dried orange peel

2 teaspoons kosher salt

1 teaspoon pumpkin pie spice

1 teaspoon freshly ground black pepper

½ teaspoon cayenne pepper

Mix brown sugar, Italian seasoning, mustard, garlic, paprika, ginger, orange peel, salt, pumpkin pie spice, black pepper, and cayenne in a bowl. Pulse in a spice grinder in a few batches until finely ground. Seal in an airtight container and store in a cool, dry place for up to 2 months.

## ■ KNOW-HOW

Our testers used dried orange peel, but you can use fresh grated orange zest—it will just shorten the shelf life of the rub.

## ■ COOK'S NOTE

When it came to concocting our favorite rubs, we were inspired by regional blends. Our Memphis Shake is elemental—sweet with heat, with a nuance only ancho chile can give. Cajun Rub is spicy with lots of high-pitched red, white, and black pepper—but it's got a veggie taste, too, from celery, garlic, and herbs. Texas Rub is smoke with sugar and spice. Prairie Rub takes its lead from the great BBQ cities of the Midwest—Kansas City and St. Louis. This rub is the tamest, but pleasingly aromatic as well.

# cajun
## RUB

Makes 1 cup

- ¼ cup firmly packed light brown sugar
- 2 tablespoons dried oregano
- 2 tablespoons dried parsley
- 2 tablespoons granulated garlic
- 2 tablespoons onion powder
- 2 tablespoons sweet paprika
- 1 tablespoon dried thyme
- 1 tablespoon freshly ground black pepper
- 2 teaspoons kosher salt
- 1 teaspoon celery salt
- 1 teaspoon freshly ground white pepper
- ¾ teaspoon cayenne pepper
- 3 bay leaves, crumbled

Mix brown sugar, oregano, parsley, garlic, onion powder, paprika, thyme, black pepper, salt, celery salt, white pepper, cayenne, and bay leaves in a bowl. Pulse in a spice grinder in two batches to a medium-fine grind. Seal in an airtight container and store in a cool, dry place for up to 2 months.

## ■ KNOW-HOW

If your spice grinder doubles as your coffee grinder, make sure you clean it well after making this rub. Place a handful of uncooked rice in the grinder, pulse to a powder, and wipe or brush the grinder clean. The rice will absorb the flavors from spices left in the grinder so your morning cup of coffee won't taste like the Bayou.

## TEXAS
# rub

Makes about 1 cup

- ¼ cup chili powder
- 3 tablespoons granulated garlic
- 3 tablespoons onion powder
- 2 tablespoons firmly packed dark brown sugar
- 1 heaping tablespoon hickory salt
- 1 tablespoon freshly ground black pepper
- ½ to 1 teaspoon cayenne pepper (use the larger amount if you want a really spicy rub)
- ¾ teaspoon pumpkin pie spice

Mix chili powder, garlic, onion powder, brown sugar, hickory salt, black pepper, cayenne, and pumpkin pie spice in a bowl. Seal in an airtight container and store in a cool, dry place for up to 2 months.

# ras al hanout

Makes about ³/₄ cup

- 3 slightly heaping tablespoons five-spice powder
- 2 tablespoons ground cardamom
- 2 tablespoons ground ginger
- 1 tablespoon ground nutmeg
- 1 tablespoon ground turmeric
- 1 tablespoon cayenne pepper

Mix five-spice powder, cardamom, ginger, nutmeg, turmeric, and cayenne in a small bowl. Store in a sealed container for up to 2 months.

**■ COOK'S NOTE**

*Ras al hanout*, which means "head of the shop," is an idiosyncratic blend of spices from North Africa. The mix can be very exotic and is reputed to include aphrodisiacs as well as aromatics. This is a streamlined version that we love on meat and chicken.

SOUTHWESTERN
# spiced salt

Makes about ¹/₂ cup

- ¹/₄ cup coarse sea salt
- 2 tablespoons cumin seeds
- 2 small dried red chiles, such as Japones or Arbol
- ¹/₂ teaspoon black peppercorns
- 2 teaspoons dried oregano, preferably Mexican

Toast the salt, cumin seeds, chiles, and peppercorns in a medium skillet over medium heat, stirring to prevent burning, until the salt is hot and spices aromatic, about 4 minutes. Cool. Pulse in a spice grinder until coarsely ground. Stir in the oregano. The spiced salt will keep about 3 months, tightly sealed, at room temperature.

**■ COOK'S NOTE**

This salt is an easy way to add flavor to grilled corn, but there are endless ways to use it. Try it on other grilled vegetables, shrimp skewers, steaks, or pork chops. You could also use it to season things off the grill, such as a bean salad or tomato salsa.

MEMPHIS
# shake

Makes about ³/₄ cup

- ¹/₄ cup sweet paprika
- 3 tablespoons firmly packed brown sugar
- 2 tablespoons dried oregano
- 2 tablespoons granulated garlic
- 1 tablespoon ancho chile powder
- 2 teaspoons kosher salt
- 1 teaspoon celery salt

Whisk paprika, brown sugar, oregano, garlic, ancho powder, salt, and celery salt in a small bowl. Store in an airtight container in a cool, dry place for up to 2 months.

## ▰SHOPSMART

Ancho powder is simply finely ground dried ancho chiles. Anchos are the sweetest of the dried chiles and are not terribly hot, so don't be put off by the amount used in this recipe.

TROPICAL FRUIT KEBABS • NECTARINE-BLACKBERRY GALETTE • MORE FOR S'MORES • HOT BUTTERED
RUM BANANA SPLIT WITH COCONUT • POACHED PEACHES WITH SABAYON • STARBERRY SHORTCAKE •
ORANGE SEMIFREDDO • PLUM FOOL • BLUEBERRY BUTTERMILK BUNDT CAKE • CHOCOLATE-CHERRY
JUBILEE • CHOCOLATE-PEANUT BUTTER PIE

# TROPICAL
# fruit kebabs

4 servings

¼ cup unsalted butter, at room temperature

1 vanilla bean

¼ cup piña colada-style sweetened coconut cream

¼ cup heavy cream

4 ounces good quality white chocolate, chopped

1 teaspoon grated lime zest

2 large red-skinned mangoes

1 large Hawaiian papaya (about 1 pound) (see ShopSmart, page 123)

**1.** Place the butter in a small skillet. Split the vanilla bean and scrape the seeds onto the butter. Mash seeds into the butter with the back of a spoon. Add the scraped pod and melt the butter over low heat. Remove from heat and set aside to steep.
**2.** Heat the coconut cream and heavy cream in a small saucepan over medium heat until simmering. Remove from heat and stir in chocolate until chocolate is melted and smooth. Stir in the lime zest. Set aside. (The vanilla butter and chocolate sauce can be made up to 3 days ahead, refrigerated, and reheated before grilling.)
**3.** If using wooden skewers, soak them in water for 30 minutes before grilling. Prepare an outdoor grill with a low-medium fire.
**4.** Prepare the fruit for the skewers according to the instructions on page 274, cutting the fruit into 2-inch chunks. Thread the fruit onto eight 8-inch skewers, alternating the mango and papaya. Brush lightly with some of the vanilla butter. Grill the fruit until lightly charred but not mushy, turning as needed, about 5 minutes per side. Pool about 2 tablespoons chocolate sauce on each of 4 plates, arrange 2 skewers on each plate, and drizzle with a bit of vanilla butter.

NECTARINE-BLACKBERRY
# galette

4 to 6 servings

DOUGH

1½ cups all-purpose flour

1 tablespoon sugar

¼ teaspoon fine salt

8 tablespoons cold unsalted
   butter, diced

¼ cup sour cream

1 teaspoon pure almond extract


FILLING

3 nectarines (about 1 pound)

1 cup blackberries

¼ cup sugar

1½ teaspoons cornstarch

¼ teaspoon pure almond extract

1 egg white, lightly beaten

1 tablespoon unsalted butter

½ cup sliced almonds

   Pinch fine salt

**1.** For the dough: Pulse the flour, sugar, and salt together in a food processor. Add the butter and pulse about 10 times until the mixture resembles coarse cornmeal with a few bean-size bits of butter in it. Add the sour cream and almond extract and pulse 2 to 4 times more. (Don't let the dough form a mass around the blade.) If the dough seems very dry, add up to 1 tablespoon of very cold water, 1 teaspoon at a time, pulsing briefly. Remove blade and bring the dough together by hand. Shape dough into a smooth disk, wrap in plastic wrap, and refrigerate at least 1 hour.

**2.** Position a rack in the lower third of the oven and preheat to 400°F. Cut the nectarines into wedges, with skin, and discard the pits. Place wedges in a bowl with the blackberries. Toss the fruit with 2 tablespoons of the sugar, the cornstarch, and almond extract.

**3.** Roll the dough on a lightly floured surface into a 14-inch circle. Transfer to a parchment-lined baking sheet. Brush dough lightly with some of the egg white. Starting 2 inches from the edge, casually arrange the fruit on dough. Dot with butter. Fold and pleat the dough over the edge of the filling; if the dough

cracks a bit, just pinch it together. Brush the folded edge of the crust with some more of the egg white.

**4.** Toss the almonds with about 1 tablespoon of the remaining egg white, the remaining 2 tablespoons sugar, and the pinch of fine salt. Lightly press the sugared almonds onto the crust. Bake until the crust is a burnished brown, about 50 minutes. Slip the galette on the paper to a rack to cool. Cut into wedges and serve warm or at room temperature.

# more for s'mores

S'mores are made-to-order fun. Sure, they start out as the kids' treat, but put out all the fixin's and see how many grown-ups get into the act.

S'mores hit every flavor and texture note just right—they're molten, mellow, gooey, and indulgent. A done-to-a-turn marshmallow countered by warm, slightly bitter chocolate sandwiched between crisp crackers is a total yum! There's a reason they're a cookout classic.

Setting up a s'mores bar can be simple—stripped down to the basics of marshmallow, chocolate, and cracker—or completely over-the-top, with choices in all categories. Marshmallows come in vanilla, chocolate, and lemon these days. Chocoholics can be satisfied in myriad ways, from intense dark to pale white and everything in between. Grahams have come a long way, too, with added flavors such as honey, chocolate, and cinnamon. Sprinkle on dried fruits, coconut, and nuts for added texture, or a smear of peanut, cashew, or other nut butter makes it that much more indulgent. Remember to have lots of long sticks or skewers for toasting the marshmallows. Kick back and let your guests go, and enjoy. You may notice you can tell a lot about people by how they prepare their marshmallows. Do they patiently turn for a perfect puffy brown or torch for the instantaneous burn? Having your way is definitely part of s'mores' appeal.

Have fun—play with your food!

# banana split with coconut

4 servings

- 8 tablespoons unsalted butter
- 3/4 cup dark brown sugar
- 1/2 cup dark rum
- 1 1/2 teaspoons ground cinnamon
- 1 1/2 teaspoons ground allspice
- 1/2 teaspoon ground cloves
- 1/2 teaspoon kosher salt
- 4 just-ripe bananas
- 2 pints coconut sorbet or your favorite ice cream

  Chocolate-Coconut Sauce

  Toasted coconut

  Maraschino cherries, for garnish (optional)

## CHOCOLATE-COCONUT SAUCE

Makes about 1 1/2 cups

- 6 ounces semisweet chocolate, finely chopped (about 1 cup)
- 1 cup canned unsweetened coconut milk, stirred
- 3 tablespoons light corn syrup
- 1 to 2 tablespoons dark rum
- 1 tablespoon unsalted butter

  Pinch salt

**1.** Bring the butter, brown sugar, rum, cinnamon, allspice, cloves, and salt to a boil in a saucepan to thicken slightly.

**2.** Halve the unpeeled bananas lengthwise. Place them peels down on a baking pan and pierce the flesh with a fork several times. Pour hot buttered rum sauce over the bananas. Cool, turn bananas over in the sauce, then cover and refrigerate until ready to grill. (This can be done up to a day ahead.)

**3.** Prepare an outdoor grill with a medium-low fire.

**4.** Grill the bananas peels down until tender and charred, about 8 minutes. Turn and cook 1 more minute.

**5.** Peel the warm banana halves, if desired. Divide them among 4 sundae boats and top with 2 to 3 scoops of coconut sorbet. Drizzle Chocolate-Coconut Sauce over the sundaes, sprinkle with coconut, and top with a cherry, if desired.

CHOCOLATE-COCONUT SAUCE
Put the chocolate in a small bowl. Heat the coconut milk, corn syrup, and rum to just below a simmer in a small saucepan. Pour over the chocolate, shaking the bowl slightly to settle the liquid. Let mixture stand a few minutes.

Add butter and whisk until the chocolate is completely melted.

## ▬ KNOW-HOW

Whether in block form or chips, semisweet chocolate is best stored tightly wrapped in a cool pantry—not in the refrigerator.

# porch
## party

**MENU**
Poached Peaches with Sabayon (page 242)
Mint Iced Tea (page 260)

*Peaches are perfect for such a short window of time, so celebrate them every chance you get.*

Poached Peaches with Sabayon (page 242)

# poached peaches
## WITH SABAYON

4 servings

PEACHES

1/2 vanilla bean

6 cups water

3 cups sugar

3 sprigs fresh mint or lemon verbena

3 coin-size slices fresh ginger, unpeeled

2 long strips lemon peel, without white pith

6 firm ripe peaches, halved and pitted

1 cup raspberries

SABAYON

4 large egg yolks

1/3 cup sugar

1 teaspoon finely grated lemon zest

2/3 cup Prosecco (a dry Italian sparkling wine)

**1.** For the peaches: Split the vanilla bean and scrape the seeds into a medium saucepan. Add the scraped pod, water, sugar, mint, ginger, and lemon peel and stir. Add the peaches skin side down. Bring to a boil. Place a circle of parchment directly on top of the fruit and adjust the heat to maintain a very gentle simmer. Cook until the peaches are easily pierced with a knife without resistance, about 5 minutes. Add raspberries and pull the pan from heat; cool. With your fingertips, pinch the skins from the peaches and discard. If they don't come off easily, don't fret. Refrigerate the fruit in the liquid, covered, until ready to serve, up to 3 days.

**2.** To assemble: Divide fruit among 4 bowls, with a splash of poaching liquid in each.

**3.** Put about 1 inch of water in a saucepan and bring to a simmer over medium heat. In a heatproof bowl that can rest in the saucepan without touching the water, use an electric mixer or whisk to beat the egg yolks, sugar, lemon zest, and Prosecco until light and foamy, about 30 seconds. Set the bowl over the simmering water and beat until the eggs thicken, about 4 minutes. Spoon the sabayon over the fruit and serve.

## ▬ COOK'S NOTE

The poaching liquid is too good to throw away. Use any leftover liquid for poaching more peaches, flavoring iced tea, or in your favorite peach cocktail. Or reduce about 2 cups of the poaching liquid until thick and syrupy; serve with the fruit and sabayon.

STARBERRY

# shortcake

8 servings

FRUIT

4 cups mixed berries, such as raspberries, blueberries, blackberries, and/or stemmed and halved strawberries

1/4 cup granulated sugar

2 to 3 tablespoons thinly sliced fresh mint leaves, plus sprigs for garnish

SHORTCAKE

2 cups all-purpose flour

1/4 cup granulated sugar, plus additional for sprinkling

1 tablespoon baking powder

1 teaspoon fine salt

6 tablespoons unsalted butter

3/4 cup half-and-half or light cream, plus additional for brushing

1 teaspoon vanilla extract

WHIPPED CREAM

2 cups heavy cream, chilled

3 tablespoons confectioner's sugar

1 teaspoon pure vanilla extract

**1.** For the fruit: Toss the berries with the granulated sugar and mint. Cover and let stand at room temperature for several hours, stirring occasionally.
**2.** For shortcake: Position a rack in the center of the oven and preheat to 450°F. Line a baking sheet with parchment paper.
**3.** Whisk flour, 1/4 cup granulated sugar, baking powder, and salt in a medium bowl. Rub in 2 tablespoons of the butter with your fingertips until no visible pieces remain. Rub in the remaining 4 tablespoons butter just until it is in even, pea-size pieces. Combine the half-and-half and vanilla and gently stir into the flour mixture to make a shaggy, loose dough.
**4.** Turn dough onto a lightly floured work surface and pat into a rectangle about 1/2 inch thick (don't worry if dough doesn't all come together). Fold dough in thirds, like a business letter, and pat lightly into an 8x4-inch rectangle that's about 3/4 inch thick. With a sharp knife, cut dough into two 4-inch squares. Cut each square into 4 triangles. Put triangles on a baking sheet, brush with half-and-half, and sprinkle generously with granulated sugar. Bake until lightly browned, 12 to 15 minutes. Cool on a rack.

**5.** To assemble the shortcakes: Whip the heavy cream in a chilled bowl until it thickens slightly; gradually add the confectioner's sugar and vanilla and beat until cream holds soft peaks. Split the shortcakes in half horizontally. Sandwich the cream and berries between the halves, positioning each triangular top to make a starlike shape. Spoon some of the berry juices around the cake, garnish with mint, and serve.

## ORANGE
# semifreddo

4 servings

  3  oranges, peeled and segmented (see page 274)

$\frac{1}{4}$  cup orange liqueur

    Finely grated zest from 2 oranges

  2  large eggs

  5  large egg yolks

$\frac{1}{2}$  cup sugar

$\frac{1}{2}$  cup vodka

$\frac{1}{2}$  teaspoon pure vanilla extract

  2  cups heavy cream, chilled

24  vanilla wafers

**1.** Dampen the inside of a 10-cup stainless steel bowl (it will be 8 inches diameter at the top), line with plastic wrap, and set aside. Put the orange segments in the orange liqueur.

**2.** Put about 1 inch of water in a saucepan and bring to a simmer over medium heat. In a heatproof medium bowl that can rest in the saucepan without touching the water, beat the zest, eggs, yolks, sugar, vodka, and vanilla with a whisk until foamy and light, about 30 seconds. Set the bowl over the water and whip with an electric mixer or whisk, moving in a circular motion around the bowl, until the mixture turns a pale yellow and an instant-read thermometer inserted into the mixture registers 170°F. Set the bowl in a bowl of ice and whisk the mixture until cooled.

**3.** Strain the liqueur from orange segments into the heavy cream. Line the prepared bowl with 8 to 10 orange segments in a pinwheel pattern. Roughly chop the remaining orange segments. Whip the heavy cream to soft peaks. Gradually fold the egg mixture and chopped oranges into the cream. Pour the cream mixture into the prepared bowl. Coarsely crumble the vanilla wafers and lightly press them onto the surface of the semifreddo to cover. Wrap in plastic and freeze until set, about 4 hours.

**4.** About 1 hour before serving, unmold the semifreddo onto a platter. Refrigerate until creamy and very cold but not frozen.

245

# plum fool

6 servings

2 pounds ripe but firm red plums, such as Santa Rosa, halved and pitted (about 6)

$^1\!/_2$ cup plus 2 tablespoons granulated sugar

$^1\!/_2$ cup water

$^1\!/_2$ cup Japanese plum wine

1 cup heavy cream, chilled

6 amaretti (Italian macaroons)

**1.** Halve and pit the plums and put in a small saucepan with the $^1\!/_2$ cup granulated sugar and the water. Simmer over medium heat just until the fruit is tender but still holds its shape, 5 to 6 minutes. Remove the 2 best-looking plum halves with a slotted spoon. Cover and refrigerate for decorating the fools before serving.

**2.** Puree remaining fruit with all the cooking juices in a food processor or blender until smooth. Return puree to pan, add the plum wine, and cook over medium-high heat, stirring occasionally, until thick and reduced to about $1^1\!/_2$ cups, about 15 minutes. Transfer plum sauce to a bowl and cool completely.

**3.** Whip the cream in a chilled bowl with the 2 tablespoons granulated sugar until stiff but not grainy. Fold half of the sauce into the whipped cream until slightly streaky. Drizzle about 1 tablespoon of the remaining sauce into each 6 parfait glasses or dessert bowls. Spoon half of the cream mixture into the glasses, then another bit of plum sauce. Top off each fool with the remaining cream mixture and finish with a bit more sauce. Cover and refrigerate for at least 2 hours.

**4.** When ready to serve, crumble cookies on top. Finish each fool with a piece of reserved plum.

## ▬ COOK'S NOTE

The fruit grabs a lovely rich color from the skin when it is cooked a day ahead and chilled before pureeing.

247

BLUEBERRY BUTTERMILK
# bundt cake

8 servings

### BLUEBERRIES

4 tablespoons unsalted butter, plus additional for pan

$^1/_2$ cup light brown sugar

Juice of $^1/_2$ lemon

1 teaspoon vanilla extract

$1^1/_2$ cups blueberries

### CAKE

$2^1/_4$ cups all-purpose flour

2 cups granulated sugar

$1^1/_2$ teaspoons baking powder

$^1/_2$ teaspoon baking soda

12 tablespoons unsalted butter, at room temperature

$^3/_4$ cup buttermilk

2 teaspoons vanilla extract

Finely grated zest of 2 lemons

5 large eggs

**1.** Preheat the oven to 350°F. Butter a 12-cup bundt cake pan.
**2.** For the blueberries: Heat the 4 tablespoons butter, brown sugar, and lemon juice in a small saucepan over medium heat, stirring occasionally, until the sugar dissolves. Remove from the heat and stir in the vanilla and berries. Spread evenly in the bottom of the prepared pan.
**3.** To make the cake: Sift the flour, granulated sugar, baking powder, and baking soda into the bowl of a stand mixer. Add the butter and beat slowly with the paddle attachment until a fine crumb forms.
**4.** Whisk the buttermilk, vanilla, and lemon zest in a liquid measuring cup. Stop the mixer and change from the paddle to the whisk attachment. While beating at a medium speed, gradually pour all the liquid into the flour mixture. Add the eggs one at a time (scraping the sides of the bowl as needed), beating until the mixture is very light, about 3 minutes. Pour batter over berries in the prepared pan.
**5.** Bake until a toothpick inserted into the cake comes out clean, 45 to 50 minutes. Cool on a rack for 20 minutes before inverting onto the rack to cool completely.

## ▬COOK'S NOTE
Don't flour the pan or the blueberries will stick. Most bundt cakes are best if allowed to ripen for a day before serving. If you make the cake ahead, wrap it tightly. The cake will keep at room temperature, tightly wrapped, for 4 days.

CHOCOLATE-CHERRY
# jubilee

8 servings

1¼ pounds sweet cherries, pitted and halved

¾ cup dark rum

½ cup granulated sugar

1 teaspoon finely grated orange zest

1 teaspoon vanilla extract

6 ounces semisweet chocolate, finely chopped

¾ cup heavy cream

2 tablespoons light corn syrup

½ gallon boxed vanilla ice cream

8 or 9 chocolate wafer cookies, coarsely crushed (2 ounces)

½ gallon boxed chocolate ice cream

**1.** The day before assembling: Put the cherries, rum, granulated sugar, orange zest, and vanilla in a small saucepan and bring to a simmer. Cook, stirring occasionally, until the cherries soften, about 5 minutes. Transfer to a medium bowl, cover, and refrigerate overnight.

**2.** Put the chocolate in a medium bowl. Bring the cream and corn syrup to a simmer in a small saucepan and immediately pour over the chocolate, shaking the bowl slightly to settle the cream. Let the mixture stand a few minutes, then stir until the chocolate is melted. Cover and refrigerate overnight.

**3.** Line a 9x5x3-inch loaf pan with a piece of parchment paper that hangs over the side by a couple inches. About 15 minutes before using, bring the chocolate to room temperature and stir until it is easily spooned.

**4.** Drain the cherries and reserve the liquid. Turn the vanilla ice cream out of the carton onto a cutting board (run the box under warm water, if necessary). Save the box. Cut a ³/₄-inch-thick slab with a warm knife from the long side of the ice cream and press it into the pan. Patch, if needed, with more ice cream to cover the bottom. Spread half the cherries on top and cover with another

³/₄-inch-thick slab of vanilla ice cream, pressing to make a snug fit. Return the remaining vanilla ice cream to the box and save for other desserts.

**5.** Scatter the chocolate cookies over the ice cream. Remove the chocolate ice cream from the carton onto a cutting board (run the box under warm water, if necessary). Save the box. Cut a ³/₄-inch-thick slab from the long side of the ice cream and press it into the pan. Scatter the remaining cherries over the chocolate ice cream and spoon about half of the chocolate mixture on top. Reserve the rest of the chocolate for sauce. Finish the terrine with another ³/₄-inch-thick slab of chocolate ice cream. Return remaining ice cream to the box. Fold the parchment over the top of the terrine and freeze 4 hours or overnight.

**6.** Simmer the reserved cherry liquid until syrupy. Remove from heat and whisk in the remaining chocolate mixture until smooth.

**7.** When ready to serve, lift the terrine out of the pan by the paper and invert it onto a cutting board. (Run warm water on the loaf pan, if necessary, to release it.) Slice into 1-inch-thick pieces and serve with the chocolate-cherry sauce.

# CHOCOLATE
# peanut butter pie

8 servings

CRUST

1¼ cups dry-roasted, salted peanuts

½ cup granulated sugar

Pinch ground cloves

¼ cup unsalted butter, melted

6 ounces bittersweet chocolate

¼ cup heavy cream

FILLING

1½ cups milk

2 large eggs

1 cup confectioner's sugar

2 tablespoons cornstarch

Pinch fine salt

4 ounces cream cheese, cut into pieces

½ cup creamy peanut butter

1 teaspoon pure vanilla extract

TOPPING

2 ounces bittersweet chocolate

1¼ cups heavy cream, chilled

1 tablespoon confectioner's sugar

**1.** For the crust: Preheat the oven to 350°F. Pulse the peanuts, granulated sugar, and cloves in a food processor until the mixture resembles coarse sand. Pulse in the butter. Press the nut mixture evenly into the bottom of a 10-inch springform pan and bake until set, about 15 minutes. Set aside to cool slightly.

**2.** Melt the chocolate with the cream in a microwave, stirring every 30 seconds, until smooth, and then spread the chocolate over the crust. Freeze the crust while making the filling.

**3.** For the filling: Whisk the milk, eggs, confectioner's sugar, cornstarch, and salt in a medium saucepan. Cook over medium heat, whisking constantly, until boiling. Continue to cook until the consistency of mayonnaise, about 2 minutes more. Transfer to a bowl. Whisk in the cream cheese, peanut butter, and vanilla. Spread evenly over the chocolate and refrigerate until cold or overnight.

**4.** For the topping: Melt the chocolate in a microwave, stirring every 30 seconds, until smooth; cool slightly. Whip the cream with the confectioner's sugar until it holds slightly stiff peaks. Stir a large spoonful of the cream into the chocolate and then fold all the chocolate into

the cream. Remove the pie from the pan. Spread the cream topping onto the pie with an offset spatula. Refrigerate for at least 30 minutes before serving.

# drinks
## ten

MANGO TANGO • WATERMELON RUM COOLER • WHITE FALL SANGRIA • POMEGRANATE MARGARITA •
BERRY-TINIS • VIETNAMESE-STYLE ICED COFFEE • ICED GREEN MINT TEA • VARIATIONS ON ICED TEA •
FRESH GINGER ALE • KEY LIMEADE

Mango Tango (page 257), Watermelon Rum Cooler (page 257), Key Limeade (page 265), Iced Green Mint Tea (page 259)

MANGO

# tango

6 servings

2½ cups mango nectar

4 ounces dark rum

2 ounces coconut rum

2 ounces Triple Sec

1½ cups pineapple juice

Juice of 1 lime (about 2 tablespoons)

**1.** Fill 2 ice cube trays with the mango nectar; freeze until solid.
**2.** Working in batches, puree the mango ice cubes, dark rum, coconut rum, Triple Sec, pineapple juice, and lime juice in a blender until smooth. Serve.

## COOK'S NOTE
At your next party, assign a single friend to bartending duties. It's a great way for him or her to meet people and a big help to the host.

WATERMELON

# rum cooler

2 servings

Ice cubes

1 cup watermelon puree (about 1⅓ cups seeded and diced fruit)

4 ounces gold rum

1 ounce Triple Sec

Juice of 1 lime (about 2 tablespoons)

Fill a cocktail shaker with ice. Add the watermelon puree, rum, Triple Sec, and lime juice. Shake vigorously. Strain into two ice-filled cocktail glasses—preferably Collins glasses.

## COOK'S NOTE
Don't forget ice; it seems there's never enough at summer parties.

WHITE FALL

# sangria

4 servings

1 bottle Sauvignon Blanc

¼ cup amaretto

Zest of ½ orange, removed in wide strips

1 red-skinned apple, such as McIntosh, Cortland, or Pink Lady

1 ripe pear, such as Anjou, Bartlett, or Comice

**1.** Put the wine, amaretto, and zest in a pitcher and stir.
**2.** Core and thinly slice the apple and pear, leaving on the skins. Add fruit to the wine and stir. Cover and refrigerate for 4 to 24 hours.

POMEGRANATE
# margarita

1 serving

Ice

2 ounces white tequila

2 ounces bottled pomegranate juice

2 teaspoons pomegranate molasses

1 ounce Triple Sec

Juice of 1 lime (about 2 tablespoons)

Fill a cocktail shaker with ice. Add tequila, pomegranate juice, pomegranate molasses, Triple Sec, and lime juice. Shake vigorously. Strain into a cocktail glass. Serve immediately.

# berry-tinis

1 serving

BERRY INFUSION

1 750-milliliter bottle vodka

1/2 cup sugar

1 whole vanilla bean

2 cups fresh blackberries

2 cups fresh raspberries

DRINK

Ice cubes

3 ounces berry infusion

1 teaspoon lemon juice

1 teaspoon sweet vermouth

Lemon twist for garnish

**1.** In a large resealable jar, shake the vodka, sugar, and vanilla bean until most of the sugar dissolves, about 30 seconds. (Save the vodka bottle.) Add berries and shake 5 times. Seal and set aside at room temperature for 2 days. Shake container after a day.
**2.** Pour the infused vodka off the berries and return to the reserved bottle. Save fruit for garnishing cocktail.
**3.** To make the drink: Fill a cocktail shaker with ice. Add berry infusion, lemon juice, and sweet vermouth. Cover and shake vigorously. Strain into a chilled martini glass. Add a couple of berries and the lemon twist. Serve immediately.

VIETNAMESE-STYLE
# iced coffee

4 servings

1 cup sweetened condensed milk

4 cups strong brewed New Orleans coffee (coffee with chicory), well chilled

Ice cubes

Briskly stir the sweetened condensed milk into the chilled coffee until blended. Fill 4 tall glasses with ice and pour in the coffee mixture.

**━━ COOK'S NOTE**
Avoid diluted iced coffee by freezing some extra coffee into cubes.

ICED GREEN
# mint tea

4 to 6 servings

6 cups water

6 green tea bags

1/3 cup sugar

1/3 cup packed fresh mint leaves

Ice cubes

Mint sprigs, for garnish

**1.** Bring 3 cups of the water to a rolling boil in a small saucepan, remove from the heat, and add the tea. Steep for about 6 minutes. Discard the tea bags and cool the brewed tea.
**2.** Meanwhile, combine the remaining water, the sugar, and mint leaves in a small saucepan. Bring to a boil, stirring to dissolve the sugar. Remove from the heat and cool.
**3.** To serve, strain the mint syrup into the green tea. Serve over ice and garnish with a sprig of mint.

## VARIATIONS ON
# iced tea

4 to 6 servings

TEA

6 cups water

8 orange pekoe tea bags or
3 tablespoons loose orange
pekoe tea

Ice cubes

Lemon, mint, or spiced simple
syrup (optional, see recipes
below)

LEMON SYRUP

Makes 1½ cups

2 lemons, coarsely chopped

1 cup sugar

1 cup water

MINT SYRUP

Makes 1½ cups

1 cup sugar

1 cup water

8 sprigs fresh mint

SPICED SYRUP

Makes 1½ cups

1 cup sugar

1 cup water

8 green cardamom pods, cracked

4 allspice berries

2 cinnamon sticks

1 whole clove

**1.** Bring 3 cups of the water to a rolling boil, remove from the heat, and add the tea. Steep for 5 minutes. Discard the tea bags or strain out the tea leaves, add the remaining 3 cups water, and cool the brewed tea.

**2.** Serve over ice with choice of flavored syrups, if desired.

LEMON SYRUP
Put lemons, sugar, and water in a small saucepan and bring to a boil, stirring occasionally. Reduce heat and simmer for 15 minutes. Cool, strain, and refrigerate until ready to use.

MINT SYRUP
Put sugar, water, and mint in a small saucepan and bring to a boil, stirring occasionally. Reduce heat and simmer for 15 minutes. Cool, strain, and refrigerate until ready to use.

SPICED SYRUP
Put sugar, water, cardamom pods, allspice, cinnamon sticks, and the clove in a small saucepan and bring to a boil, stirring occasionally. Reduce heat and simmer for 15 minutes. Cool, strain, and refrigerate until ready to use.

## STYLE

Serve these syrups in glass bottles with pouring spouts. If you are serving more than one, differentiate among them by floating a few of the syrup ingredients—a couple strips of lemon zest, a few spices, a sprig of mint—in the bottle.

Freshly Brewed Iced Tea, Spiced Syrup, Lemon Syrup, Mint Syrup

# grilling on the beach

### MENU
White Fall Sangria (page 257) ● Seafood Paella (page 176)

Set a Tuscan grill over a stack of driftwood. This one-pan paella and our white sangria make a portable party.

White Fall Sangria

White Fall Sangria (page 257), Key Limeade (page 265), Pomegranate Margarita (page 258)

FRESH
# ginger ale

8 servings

1 lemon

2 cups coarsely chopped fresh ginger with peel

2 cups water

3/4 cup sugar

Ice cubes

6 cups seltzer water

Lime wedges, for serving

**1.** Remove the zest of the lemon with a vegetable peeler, taking care not to include too much of the bitter white pith. Finely chop the lemon zest and ginger in a food processor or by hand.
**2.** Transfer the lemon-ginger mixture to a medium saucepan, add the water and sugar, and bring to a boil. Reduce heat and simmer, partially covered, for 15 minutes. Strain the mixture, pressing on the solids, and cool.

**3.** For each serving of ginger ale, pour 1/4 cup of the syrup into a tall (about 10- to 12-ounce) glass filled with ice and top with about 3/4 cup seltzer water. Serve with a lime wedge.

KEY
# limeade

4 to 6 servings

5 cups water

1 cup sugar

1 cup freshly squeezed Key lime juice, (about 16 limes)

2 whole Key limes, thinly sliced

Ice cubes

Fresh mint sprigs (optional)

Bring 1 cup of the water and the sugar to a boil in a small saucepan, stirring to dissolve the sugar. Mix the sugar syrup, remaining water, lime juice, and lime slices in a pitcher. Cover and chill. Serve over ice. Garnish with mint, if desired.

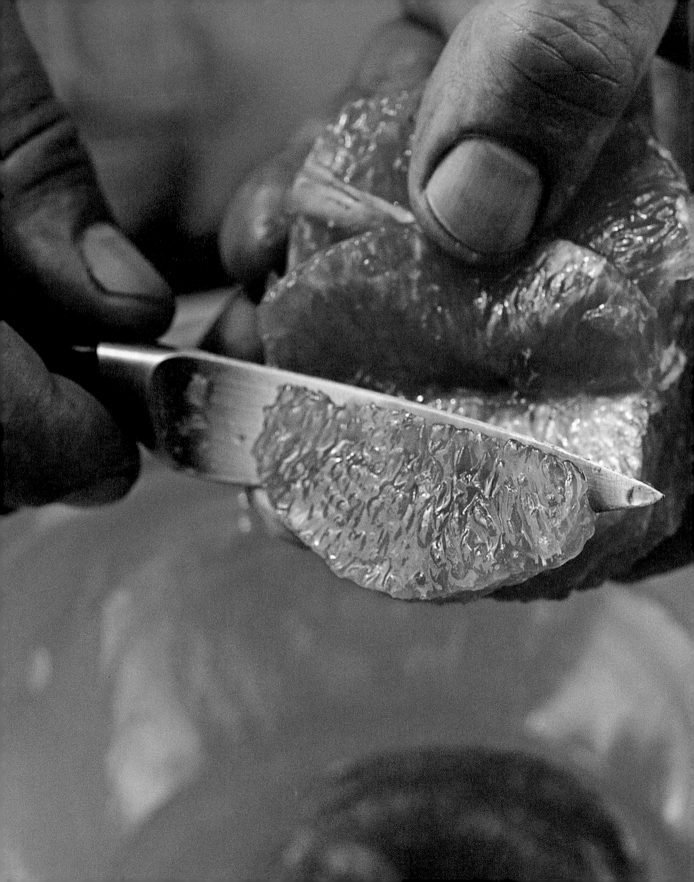

# tips & techniques

## eleven

THE SHOPPING, SLICING, DICING, AND GENERAL FOOD PREP YOU DO BEFORE ACTUALLY GETTING TO THE GRILL ARE AS IMPORTANT AS WHAT YOU DO WHEN YOU'RE STANDING BEHIND IT, SIPPING YOUR FAVORITE DRINK, AND TAKING IN THE SIZZLE. HERE'S HOW TO GET THE BEST INGREDIENTS—AND HOW TO MAKE THE MOST OF THEM.

*Whether it's a quick-grilled boneless breast or a slow-barbecued whole bird, chicken on the grill is a sure sign of summer.*

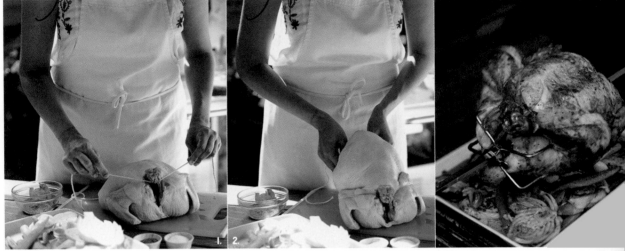

### Trussing a Chicken

The main reason to truss a chicken is to keep it compact so that it cooks evenly. This also makes it easier to handle on the grill.

I. Put the chicken breast side down on a work surface. Bring a long piece of cotton kitchen twine underneath the neck end of the bird. Bring the ends of the twine down over the wings and cross the ends of the twine underneath and around the drumstick ends. (See photo I, above.)

2. Pass the twine across the drumsticks and thighs, then pull ends of the twine snugly to draw the legs together and the wings close to the body, but not so tight that you cut into the flesh. Tie the twine tightly into a bow. (See photo 2, above.)

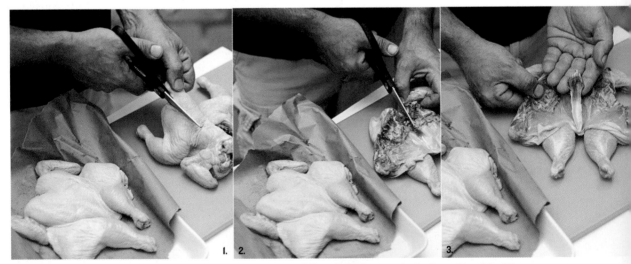

### Butterflying Cornish Hens

I. Cut the backbone out of the hen with poultry shears. (See photo I, above.)

2. Turn the bird over and snip along either side of the breast bone but not through the bird. (See photo 2, above.)

3. Lift out the breast bone. (See photo 3, above.)

# Buying Guide: Poultry

## How to Find the Freshest Poultry:
- Look for poultry that is plump and looks moist.
- Be sure packages are well sealed and not moist or leaking.
- Check expiration dates on packages to assure freshness.

## Chicken
Whether it's whole, cut up, butterflied, boneless, skin on or off—even ground—this versatile food is supremely suited for grilling.

Don't be restrained by packages that define chicken as fryers or broilers—they are perfect for grilling. (These distinctions refer to their size, which ranges from 2 to 4½ pounds.)

Large roasters, 6- to 7-pound birds, are great on a rotisserie or cooked by indirect heat. Capons—young roosters that have been castrated, fattened up, and sent to market before turning 10 months old—are especially delicious, and can be used in recipes that call for large chickens or small turkeys.

## Cornish Game Hens
When butterflied, Cornish hens are a fantastic quick grill. These petite, I- to 2-pound birds make for a generous single serving but are also great halved if your friends have more restrained appetites. The "game" in their name refers to the name of the breed, Cornish

Game Hen, not to the flavor of the bird or the way it is caught.

## Turkey
Fresh turkeys come in a wide range of sizes. For grilling, we prefer the more moderately sized hens that weigh between 10 and 12 pounds. We love the improved flavor and overall juiciness of a brined fresh turkey. However, if your market stocks only self-basting or kosher birds, skip brining. The processing of these birds includes salting, and brining would be overkill.

## Duck & Quail
The most readily available game birds are ducks and quail. Most supermarkets stock Pekin, a.k.a. Long Island ducks, in the freezer section. As with all meat and poultry, defrost these birds in the refrigerator. Never defrost at room temperature.

## Poultry Safety
According to the USDA, there is no benefit to washing poultry and meats. Washing might, in fact, spread bacteria to other ready-to-eat foods. Do, however, always remember to wash your hands with soap and hot water after handling raw poultry. Any bacteria that are present on the poultry will be destroyed by cooking to a temperature of 160°F.

## General Shrimp Prep

- Pinch off the short swimmerets on the underside of the shrimp.
- Peel off the shell, beginning at the thicker end and moving toward the tail. If shrimp are to be served as a finger food that needs a "handle," leave the tail's shell intact with one segment of shell attached. Otherwise, pull off the tail shell, taking care to leave the morsel of meat inside the tail on the shrimp. This extra effort is worth it; because the "tail feathers" are completely edible, it wastes less shrimp, and looks better.

## Deveining Peeled Shrimp

Removing the vein that runs along the top of the shrimp is a matter of preference. There is no need to remove the very thin vein from the underside of the shrimp.

- Snip along the curve of the shrimp with scissors to expose the vein.
- Lay the shrimp on its side and, with a paring knife, make a shallow incision along the top to expose the vein, then rinse. (See photo, below.)

## Butterflying Shrimp in the Shell

Follow the instructions for deveining, but slice about ¾ of the way through the shrimp to open it up, like a butterfly. (See photo, above.)

## Preparing Soft-Shell Crabs

If you're squeamish about preparing crabs, you can have your fishmonger do it; just cook them immediately.

1. Trim the eyes and mouth of the crab with cooking shears or a sharp knife. (See photo 1, above.)
2. Fold back tips of shell; snip out gills. (See photo 2, above.)
3. Remove the pointed or dome-shaped "apron" from the pale underside of the crab. Pat dry. (See photo 3, above.)

## Preparing Lobster

1. Place the live lobster on a cutting board. Hold it by the tail. Insert the tip of a heavy knife into the cross mark in the center of the body. Push the knife through the head down to the board. (See photo 1, above.)
2. Split the tail through the underside of the shell to expose the meat, but leave the shell connected along the back. Gently pry the shell open. (See photos 2 and 3, above.)
3. Slip a skewer lengthwise through the tail into the head to keep it from curling during grilling. Remove the vein.
4. Crack the lobster claws with the backside of a heavy knife before grilling.

## Preparing Mussels

- Place the mussels in a colander in the sink and rinse with cold water, scrubbing with a brush if the mussels are very dirty.
- If there are barnacles on the mussels, knock them off on the side of the sink.
- Tug off the beard—the dark wiry tuft that protrudes from the shell—if it is still attached.

## Preparing Scallops

Whether using large sea scallops or medium-size to tiny bay scallops, remove the small tough muscle on their sides. Simply pinch it off and discard.

# Buying Guide: Fish & Shellfish

## How to Find the Freshest Fish:
• Look for fish that smells fresh, not at all fishy.
• Look for fillets that are moist with no gaps between the muscles. On whole fish, the eyes should be clear and gills red. The skin should shine as if the fish were just pulled from the sea.
• Consider fish fillets for grilling that are dense and meaty, such as salmon, swordfish, tuna, Arctic char, halibut, or mahi mahi. Avoid flaky fish such as cod, flounder, orange roughy, or skate; they tend to fall through the grill grate. Whole dressed fish are fantastic grilled. Consider trout, snapper, sea bass, or small bluefish or mackerel.

## Shellfish
Buy bivalves—which include mussels, clams, and oysters—that are still alive; look for closed shells or those that close when tapped.

## Lobster & Crab
Lobsters should be feisty and very much alive. Lobsters held in tanks for too long have less meat, so buy from a fishmonger that does a brisk business.
The best-tasting soft-shell crabs are purchased live and cleaned right before cooking. (If you are squeamish about dispatching the crabs yourself, choose frisky ones, then have your fishmonger clean them for you.)

## Shrimp
Don't be afraid of frozen shrimp. Most "fresh" shrimp in markets have been frozen and defrosted. Frozen peeled and deveined shrimp are convenient and great to have in your freezer. Check the numbers on the bags to know the size of the shrimp. For example, $^{16}/_{20}$ are jumbo shrimp with 16 to 20 shrimp per pound; the higher the numbers, the smaller the shrimp.
Defrost shrimp in a bowl of cold water for about 20 minutes.

## Scallops
Always look for "dry," unadulterated scallops. Dry scallops have a creamy opalescence and tend to clump together. Wet scallops, which are treated with a chemical phosphate to extend shelf life, are uniformly white, unusually plump, and puddle water.

## When You Get Home
Seafood stays freshest when kept chilled. Fill a plastic bag with ice and lay fish or shellfish on top. Open up sealed bags of mussels and clams.
Lobsters and crabs should be kept moist, but don't put them in fresh water. To prevent them from drying out, transport and keep them wrapped in moist paper towels, newspaper, or seaweed. Cook live shellfish within a day; fresh fin fish within 2 days.

# Rib Primer

Although all types of ribs are satisfying, there are differences between pork ribs—spare, baby back, or country—and beef short ribs.

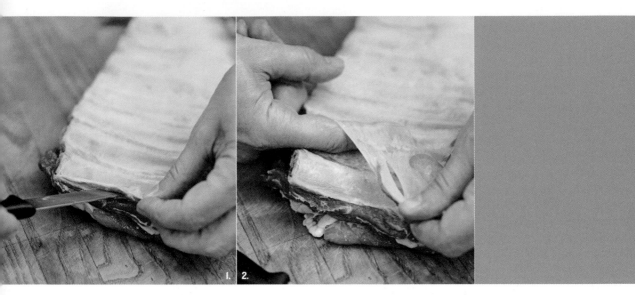

## Removing the Rib Membrane

All ribs have a thin membrane attached to the underside of the bones, which should be removed before cooking. To remove it:

1. Slip a knife between the bone and the membrane. (See photo 1, above.)
2. Once enough of the membrane has been released, slip your finger between the ribs and membrane as you gently pull it free from the bones. (See photo 2, above.)

## Baby Back Ribs

The popular baby back ribs, contrary to their name, are not from baby pigs. They are the eight ribs that hug the central section of a pork loin, a.k.a. the chop bones, which are shorter, leaner, and less meaty than classic spareribs. Their diminutive size makes them ideal as finger food and for cooking on smaller grills.

## Spareribs

Spareribs always mean pork. These are the 11 ribs from the belly and, ideally, weigh 2 to 3 pounds. They're often sold with a meaty section of the flank attached. When this is trimmed, they are known as St. Louis-style ribs. Spareribs can have a flap of meat on the underside, which should be trimmed.

## Country Ribs

Country-style ribs vary from butcher to butcher. They are cut from either the sirloin or the blade end of the loin. They can be butterflied chops or well-marbled meaty portions with blade bones but no ribs—or even boneless sections of the loin that require a knife and fork for eating. If you have a particular way you want them cut, it pays to be specific with your butcher.

## Beef Ribs

Beef short ribs, from the short plate, are very, very meaty. When cooked long and slow, they are tender and rich—but they can be butterflied and grilled as well. Short ribs can come in dinosaur-size slabs or can be cut into more manageable 2-inch sections.

# Buying Guide: Meat

### How to Find the Freshest Meat:
- Look for red meat that has a rosy cast. Packages should be well sealed and not leaking.
- Check expiration dates on packages to assure freshness.
- Keep raw meats separate from produce in your cart.

### Steaks Defined
"Let's grill a couple steaks" is the perfect call for a thoroughly satisfying no-fuss meal. All steaks are not created equal, however. Some are tender with mild taste; others have more chew but great taste. Tender steaks usually cost more, but don't let price alone be your guide. Affordable cuts often pay off with big beefy flavor. Steaks cooked on the bone are especially delicious.

### Most Tender
Filet of beef: A.k.a. tenderloin, medallions, tournedos, or filet mignon; these define melt-in-your-mouth meat.

### Tender with Lots of Beef Flavor
This category includes loin steak, shell steak (a.k.a. New York strip), and top loin—bone-in or boneless.
   These steaks have a perfect balance of tenderness and taste.
Porterhouse: The best of all worlds. A healthy portion of the shell on a T-bone with a large eye of fillet.
T-bone: Like a porterhouse, but the eye of the tenderloin is smaller.

Rib steak: Rib-eye, bone-in or boneless; this steak comes from the same cut as a standing rib roast, sort of like a huge beef chop or medallion.

### Great Beef Flavor But Not as Tender
Flank steak, sirloin, tri-tip, and top round: These steaks take to marinades and are best grilled medium-rare. They should always be cut against the grain.
Skirt steak: Long, very thin steak that is best seared over high heat and almost always sliced against the grain.

### Prime Time
The finest beef gets the rare designation of Prime from the USDA. These steaks have a fine network of fat throughout the meat—known as marbling—that assures both flavor and juiciness. The majority of Prime meat gets snapped up by restaurants, but if you have access to a butcher that carries Prime meats, these steaks are a sublime treat. Most beef falls into the subsequent categories of Choice or Select, with a diminishing amount of marbling in each class. Less fat means less cooking because these meats can dry out if overcooked.

### When You Get Home
Store meats in the coolest spot of the fridge—lower shelves near the back are often best.
   Ground meat keeps for 2 days; roasts, chops, and steaks for 3 to 5 days.

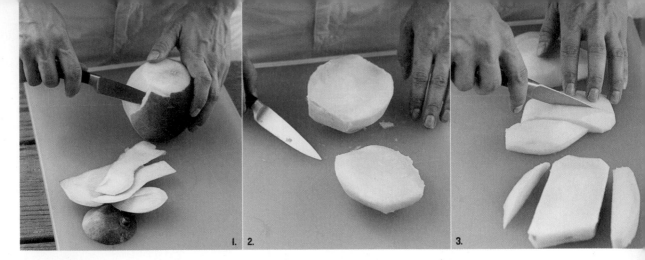

## Preparing Mango

1. Set the mango on its side and slice ½ inch from each end. Stand mango upright, look down over it, then sliver away skin from top to bottom. (See photo 1, above.)
2. Slice away the two fat sides by running your knife along the pit. Repeat with edges of mango. (See photo 2, above.)
3. Chop or slice as needed for recipe. (See photo 3, above.)

## Preparing Papaya

• Follow Steps 1 and 2 for preparing a mango, then cut papaya in half lengthwise from top to bottom.
• Using a spoon, scrape out the seeds from each papaya half.
• Chop or slice as needed for recipe.

## Preparing Pineapple

• Slice off the crown and the bottom of the fruit.
• Quarter the pineapple lengthwise.

• Stand the sections up and slice downward to cut off the hard pointed core from each piece.
• Lay the section of pineapple on its side and remove the fruit in one piece with a flexible knife or grapefruit knife. Dice or slice as needed for recipe.

## Pitting Cherries

• If possible, leave cherries on the stem.
• Use the stem to position the cherry in a cherry/olive pitter. Press or poke, depending upon the kind of cherry pitter you are using.
• Alternatively, position a cherry under the broad side of a cook's knife. Briskly press with your fist or the heel of your hand onto the knife to open the cherry. Pop out the pit.

## Sectioning Citrus

1. Cut the ends off the fruit. (See photo 1, above.)
2. Remove remaining peel by cutting down fruit from one end to the other. (See photo 2, above.)

3. Working over a bowl, cut between the sides of each section and the membrane to the center of the fruit. (See photo 3, above.)

274

# Knife Skills

## Chop, Chop

It's best to always prepare food on a cutting board rather than directly on the counter; it's kinder to a knife's sharp blade and more hygienic. To keep the cutting board from slipping around, lay a dampened towel under the board. For a reusable slip guard, cut a square of plastic mesh shelf liner—about half the size of the board—and position it under the board.

You will have more control cutting a tomato or onion if you halve it, then cut or trim an edge to make it flat so it won't roll around as you cut. When preparing multiple pieces, instead of peeling, seeding, and chopping each piece, peel them all first. Then seed all and chop all.

## Cuts Defined

Mince, chop, dice, julienne: Is there a difference, and does it really matter? The simple answer: yes on both counts. The cut affects how long food takes to cook and sometimes how it tastes. The flavor of garlic in a salad dressing is more balanced if it's finely minced than if it's in large pieces.

Slice: Thin pieces that usually keep the shape of the vegetable intact, such as rounds of carrot, zucchini, cucumber, or tomato. For a bias cut, slice on an angle.

Shred: Vegetables cut into long, narrow, rough pieces. Generally done on a grater. Candidates for shredding include lettuce, cabbage, and potatoes.

Chop: A large casual cut that is somewhat square or chunky. Perfect for carrots, apples, or onions. Bigger than a dice or a mince and not uniform.

Dice: Even cubes, about ¼ to ¾ inch square. More exact than a chop.

Mince: The finest cut of all. Parsley should be like fine confetti, garlic tiny, and citrus zest minuscule.

Julienne: Narrow, fine sticks of vegetables or fruit that are 2 to 3 inches long and ⅛ inch square. A finer julienne measures 1/16 of an inch square.

Chiffonade: A fancy term for cutting leafy vegetables or herbs such as basil into strips or ribbons. The best way to do this is to roll the leaves up into a cylinder before slicing into thin strips.

## A Knife Can Do More Than Cut

The broad blade of a chef's knife can be used for other things besides cutting.

Turning the blade flat presents a broad surface that is perfect for pounding or smashing. Use the knife this way to loosen a clove of garlic's papery skin. Hold the knife flat, place the garlic under the widest part of the blade, and then pound the blade with your fist. Do the same thing to pop the pits out of olives or cherries. You can also use the knife broadside to pound boneless chicken breasts to a uniform thickness.

## Against the Grain

The grain in meat is the direction the fibers in the muscle run. With a cut of steak such as a flank steak or brisket, it is important to cut the meat against the  grain. If you cut the meat parallel to the grain, it will be stringy and fibrous in the mouth. To get nice, thin but broad slices, hold a fork at about a 45-degree angle to the meat and make cuts across the grain with a slicing knife, using the fork as a guide for the angle of the cuts.

index

Food photographs are noted in colored numerals.

# a

Ancho powder, about, 231
Annato paste
  about, 106
  Yucatan Rub, 106
Antipasti Salad, 193
Appetizers. See also Little dishes
  Edamame Hummus, 16
  Extreme BBQ'd Nachos, 26, 27
  Guacamole, 20, 23
  Jicama Sticks, 20, 28
  New Orleans-Style BBQ Shrimp, 29, 44
  Oysters on the Half-Shell with Two Sauces, 30, 31
  Skordalia (Greek Potato-Garlic Dip), 20, 24
  Smoky Eggplant Dip, 17, 190
  Spicy Thai-Style Pineapple Wraps, 18, 19
  Spinach & Artichoke Dip, 25
  Summer Rolls with Chile Dipping Sauce, 14, 15
  Summer Salsa with a Shot, 20, 22
Apples
  Apple-Cranberry Chutney, 136
  Confetti Coleslaw, 180, 183
  Grill-Smoked Trout with Apple-Beet Salad, 166, 167
  Quick Cranberry-Apple Relish, 108, 109
Artichokes
  Antipasti Salad, 193
  Baby Artichoke & Potato Salad, 50, 51
  Spinach & Artichoke Dip, 25
  trimming, 50
Arugula
  Antipasti Salad, 193
  baby, about, 193
  Fattoush (Middle Eastern Bread Salad), 190, 192

Roasted Garlic & Arugula Pizzas, 48, 49
Watermelon & Baby Arugula Salad, 194, 195
Avocados
  Guacamole, 20, 23
  ripening, 23
  Spicy Shrimp & Avocado Salad with Grapefruit Dressing, 168, 169

# b

Bacon
  Bacon-Wrapped Dates with Manchego, 36
  BLT Crostini, 36
  Chicken Liver, Pancetta & Lemon Kebabs, 37
  Chicken Spiedini, 91
  Hog-Tied Cheese Dogs, 70
  Hot German Potato Salad, 180, 182
  Matambre (Hunger Killer), 122
  Southern Greens with Whole Spices, 189, 197
Banana leaves
  buying, 41
  Thai Curried Scallops in Banana Leaves, 40, 41
Banana Split, Hot Buttered Rum, with Coconut, 239
Barbecue-sauced recipes
  Backyard BBQ'd Spare Ribs, 140, 141
  Extreme BBQ'd Nachos, 26, 27
  K.C.-BBQ'd Glazed Chicken, 103, 104
  North Carolina-Style BBQ Pulled-Pork Sandwiches, 80, 81
  Texas BBQ Braised Beef Brisket, 128, 129
Barbecue sauces
  Chile-Coffee BBQ Sauce, 223
  Cider Mop, 219
  Cola Barbecue Sauce, 216, 217
  Kansas City-Style BBQ Sauce, 218

  mopping with, 103
  North Carolina-Style Vinegar BBQ Sauce, 218
  Peach-Mustard BBQ Sauce, 220
  Sweet & Sour BBQ Sauce, 221
  Tamarind Barbecue Sauce, 224
Basil
  Chicken Paillards with Herb-Tomato Salad, 94
  chopping, 201
  Pesto-Stuffed Salmon with Tomato-Corn Salad, 156
  Tomato & Basil Dressing, 198, 201
Beans
  Antipasti Salad, 193
  Black-Eyed Pea Salad, 196, 197
  Chili for Dogs, 65, 68
  Edamame Hummus, 16
  Extreme BBQ'd Nachos, 26, 27
  Seafood Paella, 176, 177
  Spicy Baked Beans, 204
  Summer Salad with Tuna, 162
Beef
  Beef Satay, 42
  brisket, slicing, 275
  buying, for burgers, 57
  Chili for Dogs, 65, 68
  Classic Burgers, 56, 57
  Fajitas, 78
  Fiery Flank Steak & Papaya Salad, 123
  fillet (tenderloin), cuts from, 273
  flank steak, about, 273
  flank steak, slicing, 42, 275
  Hog-Tied Cheese Dogs, 70
  hot dogs, types of, 70
  Korean Short Ribs with Cucumber Kimchee, 130, 131
  London Broil with Onion Marmalade, 79
  Matambre (Hunger Killer), 122
  Medallions of Beef with Chile-Coffee BBQ Sauce, 124, 125
  Mixed Grill with Chimichurri Sauce, 132
  Pepper-Crusted Strip Loin Roast with Chimichurri, 120, 121
  Porterhouse steak, about, 119, 273